Political élites in the USSR

Political Elites in the USSR

Central leaders and local cadres
from Lenin to Gorbachev

T. H. Rigby

Professor of Political Science,
Research School of Social Sciences,
The Australian National University

Edward Elgar

© T. H. Rigby 1990

Published by
Edward Elgar Publishing Limited
Gower House
Croft Road
Aldershot
Hants GU11 3HR
England

Gower Publishing Company
Old Post Road
Brookfield
Vermont 05036
USA

British Library Cataloguing in Publication Data

Rigby, T. H. (Thomas Henry, *1925–*)
  Political élites in the USSR : central leaders and local cadres from Lenin to Gorbachev.
  1. Soviet Union. Political élites, History
  I. Title
  322.4'3'0947

  ISBN 1-85278-303-6

Printed in Great Britain by
Billing & Sons Ltd, Worcester

Contents

Preface

I am grateful to the editors and publishers of the following journals for permission to reproduce articles which appear in this volume: *Soviet Studies* (for Chapters 3, 4, 6, 8 and 9), *British Journal of Political Science* (for Chapter 2), *Australian Outlook* (for Chapter 7) and *Slavic Review* (for Chapter 10).

Passages containing evaluations or speculation specific to the periods when they were first published have been retained in their original wording. While in certain instances, notably in chapters 7 and 9, they now read somewhat anachronistically, their inclusion should contribute to a livelier sense of the contemporary significance of past changes affecting the character of Soviet political élites.

1. Introduction

The leading officials of party and state at the centre and throughout the country are the key element in socio-political systems of the
Soviet type. It is therefore of the utmost importance to understand
what kind of people they are, how they achieve office, and
what factors determine their mutual relationships. These are the
questions addressed in this book.

At the outset we encounter a seeming paradox. How is it that
Soviet officialdom, collectively so dominant, are personally so
vulnerable, expendable and ultimately powerless? And here we
recall that it was Stalin, whose oft-quoted aphorism 'cadres decide
everything' (*Kadry reshayut vsë*) is the supreme testimony to the
social and political dominance of party–state officialdom, who
sent hundreds of thousands of them to their deaths, without
encountering a single act of individual or collective resistance.
And we ask why it is, if the central ministries and regional party
machine remain as powerful and as opposed to reform as most
observers believe, that they have been unable to prevent Gorbachev
from introducing ever more radical changes and from pensioning
off a steady stream of their leading representatives.

Perhaps there is a simple answer here: surely the members
of ruling classes always and everywhere are peculiarly liable to
fall personally victim to the very practices through which their
collective dominance is ensured. It is the feudal lord, not his serf,
who falls in battle. It is the 'bourgeois', not the 'proletarian', who
goes bankrupt. Similarly, it is the 'leading cadre' in a communist
country, raised to power and privilege through participation in the
administrative process, who stands to lose most as a consequence
of that process.

Yet there is evidently more to it than this. Past ruling classes
have always had a privileged relationship with the state, but individual membership has not been something granted or withheld by

1

the state; rather, as a rule, it has been conferred by ascribed or achieved social status: by noble birth, by ownership of land, or through commercial or industrial wealth. In Soviet-type societies, the ruling class of officials *constitutes* the state. Thus on the one hand they enjoy an extraordinary *independence* of the rest of society, but on the other they are subject to an extraordinary *dependence* on the state, in the person of its top officials, its inquisitorial and coercive agencies and their own hierarchical supervisors.

The key to this paradox lies in the 'mono-organizational' character of Soviet society which resulted from Lenin's concentration of absolute power over all spheres of life in the hands of his Communist Party leadership, a concentration he deemed necessary in order to effect that total transformation of society towards the Utopian goal of 'communism' for the sake of which he had led his Bolsheviks to take power. For this sublime goal, he believed, required the establishment of a 'dictatorship of the proletariat', a dictatorship defined as 'power unlimited by any laws', and in practice exercised, as Lenin frankly admitted, by the proletariat's 'organized vanguard', that is, by his communist (till 1918, 'bolshevik') followers. Within the Communist Party itself power was ideally to be exercised on the basis of 'democratic centralism', but the centralism always took precedence over the democracy, and the latter, while a genuine ingredient in the party's original tradition, soon withered under the desperate stresses of winning and holding power while carrying through revolutionary social changes that alienated nearly all sections of society.

The great historic task of the 'dictatorship of the proletariat' was to crush and sweep away all that stood in the way of 'socialism' (defined as the first or lower phase of 'communism'), and this meant not just overt political opposition, but all rights, immunities and autonomies that set limits to the 'vanguard's' prerogatives, to its power to command obedience in all things small and large: be these property rights, rights to due process under law, immunity from arbitrary arrest or from 'mobilization' for unpaid labour, or free association in pursuit of shared economic, cultural, religious, ethnic or other concerns.

There is no evidence that Lenin aimed to convert his 'organized revolutionary vanguard' into a bureaucratic machine, but once the traditional and market procedures through which much of the business of society had till then been conducted were largely dismantled as obstacles to the revolution, no mechanism was left to him for keeping things running except chains of naked command, transmitted through hierarchies of full-time officials. Progressively, every sphere of activity was made the monopoly of a particular bureaucratic organization (a people's commissariat or later ministry, state committee, and so on,), while voluntary associations such as trade unions, youth organizations, writers' and artists' fellowships, were converted into official agencies for enforcing the party's policies in the context concerned. The party itself became an appendage of its own full-time officialdom, who had the daunting task of directing, co-ordinating and monitoring the plethora of specialized bureaucracies, binding them together into a single, vast, organizational system. The first, giant studies towards such a mono-organizational society were taken under Lenin, in the period of so-called 'War Communism'; there was a partial retreat under Lenin's 'New Economic Policy', and it reached its full development under Stalin in the 1930s. With some important modifications this system persisted into the era of Gorbachev's *perestroika*.

The peculiar situation of the bureaucratic 'class' (some sociologists prefer other designations for this social category) within mono-organizational societies of the Soviet type should now be clearer. On the one hand its dominance is uncontested, indeed virtually unqualified, by any other social group drawing power and authority from some resources other than administrative resources. But on the other its members themselves have no social basis outside the administrative command-structure from which they can draw material support, authority and standing, and so their own future is entirely dependent on administrative decisions taken within that structure.

These two related aspects of Soviet society–its bureaucratic ruling class and its mono-organizational structure – have occupied much of my attention during close on four decades of studying the Soviet political and social order, and this book and a companion volume entitled *The Changing Soviet System: Mono-organizational Socialism from its Origins to Gorbachev's Restructuring* bring together and seek to carry forward some of my principal writings on these matters. In the present book I examine several basic topics necessary for understanding the character and internal relationships of the Soviet ruling bureaucracy. Most of these I looked at for the first time in my doctoral thesis, 'The Selection of Leading Personnel in the Soviet State and Communist Party', written in London in the early 1950s, when the relevant scholarly literature was scanty in the extreme.[1] Its chapters dealt with such matters as the recruitment and composition of the Communist Party membership, the formal and actual procedures for the appointment of party and government officials at all levels, the social composition of central, regional and local soviets and party committees and their executive bodies, and patterns of career-making within the party–state bureaucracy. Since then a considerable scholarly literature has grown up around these topics, much of which is drawn on in the chapters that follow. In introducing these matters here, I shall seek to bring in findings from parts of my own research not included in this volume.

The party membership is one subject that space does not permit us to consider in detail, but some major aspects of it deserve to be noted at this point.[2] First, while the early decades of its post-revolutionary history, up to the death of Stalin, were marked by alternating periods of rapid expansion and contraction, reflecting the cataclysms of civil war, crash industrialization, Stalin's purges and the Second World War, it has since shown a continuous, though fluctuating, pattern of growth. Secondly, although the Bolshevik Revolution paved the way for party members to take over nearly all important positions in the state and other official organizations, at no time has the CPSU membership simply been identical with Soviet officialdom. The reason for this lies in the varied political roles for which members are required: not only to staff key positions, but also to provide a strong party presence in all influential professions, from school teachers to factory management to army officers, and to serve as the party's eyes, ears and voice in all work groups and other organized social settings, and as its 'vanguard' in 'mobilizing the masses' for successive programmes and campaigns. Thirdly, the varying priorities given to these roles under different historical circumstances have led to marked changes in the social composition of the party, although at all times there has been a far stronger representation of men than women, the better than the worse educated, the desk worker than the manual worker, the urban than the rural, and some ethnic groups than others. And finally, there has been a secular trend for the party to incorporate a higher and higher proportion of the active adult population, owing mostly to the social effects of modernization and to the tendency of manual worker communists to transfer to desk jobs, thus requiring the recruitment of replacements in order to retain some credibility as a 'proletarian' party and maintain a shop-floor presence. Membership trebled between the 1950s and the 1980s and now embraces about one in nine of the adult population. Nevertheless, recognizing the crucial importance of the above-mentioned party membership roles for the maintenance of the mono-organizational system, the leadership has been concerned that this trend should not get out of hand, thus threatening the leading role of the 'vanguard' *vis-à-vis* the 'masses', and party growth has tended to round off since the 1960s.

It is from party's ranks that the overwhelming majority of 'leading cadres' in all organizations, both at the centre and around the country, are chosen. But how are they chosen? According to the federal and republic constitutions, and the rules of the CPSU, of mass organizations like the Young Communist League (the *Komsomol*) or the trade unions, and indeed all ostensibly voluntary associations, the leaders at every level are elected by the soviets (councils), committees, conferences and so on, to which they are formally responsible, and the latter are in turn elected by the rank-and-file membership (or the public at large in the case of the soviets), either directly or in a multi-stage process. This stems from a genuine democratic strain in the early tradition of Russian marxism, but the reality rapidly faded during the earliest years of communist power, and these ubiquitous elections were reduced to the role of legitimating rituals, in which the 'electors' endorsed unopposed 'candidates' selected by those administratively responsible for doing so.[3]

But who precisely is 'administratively responsible', and how do they go about exercising their responsibilities? Long before the revolution the principle was well established within the Bolshevik ranks that the Central Committee bore the major responsibility for 'distributing forces', while local committees were supposed to assign members to specific functions. The hierarchical principle of personnel direction, however, was never embodied in effective structures, and was offset by a considerable level of *de facto* local autonomy and by some commitment to operating democratically.[4]

This mixture of the hierarchical with often clique-dominated local-ism and with residual democracy persisted in the early years of Bolshevik power, when the membership multiplied at breakneck speed and 'cadres' had to be found for tens of thousands of official posts at all levels. Between 1919 and 1921, with the establishment of a full-time party bureaucracy, a degree of order was introduced into the initial near-chaotic improvization, and the first years of NEP saw a progressive refinement and regularization of assignment procedures.

It was at this time, as we see in Chapter 3, that the *nomenklatura* system emerged. The essence of this system was simply the official designation of those posts (in government bodies, the economy, 'voluntary' associations and the party itself) for which each level and sector of the party apparatus was responsible for selecting or approving personnel. It included nominally elective posts along with officially appointive ones. Under Stalin this system became deeply entrenched and a key element in the whole socio-political order. Chapter 4, although written some 36 years ago and not previously published, remains the only extended account of the operation of the nomenklatura system in the late Stalin era. That system persisted with little change into the 1980's and as we observe in Chapter 10 it poses fundamental problems for the Gorbachev leadership in the context of their proclaimed policy of democratization.

For the nomenklatura system is far from being a mere adminis-trative device: it is a basic factor in the distribution and exercise of power and privilege in Soviet society. From its inception it was a crucial instrument in reinforcing central control over the provincial mutual-protection cliques described in Chapter 2. At the same time, however, it enabled the regional and republican bosses installed by Moscow to progressively pack the leading positions in all local organizations with 'cadres' personally beholden to them. The monopoly which the latter collectively enjoyed and mutually shared over access to jobs, goods, services and privileges of all kinds turned them into a myriad of interlocking charmed circles, the totality of which are often seen as constituting the dominant social group in the USSR – 'the nomenklatura'.[5]

The concept of 'the nomenklatura' as a social category has considerable validity, which is implicit even in some official Soviet uses of the term 'nomenclatured workers' (*nomenklaturnye rabotniki*). Yet there are problems; first and foremost, the problem of boundaries. Whose nomenklatura do you have to be on to be a member of *the* nomenklatura? That of the Central Committee (CC) of the CPSU, making you one among some tens of thousands? Or should we widen it to include the *nomenklatury* of the republic CCs and the territorial and regional committees (*kraikoms* and *obkoms*), making you one of perhaps a quarter of a million? Or should we take in a further echelon, the nomenklatury of the city and district party committees (*gorkoms* and *raikoms*), giving you around two million fellow nomenklatura members?[6] Nor need we stop here. Other organizations, such as the industrial ministries, the armed forces and the KGB, also have their nomenklatury, and if we were to include all individuals figuring on these we should have to add at least a couple more millions. Describing the dominant social category as 'the nomenklatura' then, does not overcome the vagueness of such alternative descriptions as 'the bureaucracy', 'partocracy', 'new class' and so on. In contexts where we wish to define its boundaries more precisely, we have to elaborate our definitions accordingly. More fundamentally, such definitions will tell us little unless they are embedded in some general understanding of the nature of Soviet society.

In whatever way we define the dominant social category, should we think of it as a 'class' at all? If we understand 'class' in narrowly marxist terms as determined by 'relations of production' seen as property relations, 'class' would seem to have limited analytical value for a society in which private ownership of the means of production has been marginalized. There have been efforts to salvage its use through the device of deeming the means of production to be *collectively* owned by the ruling class, but the concept of ownership thereby becomes so attenuated as to be emptied of explanatory potential. Given the abundant evidence that a certain category of Soviet society enjoys a highly privileged position with respect to power, status and access to goods and services, the obvious conclusion must surely be that this rests on resources *other than* property resources. Property, for example, slaves, herds, land or capital, frequently constitutes the main basis on which the power and privilege of a ruling class rests. But it is not the *only* possible basis. In Soviet society it is access to administrative resources, by virtue of office in one or other of the command hierarchies through which the whole business of society is conducted, that forms the main basis of power and privilege. Whether the hierarchy in question is that of the party apparatus, a government ministry, the army, the KGB, a provincial soviet or whatever, such office can therefore be regarded as bestowing membership of the 'ruling class'.

Certainly, the upper echelons of the several hierarchies can usefully be seen as constituting, in Suzanne Keller's term, so many 'strategic élites',[7] but this does not invalidate or make redundant the concept of a 'bureaucratic' ruling class in the USSR and other mono-organizational societies modelled on it. For what they all share is access to the crucial resource conferring power and privilege in such societies. And this community of objective interest is reinforced by common membership in the ruling Communist Party, prolonged political socialization within its ranks and shared participation in party conferences, *aktiv* meetings, conferences and other activities. This is not to say, of course, that no important differences and potential conflicts exist among the several hierarchies and their dominant élites. But conflict between them does not assume the salience in Soviet political life that one might expect. Political cleavages tend to cut across them, and the informal patronage groupings that strongly influence political alignments in the USSR characteristically include office-holders in several such hierarchies.

The study of Soviet political élites has understandably attracted a great deal of scholarly interest. By examining the background, education, career experience and other characteristics of those staffing the various echelons of the party and other hierarchies we can learn much about the social, intellectual and value context of Soviet politics and administration, and about how this has changed over time. Even the membership of such largely symbolic pseudo-elective bodies as the soviets can be instructive in this respect. I have been an energetic participant in this line of research, and this is reflected in several chapters in the present volume.[8] This literature could be criticized for its inconsistent and eclectic use of the 'élite' concept, not only as between scholars but even within the writings of particular individuals, myself included, although arguably such inconsistency is acceptable provided one is careful to describe the analytical purpose in hand. There is also, however, a danger of presenting élite data as if their implications were self-evident, or alternatively of making unwarranted assumptions about the attitudinal or behavioural consequences of various background factors or career experiences. If we have a deep enough knowledge of the Soviet system, we can learn important things from such data, but not with the 'scientific' certainty or precision that some have imagined.

The three hundred or so (it used to be far fewer) members of the CPSU Central Committee, comprising as they do not only the chief party leaders at the centre and in the provinces, but also leading figures in the various branches of government and other specialized élites, are often treated as *the* political élite in the USSR. It is of course perfectly valid, however, to interpret this concept either more generously or more narrowly, and it has even been applied to the dozen-or-so-strong Political Bureau (Politburo) of the Central Committee. But the Politburo, as the core of the Soviet political executive, attracts scholarly interest not only for the background and experience of its members, but also for its internal power relationships, mode of operation, and connections with other executive bodies and organizations. These two aspects are examined respectively in Chapters 7 and 8 of the present volume.

There is also a third aspect, namely, the informal elements of power, authority and leadership at the summit, and although assumptions and speculations about these inform the constant stream of discourse among scholars, journalists and officials concerned with Soviet politics, we are often desperately short of hard information and lacking in tried and trusted conceptual and analytical tools. The structure of supreme power in the USSR has always been fluid and weakly institutionalized, and it remains a *problem*, rather than a *given* of the system, even under Gorbachev. The phrase *under* Gorbachev points up one of the central issues: *is* there at any particular time a single dominant leader, a 'boss' (*khozyain*), and if so what are the formal and informal bases of his power within the top political executive and *vis-à-vis* the wider political élite at the centre and in the provinces, and its effects on the operation of the socio-political system generally? This is a recurrent theme of this book.[9]

The breadth and complexity of our topic will now be apparent, and in selecting material for this volume I have been aware of the opposite dangers of over-generalization and of overwhelming the reader with empirical detail. The search for an adequate conceptual framework for understanding the key elements of the Soviet socio-political order is of the utmost scholarly and practical importance, but we should not let it blunt our sensitivity to the rich variety and unpredictability of human behaviour. In seeking to uncover persistent underlying patterns, we must avoid too static an analysis. With this in mind, I have chosen material drawn from all major periods of Soviet history, and in the final chapter I have carried our main themes forward to the eve of the 1990s, and sought to answer the question whether this central element in Soviet mono-organizational socialism has undergone radical change in the course of Gorbachev's *perestroika*.

NOTES

1. The first edition of Merle Fainsod's *How Russia is Ruled*, (Harvard University Press, Cambridge, Mass.,1953), a landmark in this as in many other fields of Soviet political studies, came out about the time my thesis was completed. There was also some material of interest in Julian Towster's *Political Power in the USSR, 1917–1937*, (Oxford University Press, New York, 1948), and Barrington Moore, Jr, *Soviet Politics: The Dilemma of Power* (Harvard University Press, Cambridge, Mass., 1950), but in general earlier textbooks on Soviet politics and government paid little attention to its personnel aspects. In Germany pioneering work of permanent value was being done by Boris Meissner; see, for example, his 'Der Wandel im sozialen Gefüge der Sowjetunion', *Europa-Archiv*, no. 9, 1950, 'Das Generationsproblem im Kreml', *Der Monat*, June 1953, and his earlier three-part study 'Die Entwicklung der Ministerien in Russland', *Europa-Archiv*, nos 2–4, 1948. In America there was Louis Nemzer's article 'The Kremlin's Professional Staff: the Apparatus of the Central Committee, Communist Party of the Soviet Union', *American Political Science Review*, March 1950. The one topic that was well served was political biography of Stalin, the literature on whom already included the most influential works by Leon Trotsky, *Stalin: An Appraisal of the Man and his Influence*, (Hollis and Carter, London, 1947), Boris Souvarine, *Stalin: A Critical Survey of Bolshevism*, (Angus and Robertson, London and Sydney, 1940; originally published in French in 1935) and Isaac Deutscher, *Stalin: A Political Biography*, (Oxford University Press, London, 1949).

2. See my *Communist Party Membership in the USSR, 1917–1967* (Princeton University Press, Princeton, N.J., 1968); 'Social Orientation of Recruitment and Distribution of Membership in the CPSU', *American Slavic and East European Review*, vol.*XVI* (1957) no. 3; 'Soviet Communist Party Membership under Brezhnev', *Soviet Studies*, vol. 28, no. 3 (1976) pp. 317–37; Robert F. Miller and T. H. Rigby, *26th Congress of the CPSU in Current Political Perspective* (Australian National University, Canberra, 1982) pp. 65–71; and 'The CPSU from Stalin to Chernenko: Membership and Leadership', in Georg Brunner *et al.* (eds), *Sowjetsystem und Ostrecht* (Duncker and Humblot, Berlin, 1985) pp. 143–58.

3. T. H. Rigby, 'Party Elections in the CPSU', *Political Quarterly*, vol. 35,

no. 4, (1964) pp. 420-43; 'The Selection of Leading Personnel in the Soviet State and Communist Party', chaps Two and Seven (PhD Thesis, University of London, 1954).

4. I examine this in 'A Dictatorship for Communism', ch. 1 of *The Changing Soviet System. Mono-organizational Socialism From Its Origins to Gorbachev's Restructuring* (Edward Elgar, Aldershot, Forthcoming).

5. Further to chs. 2-6 in the present volume, see T. H. Rigby and Bohdan Harasymiw (eds) *Leadership Selection and Patron-Client Relations in the USSR and Yugoslavia*, (Allen and Unwin, London, 1983); T. H. Rigby, 'Khrushchev and the Rules of the Game', in R. F. Miller and F. Fehér (eds), *Khrushchev and the Communist World*, (Croom Helm, London and Sydney, and Barnes and Noble Books, Totowa, N.J., 1984), pp. 39-81; idem, 'Crypto-Politics', *Survey*, no. 50 (January 1964), pp. 183-94: reprinted in Walter Laqueur, (ed), *The State of Soviet Studies* (MIT Press, Cambridge, Mass., 1965), and Frederic J. Fleron Jr (ed.), *Communist Studies and the Social Sciences: Essays on Methodology and Empirical Theory*, (Rand McNally, Chicago, 1969); idem, 'The Need for Comparative Research', *Studies in Comparative Communism*, vol. *XII*,, nos. 2-3, (1979), pp. 204-11; idem, 'How the Obkom Secretary was Tempered', *Problems of Communism*, vol. *XXIX*, no. 2 (March-April 1980), pp. 57-63; and idem, 'Political Patronage in the USSR from Lenin to Brezhnev, *Politics*, vol. 18, no. 1 (May 1983), pp. 84-9.

6. See Rigby and Harasymiw, op. cit., p. 9.

7. See Suzanne Keller, *Beyond the Ruling Class. Strategic Elites in Modern Society* (Random House, New York, 1963).

8. There was much of relevance in my doctoral thesis, op.cit. See also 'Changing Composition of the Supreme Soviet', *Political Quarterly,*vol. *XXIV*, no. 3 (July-September 1953) pp. 307-16; 'Soviet Government Changes since Stalin', *Australian Outlook*, vol. 9, no. 3 (September 1955) pp. 165-71; 'The CPSU Elite: Turnover and Rejuvenation from Lenin to Khrushchev', *Australian Journal of Politics and History*, vol. XVI, no. 1 (April 1970) pp. 11-23; 'The Soviet Government since Khrushchev', *Politics*, vol. *XII*, no. 1 (May 1977) pp. 5-22; *Lenin's Government. Sovnarkom 1917-1922* (Cambridge University Press, Cambridge, 1979) ch. 11; and 'The CPSU from Stalin to Chernenko', in Brunner *et al* (eds), op. cit.

9. Other writings in which I consider this question include *Lenin's Government: Sovnarkom 1917-1922; Stalin* (Prentice-Hall, Englewood Cliffs, N.J., 1965); 'Stalinism and the Mono-organizational Society', in *The Changing Soviet System*, originally published in Robert C. Tucker (ed), *Stalinism. Essays in Historical Interpretation* (Norton, New York, 1977) pp. 53-76; 'The CPSU from Stalin to Chernenko', loc. cit.; 'How Strong is the Leader?', *Problems of Communism*, vol. *XI*, no. 5 (1962), pp. 1-8; 'The Extent and Limits of Authority', *Problems of Communism*, vol. *XII*, no. 5 (1963), pp. 36-41; 'A Behavioural Symposium', *Soviet Studies*, vol.XXVI, no. 3 (July 1974), pp. 446-9; 'The Making of the President - Soviet Style', *Quadrant* (Sydney), August 1977, pp. 64-67; 'Personal and Collective Leadership: Brezhnev and Beyond', in Dimitri K. Simes *et al.*, *Soviet Succession: Leadership in Transition, Washington Papers*, vol. *VI*, no. 59, (1978) pp. 41-58; 'A New Soviet Succession Crisis?', *World Review* (Brisbane), vol. 19, no. 2, (June 1980) pp. 17-20; 'Khrushchev and the Rules of the Game', in Miller and Fehér (eds) op. cit., pp. 39-81; 'The Soviet Political Executive, 1917-1986', in Archie Brown (ed), *Political Leadership in the Soviet Union*, (Macmillan, London, 1989) pp. 4-54.

2. The Soviet political élite under Lenin*

> Founded by V. I. Lenin as the advanced detachment of the working class, the Communist Party . . . led the working class and the labouring peasants to victory in the Great October Socialist Revolution, and established the dictatorship of the proletariat in the USSR.
>
> CPSU Rules, 1966

> Russia was ruled after the 1905 Revolution by 130 000 landowners . . . and it is alleged that the 240 000 members of the Bolshevik Party will not be able to rule Russia . . .
>
> Lenin, 'Will the Bolsheviks Retain State Power?', October 1917

> . . . the working class no longer feels itself at home in our party.
>
> Alexandra Kollontai, XI CPSU Congress, 1922

Revolutions characteristically effect more or less radical changes not only in the political order but also in the composition of those staffing it. This usually involves more than an influx of 'new men'; the socio-political factors determining access to office also change. In the revolutionary rhetoric such changes are usually represented as ending political and social privilege and equalizing opportunities, although notoriously they tend to substitute new forms of privilege for the old – wealth for birth, education for wealth, and so on – as well as affecting differentially the chances

*'The Soviet Political Elite, 1917–1922', *British Journal of Political Science*, vol. 1 (1971) pp. 415–36.

of various ethnic, religious, associational and other groups. Furthermore, the break in continuity of the political élite is rarely if ever complete. Sometimes the determinants of access to the élite are not so much changed as reshuffled and reweighted, with many of the same individuals retaining office, albeit in more subordinate posts. Even when the structural changes are more far-reaching and few of the old élite survive, the new political élite will tend to incorporate considerable elements drawn from relatively privileged milieux under the old order, partly as members or even leaders of the revolutionary movement itself, and partly as post-revolutionary recruits possessing skills valued by the new regime. Finally, the new élite in its initial, post-revolutionary, phase is frequently disturbed by tensions between the emergent privileged strata and the groups in whose name the revolution has been made, and between the old revolutionaries and the Johnny-come-lately and Vicar of Bray experts and administrators.

IDENTIFYING THE ELITE

The 'élite' concept is most useful and least fraught with theoretical difficulties when employed relatively, to embrace those individuals manifesting in relatively high degree attributes valued by the group concerned and unequally distributed amongst its members. Given this approach, which does not necessarily commit the researcher to an 'élitist' view of society or of politics, how broad the stratum of 'top people' he chooses to define as the 'élite' becomes a matter of analytical convenience. In complex societies members rank differently with respect to different socially-valued attributes, giving rise to a number of separate though often overlapping élites: political, economic, religious, artistic, sporting, military and so on. In distinguishing and identifying these élites serious definitional problems arise, especially when cross-societal comparisons are being attempted.

Our approach to locating the boundaries of the political élite is essentially that proposed by Geraint Parry and summarized in his phrase 'élites in politics',[1] which means that we are prepared to include in the political élite persons whose primary identification is with some sphere other than the political when they manifest a secondary political involvement of sufficient importance. By 'political' here we mean 'pertaining to authoritative and enforceable decisions for the society at large or some local division of it'.

Scholars have tackled the problem of identifying élite members in a number of different ways: in terms of formal rank, office or title, by establishing who have a reputation for being top people in the society concerned, by studying who most influence major political decisions, and so on. For students of party–state bureaucratic polities of the Soviet type several approaches are ruled out by the conditions of research. The role and structure of the party in such polities, however, offer a ready-made solution to the identification problem. In Soviet-type systems there is no institutionalized distinction between politics and administration, but there is a close relationship between the political importance of an office and the party standing of its incumbent. By the same token, party standing is usually a reliable index of the political significance of members of the economic, military and other élites. Thus the Soviet political élite in its broadest sense can be identified with the totality of party members, and in its narrowest sense with the members of the Political Bureau of the Party Central Committee. Similarly, depending on how broad the stratum we are interested in and whether we wish to focus on the national, regional or local level, the delegates to party conferences and congresses and the members of party committees and their bureaux at different echelons provide us with a generally reliable indication of who the political élite are. It is true that in the late Stalin era and especially since Stalin's death this identification has been somewhat blurred by the inclusion among conference delegates and even committee members of a certain amount of political 'ballast' – individuals of marginal political significance added to provide a measure of 'virtual representation' for various politically 'under-privileged' groups. This particular hypocrisy, however, was in little evidence in the early post-revolutionary period.

The data employed in this paper are drawn from official analyses of party congress delegates and the members of *gubernia* (provincial) and *uyezd* (district) committees (*gubkoms* and *ukoms*) supplemented by some additional party statistical information relating to broadly the same segments of the membership. Our attention will thus be focused on levels intermediate between the narrowest élite as represented by the Politburo and Central

Committee members and the broadest élite as represented by the party membership as a whole, both of which have been the object of considerable earlier research,[2] but some comparisons with these levels will be noted.

What can one hope to learn from such a study? Our opening paragraph embodies a number of hypotheses about the character-istics of the post-revolutionary Soviet élite – the reader has been spared the pedantry of having them formally set out as such – and an attempt will be made to test these against our data. Still, so what? It would be naïve in the extreme to assume that knowledge of the social background and characteristics of politicians will enable us to predict their political behaviour, or that changes in the relative frequency of different social characteristics in the political élite – class, occupational, ethnic, educational, etc. – can be taken as a measure of the shifting relative power of the social groups sharing these characteristics.[3] Yet few would go to the opposite extreme of asserting that such factors are always, or even usually, irrelevant to the operation of political systems and the performance of political actors: scarcely a day goes by on which news reports from some country or other fail to provide dramatic evidence to the contrary. In this respect knowledge of the composition of the political élite shares the same logical status as knowledge about other structural dimensions of the political system – institutional, ideological, and so on. Political science and political sociology cannot substitute for political history, yet the political historian will ignore their findings at his peril.[4]

In the case of the USSR the findings of research on the political élite has further significance in a number of distinct contexts: (*a*) in drawing out the implications of Soviet developments for certain assertions of Marxist and Leninist theory; (*b*) in evaluating 'bureaucratic degeneration' and 'new class' theories of the Soviet socio-political system; (*c*) in elucidating the factual basis of dis-putes between the ruling group and various opposition groups over the social character of the regime, beginning with the Workers' Opposition in 1920–1; (*d*) in providing data for comparative élite research. To explore all these lines of relevance would obviously be beyond the scope of a single chapter. Still, in setting ourselves the modest task of identifying some of the salient features of the Soviet political élite in the early post-revolutionary period, we hope that, in addition to any intrinsic interest our findings may have, they may also be of use to students of these broader problems, and this has influenced the questions we have addressed to our data.

OLD AND NEW BOLSHEVIKS

It was the Bolsheviks who seized power in October 1917, though they did so in the name of the workers and peasants and sought to enhance the legitimacy of their rule by channelling it through the soviets. Our first question, then, is how far these pre-October Bolsheviks served as the reservoir from which the new political élite was recruited in the first five years of the regime. Here we shall need to make some distinctions. The party underwent two periods of illegality. The first preceded the 1905 Revolution. In 1905 there were only 8400 Bolsheviks and many of these had dropped out and some had died before 1917. During the 1905 Revolution and the shortlived phase of legality that followed it tens of thousands of recruits entered the party, but the majority of these fell by the wayside when official repression resumed in 1907. In the difficult years before and during the First World War, however, numbers picked up again, and the estimated membership at the beginning of 1917 was 23 600.[5] It was these that constituted the genuine 'undergrounders' (*podpol'niki*) of the Bolshevik Party. With the downfall of the Tsarist regime the Bolsheviks, like the other opposition parties, recruited apace, and their numbers may have exceeded 400 000 by the time they took power.[6] Despite Civil War losses, the party still retained about 12 000 'undergrounders' in 1922 and over three times that number who had joined between the February and October Revolutions[7] – more than enough, one might have supposed, to have fully staffed the upper and middle levels of the new political élite even though they now constituted only a small minority of the total party membership.

As we see from Table 2.1, pre-October Bolsheviks did indeed monopolize the upper levels of the emergent political élite in the first two years of the new regime. Between 1919 and 1921, however, their numbers were heavily diluted with newcomers, and meanwhile the relative representation of *podpol'niki* and 1917 recruits also shifted sharply, the former dropping from three-quarters to little over one-third of Congress delegates. At the end of the Civil War there was a significant resurgence of *podpol'niki* at the expense of post-October recruits, owing largely to the return of prestigious Old Bolsheviks from the Red Army to the civil administration, and backed up by new personnel policies requiring specified periods of party membership for appointees to certain senior posts – policies reflecting for the first time sharp generational tensions within the new élite.

Table 2.1   *Analysis of voting delegates to party congresses, 1917–22, by time of joining party**

Year joined Party	6th Congress 1917		8th Congress 1919		9th Congress 1920		10th Congress 1921		11th Congress 1922	
Before 1905	24	97%	27	77%	16	49%	9	36%	13	48%
1905–16	73		50		33		27		35	
1917	3		23		24		26		26	
After October 1917	—		—		27		38		26	

*Based on figures in *Deviatyi s''ezd RKP (b) Mart-Aprel' 1920 goda: Protokoly* (Moscow, 1960), p. 481 (referred to hereafter as *IX s''ezd RKP(b)*), *Desiatyi s''ezd RKP(b) Mart 1921 goda: stenograficheskii otchët*, (Moscow, 1963) p. 762 (referred to hereafter as *X s''ezd RKP(b)*); *Odinnadtsatyi s''ezd RKP(b) Mart-Aprel' 1922 goda: Stenograficheskii otchët* (Moscow, 1961) p. 715 (referred to hereafter as *XI s''ezd RKP(b)*). The figures for those joining in 1917 given at the Tenth and Eleventh Congresses appear to include recruits in November–December.

During the Civil War there had been an influx of young recruits to local party posts, as the establishment of a full-time party apparatus coincided with the massive mobilizations of Bolsheviks for the front; the majority of *ukoms*, for instance, lost most of their more senior Old Bolsheviks, and as early as mid-1919 three-fifths of their membership were young men who had joined the party since the October Revolution.[8] Between 1919 and 1921 the party apparatus, and particularly its hierarchy of secretaries, established itself as the key organ of rule in the Soviet regime, and many of the young *apparatchiki* recruited in 1919 rose to high office. This is the situation that confronted the Old Bolshevik veterans of the

Civil War as they were demobilized in 1921–2. Naturally, pressure arose for a reshuffle of apparatus posts that would give due weight to the services of older members. The issue came to the surface at a conference of *gubkom* secretaries held in December 1921, and resulted in a Central Committee decision that *gubkom* secretaries must be Bolsheviks of pre-February Revolution standing and *ukom* secretaries members of at least three years standing. At the Eleventh Congress four months later, the prescription regarding *gubkom* secretaries was eased by making all those who joined before the *October* Revolution eligible.[9] Even then, however, no less than eighteen *gubkom* secretaries (over a quarter) were found to lack the prescribed length of service in the party, and the Personnel (*Uchraspred*) and Organization Departments of the Central Committee were instructed to replace them.[10] By mid-1922 candidates for seven of these posts had been nominated, but it was stated that suitable Old Bolsheviks were proving very hard to find, and it was estimated that it would take several months to fill all eighteen posts.[11] In fact this issue was destined to persist into the middle 1920s. Since there were still several thousand *podpol'niki* and tens of thousands of 1917 Bolsheviks to choose from, it would appear that the qualities required to staff the victorious communist regime were very rare among the surviving revolutionaries.

Looking a little more closely at those few hundred members of the post-revolutionary political élite important enough to gain election to party congresses, a further fact emerges about the *podpol'niki* among them: few of them had been prominent in party affairs before the Revolution. Only 13 per cent of the delegates to the Ninth Congress had attended party congresses before the October Revolution,[12] and at the Tenth Congress the proportion dropped to 5 per cent.[13] In view of the relatively small size and the peculiar circumstances of pre-revolutionary congresses, these figures may not be entirely conclusive, but there is other corroborative evidence on this point. Over two-thirds of the delegates to the Ninth Congress claimed to have had some experience of illegal work under the Tsarist regime and well over half of them had suffered arrest by the Tsarist police.[14] However, only 110 of the 530 delegates were actually engaged in illegal work or were in prison, exile or abroad at the time of the February Revolution,[15] and few of the remainder can have held positions of much influence in the revolutionary movement. Thus, within three years of the October Revolution, not only was a quarter of the emergent political élite drawn from adherents who joined after the party took power and a further quarter from the mass recruitment that followed the collapse of the Tsarist regime, but the majority of the remaining half, whose adherence to the party went back to its 'underground' days, had been relatively obscure or inactive before 1917, and rose to positions of prominence and authority only after the Revolution.

Moving down to the next broad stratum in the new political élite – the several thousand persons of sufficient political standing to earn places in the *gubernia* and *uyezd* committees of the party – we observe the same process of dilution of the revolutionaries by 'new men', but predictably moving farther and faster, so that by 1922 the latter constituted nearly half at the *gubkom* level and nearly three-quarters at the *ukom* level, while the *podpol'niki* had contracted to 16 per cent and 6 per cent respectively (see Table 2.2).

At the same time, there is ample evidence that *podpol'niki* became more and more common the closer one moved to the centres of power. This comes out clearly in Table 2.3, which compares the representation of different party membership generations at successively more senior levels of the *gubernia* level élite.

To complete the picture, we must note that far from all the

Table 2.2   *Analysis of* gubkom *and* ukom *members, 1919 and 1922, by time of joining party**

	Gubkoms		Ukoms	
Year joined party	1919	1922	1919	1922
Before 1917	31.2%	27.6%	16.3%	6.1%
During 1917	37.7	26.1	24.2	18.6
After 1917	22.9	44.0	54.8	70.5
Not Known	8.2	2.3	4.7	4.8

*Based on figures appearing in *Izv Ts K,* no. 9, December 1919, and no. 42, June 1922. The figures for 1919 are averages for 14 *gubkoms* and 144 *ukoms*, those for 1922 for 43 *gubkoms* and the *ukoms* contained in them.

Table 2.3   *Analysis of* gubernia *leadership in 1921 by time of joining party**

	Before 1917	1917	After 1917
All major *gubernia*			
level officials	10%	19%	70%
Members of *gubkoms*	37	27	36
Members of bureaux			
of *gubkoms*	44	23	33
Secretaries of *gubkoms*	52	21	27

*Based on figures appearing in *Izv Ts K,* no. 39, March 1922.

new recruits to the Bolshevik Party were political innocents. A significant number of recruits at all stages up to the Civil War were former members of other revolutionary parties. Some of those who transferred their allegiance during 1917, such as Trotsky and his small group of adherents, played a prominent part in the Revolution and occupied important posts in the new regime. Others threw in their lot with the Bolsheviks in the initial stages of the new regime. Analysis of a large sample of party members in October 1919 showed that 4.5 per cent had transferred from other parties – about half of them from the Socialist Revolutionaries and nearly a third from the Mensheviks.[16] This percentage declined during subsequent mass recruitment campaigns, but transferees from other parties remained a significant element in the Soviet political élite throughout the period under consideration.[17]

Interestingly, former members of other left-wing parties were far more common in the party élite than in the rank-and-file, and their numbers increased at successively higher levels. Thus a 1921 census of party members holding official posts in the provinces showed that 16 per cent at *uyezd* level and 24 per cent at *gubernia* level were former members of other parties.[18] Moreover, such converts tended to increase their share of the party élite throughout the early post-revolutionary period. Data on about three-quarters of the delegates to the Eighth Congress indicates that some 18 per cent were ex-members of other parties,[19] compared to 20 per cent of delegates to the Ninth Congress[20] and 25 per cent of those to the Tenth.[21] Ex-Socialist Revolutionaries and ex-Mensheviks were roughly equal in number, and between them provided the overwhelming majority. At the same time there were marked differences as between the main institutional divisions of the political élite in the relative weight of former members of different parties, as the breakdown of 'converts' among *gubernia* level officials shown in Table 2.4 indicates. One is struck here by the large proportion of ex-Mensheviks in the trade union apparatus, and there is evidence that nearly two-thirds of these joined the Bolsheviks as late as 1918–20.[22] The relatively low proportion of converts, particularly ex-Mensheviks, among those who acquired prominence in the military is also worth noting. On the other end, both ex-Anarchists and former liberals – though in both cases the numbers involved were very small – were relatively more common among the military than among other sections of the élite.

Table 2.4   *Former members of other parties among* gubernia *level officials, 1920**

	Mensheviks and other Social Democrats	Socialist Revolutionaries	Anarchists	'Bourgeois' parties
Party officials	17.0%	6.7%	0.6%	0.1%
Soviet officials	17.1	8.4	0.7	0.2
Trade union officials	23.2	8.5	0.8	—
Military officials	7.6	7.6	1.5	0.7

**Izv Ts K,* no. 29, 7 March, 1921.

The political élite that formed in the first years of the Soviet regime, then, was drawn from three sources: persons who had been active in the new ruling party before the Revolution, converts from other opposition (mainly revolutionary) parties, and persons who became active politically and identified themselves with the Bolsheviks only after they took power. Predictably, the first group was predominant immediately after the Revolution, but their dilution by members of the other two groups, and particularly the last, set in very quickly, so that within four or five years of the establishment of the new regime the revolutionaries were heavily outnumbered by 'new men' on all but the topmost levels of the élite. While it is true that the 'Old Bolsheviks' remained greatly over-represented in the élite in proportion to their numbers, it is obvious that a large proportion of them remained in humble positions. The requirements of rule thus evidently imposed principles of recruitment to the élite that cut across considerations of past loyalty and service. We move, then, from the political background of the members of the new élite to a consideration of their personal and social characteristics.

CHARACTERISTICS OF THE NEW ELITE

If the Communist Party in these early years was overwhelmingly a party of young men,[23] this was scarcely less true of the emergent political élite. It was only at the very summit that the younger middle-aged (35–50) prevailed.[24] Only 12 per cent of the delegates to the Eighth Congress were aged over forty,[25] 7 per cent of those to the Ninth congress[26] and 8 per cent of those to the Tenth Congress.[27] Between 1917 and 1921 the average age of Congress delegates remained steady at about thirty.[28] This indicates the constant rejuvenation of the political élite during these years. With the reincorporation of many Old Bolsheviks into the regional leadership at the end of the Civil War, however, a significant shift in the age-structure of the political élite became apparent: between the Tenth and Eleventh Congresses, delegates aged in their twenties decreased from 52 to 44 per cent, while those aged in their thirties increased from 40 to 46 per cent.[29] Even then, however, with only 45 of the country's top 520 political figures aged over forty, the youthfulness of the Soviet political élite remained very striking. Similar patterns prevailed at subordinate echelons. In 1921 communists under the age of thirty made up 43 per cent of *gubernia* level officials and 45 per cent of *uyezd* level officials.[30] Again, however, there were marked differences as between the major divisions of the élite. A survey of *gubernia* level officials in 1920 showed the average age of trade union and soviet officials to be considerably higher than that of party and military officials. Fifty-seven per cent of the party officials were aged under thirty, compared with 47 per cent of the soviet officials, while the proportions aged over forty were 6 per cent and 12 per cent respectively.[31] As we noted earlier, the relative youthfulness of those staffing the new but increasingly crucial party apparatus became a source of intra-élite tension at the end of the Civil War.

Despite a feminist strain in their tradition which the Bolsheviks shared with other revolutionary parties and which has prompted the CPSU to constantly strive to increase its female membership, male predominance has always been very marked, and this predominance was imparted to the Soviet political élite in its formative phase. While a few women like Alexandra Kollontai lent colour to the Bolshevik leadership, and others like Elena Stasova and Lidia Fotieva served the top leaders faithfully behind the scenes, no woman ever gained a place in the Politburo, while Stasova was the only one to enter the Central Committee, and that only for two years.[32] There was a tendency for the number of women to decrease at successively higher levels of the élite. While women constituted about 8 per cent of the total party membership,[33] their share of official posts at the *uyezd* level in 1921 was 4.9 per cent and at *gubernia* level 3.6 per cent, [34] while they supplied only 2.7 per cent of the delegates to the Tenth Congress.[35] The party apparatus contained the largest proportion of women officials. Among *gubernia* level officials in 1920, 10 per cent of those in party posts were women, compared with 5 per cent in trade union posts, 4 per cent in the Soviet apparatus and 1 per cent in the military.[36] Modest though it was, the female element in the new political élite steadily declined as the regime entrenched itself. About 5 per cent of the delegates to the Ninth Congress were women,[37] 3 per cent to the Tenth,[38] and 2 per cent to the Eleventh.[39] The pressure on senior posts in the party apparatus as male 'Old Bolsheviks' were discharged from the Red Army seems to have told very heavily on the women *apparatchiki*: between July 1921 and February 1922 the proportion of female members of *gubkoms* fell from 3.0 per cent to 0.7 per cent.[40] Thus opportunities for women in the élite sector where they had most established themselves during the Civil War were drastically narrowed.

Politico-administrative careers in the Tsarist bureaucracy, as in the other state machines of Europe at that time, were open only to men. Thus the appearance of a few women in the Soviet political élite at all levels below the summit must have seemed rather revolutionary to many contemporaries. Seen in statistical terms, however, Russia's new political élite was scarcely less of a man's preserve than the one it replaced.

That half of the Russian Empire's population who were not Russians generally enjoyed very limited opportunities of entering the political élite, though there were some conspicuous exceptions. Resentment and bitterness bred by national discrimination and repression ensured that many young non-Russians gravitated to the revolutionary parties, and the Bolsheviks recruited a good share, many of whom played a leading role both in the underground organizations and the *émigré* leadership. It is not surprising, therefore, that non-Russians, particularly Jews, Poles, Latvians and Georgians, were prominent in the new Bolshevik regime,[41] and that ethnic Russians formed little more than half of the new political élite in its initial phase – a proportion, it bears mentioning, which more than corresponded with their percentage in the country's population. However, while non-Russians held their own in the inner executive bodies of the party and the state, there was a marked Russification of the political élite as a whole in the years 1917–22, owing largely, no doubt, to the fact that the main area of effective Soviet rule throughout most of this formative stage consisted of the central regions of European Russia, roughly corresponding with sixteenth-century Muscovy.

In the party at large, nearly three-quarters of all members were ethnic Great Russians by 1922.[42] As we see in Table 2.5, the same trend was apparent in the ethnic composition of the top few hundred of the political élite. There was, however, some reversal of this trend in 1921–2, owing primarily, it would seem, to the consolidation of Bolshevik authority in the largely non-Russian southern and eastern areas of the country at this time. Table 2.5 also reveals substantial changes in the relative representation of different non-Russian nationals, notably the sharp decline in the number of Poles and Latvians, the slight falling-off in Jewish representation, and the emergence of a significant Turco-Tatar group. Unfortunately, our picture of the representation of Ukrainians and Belorussians is incomplete. It is not clear whether or not delegates of these nationalities at the Tenth and Eleventh Congresses were classified as Russians, though in the former case at least they almost certainly were.

Table 2.5   *Nationality of CPSU Congress delegates, 1917–22**

	Population 1926	Congress Delegates				
		Sixth 1917	Eighth 1919	Ninth 1920	Tenth 1921	Eleventh 1922
Russians	53%	54%	62%	70%	72%	65%
Ukrainians	21	4	4	3		
Belorussians	3	1	1	2		
Jews	2	17	16	14	14	15
Latvians }	1	10	7	6	5	4
Poles }		5	3	2		
Turco-Tatar Nats.	12			1	4	4
Georgians	1	4	1		1	2
Armenians	1	1	1		1	2
Others	6	5	5	2	3	8

*Based on figures in *Shestoi s"ezd RSDRP(b) August 1917: Protokoly* (Moscow, 1958) p. 294 (referred to hereafter as *VI s"ezd RSDRP(b)), VIII s"ezd RKP(b),* p. 451, *IX s"ezd RKP(b),* p. 480, *X s"ezd RKP(b),* p.760, and *XI s"ezd RKP(b),* p. 716. The analysis for the Sixth Congress is based on data on approximately two-thirds of all delegates, voting and non-voting, that for the Eighth Congress on about three-quarters of all delegates, and those on the Tenth and Eleventh Congresses on between 96 and 99.6 per cent of voting delegates only. Population figures adapted from Frank Lorimer, *The Population of the Soviet Union* (League of Nations, Geneva, 1946) p. 51.

The Great Russian predominance became even more marked in lower élite strata. In 1921 79 per cent of *gubernia* level officials and 89 per cent of *uyezd* officials were Russians. Jews, who were the next most numerous nationality, were only half as common among *uyezd* officials as they were among *gubernia* officials.[43] It is clear that, in contrast to the ethnically very mixed Old Bolsheviks whom they were coming increasingly to replace, and to the cosmopolitan ex-*émigré* element in the inner leadership, the 'new men' recruited to the party and co-opted to the élite after the Revolution were overwhelmingly Great Russian in nationality, and there is some evidence that this brought a resurgence of traditional Russian political and social attitudes and thought-patterns, as well as a strong current of 'great power chauvinism', within the Soviet political élite. The concern which Lenin began to express on this score in 1922 is well known.[44] In a number of non-Russian areas, ethnic tensions within the communist political élite were apparent as early as 1921. In Bashkiria enmity between Russians and natives in the local party machine was said to have reached such a pitch that party activities in the region were virtually paralyzed.[45] It is perhaps not too fanciful to suggest that the human foundations were being laid during this period for that identification of the Soviet political élite with past emanations of the Russian state, which was to come out into the open in the later 1930s.

WORKERS, PEASANTS – AND OTHERS

The Bolsheviks claimed, and Soviet spokesmen have continued to maintain, that the October Revolution placed political power in the hands of the workers and (more ambiguously) of the poorer peasants. The relationship between class, party and regime has always been rather obscure in Soviet political theory, which has operated with vague and often conflicting notions of representation and participation and manifested an ever-growing hypocrisy in its discussion of this issue. Yet whether or not one finds a class-reductionist view of politics convincing, it would seem that any meaningful vindication of this claim would have to show that the 'hands' of those exercising power, that is, of the new political élite, were in their great majority the hands of workers and poorer peasants. After all, Lenin defined the 'dictatorship of the proletariat' as meaning 'in essence' dictatorship by the Communist Party, while it was frankly admitted up to 1921 that military-style discipline prevailed in intra-party relations, the upper ranks being chosen predominantly by appointment and co-option rather than by election, and decisions being taken executively with little or no consultation of the 'party masses' – these things being justified by the demands of the Civil War. If, in these circumstances, workers and poorer peasants did not predominate in the upper circles of the party, it is difficult to see in what sense these social groups could be said to 'rule'. This, of course, would still leave open the question whether those who *did* rule could fairly be said to do so on behalf of, or in the interests of, these social groups.

One does not need to subscribe to the Utopian notions evident in Lenin's *The State and Revolution* ('any housewife can manage the State', etc.) to suppose that the many thousands of workers in the Bolshevik movement *might well* have included enough self-taught men of intelligence and ability to staff the new political élite. After the Revolution, and particularly as the Civil War got under way, Lenin became convinced that experts were necessary after all in various fields of administration, but they could be effectively controlled by placing Bolshevik workers in key posts. Experience in various Western countries, where working-class politicians with little formal education have often shown themselves perfectly capable of providing intelligent and effective leadership and of keeping their experts in their place, suggest that this picture was entirely feasible. In the Soviet case, the institutional device of the full-time party apparatus, supervising and co-ordinating all other organizations, seemed further to enhance the probability that proletarian 'red' might succeed in mastering bourgeois 'expert'.

There was, however, a complication scarcely evident in the Western cases – at least those in the English-speaking world: the tradition of a revolutionary movement whose leadership was drawn from the 'intelligentsia' and which placed a great store by verbal and literary facility and a sophisticated knowledge of 'theory'. Despite Lenin's frequent strictures on the intelligentsia, it was this group that gave the tone to at least the upper levels of the Bolshevik movement in the pre-Revolutionary period. At the top the 'intelligentsia' domination of the leadership was very striking even in numerical terms, and remained so after the Revolution. It was not till the Fifth Congress that the first worker entered the Bolshevik Central Committee. Only three of the twenty-five full members of the Central Committee chosen at the Sixth Congress in August 1917 had been workers, and five of the twenty-three chosen at the Seventh Congress in March 1918. Thereafter, with the rapid expansion of Central Committee membership, the proportion of workers increased, and reached 44 per cent by 1922.[46] Meanwhile, however, the new inner bodies in which the Bolshevik leadership institutionalized itself after 1919, in particular the Politburo, continued the same pattern of intelligentsia domination as the Central Committee itself had shown when it was the effective ruling body. The question then, is whether, despite their rarity at the summit, workers and poorer peasants were sufficiently predominant in wider circles of the political élite to lend some plausibility to the notion of these social groups as 'ruling'.

The two terms applied in party statistics for this period to persons who were *not* manual workers or peasants, namely *intelligentsiia* and *sluzhashchie* (roughly: 'officials'), were neither clearly distinguished nor used consistently by different sources. Although they originally carried very different connotations, the two terms ultimately converged in usage. This terminological confusion is a source of frustration to the researcher, for whom it is often a matter of importance whether a particular group referred to by one of these terms was made up more of *intelligenty* or of office-workers. None the less, the confusion is itself a fact of some political significance, since it appears to reflect an assumption of basic affinity between all non-manual employment groups. While this whole question remains obscure and requires much further study, it seems clear that this affinity was not seen as resting on family background or strictly occupational factors so much as on more general characteristics of personal and social style and attitudes. Since one of the most important formative influences here was probably formal education, and especially education beyond the elementary level, it may be instructive to look first at the educational profile of the new political élite before going on to investigate their occupational background.

Of the ten leaders who served on the Politburo during our period, six had received a higher education and the remainder a secondary school education (including one seminarist).[47] At the other extreme, in the party at large, while only 7 per cent in 1922 had completed a secondary or higher education,[48] this was still some 20–30 times the percentage in the population at large.[49] At this time a good half of Soviet adults were illiterate, whereas the percentage of illiterates in the party was inconsiderable.[50] There was evidently, then, a powerful tendency to educational selectivity at work in the formation of the Soviet political élite. Thus a sample of party committee members in 1919 showed that 18 per cent at *uyezd* level and 38 per cent at *gubernia* level were secondary school or university graduates.[51] In 1921 an analysis of *uyezd* and *gubernia* level officials (a considerably broader group than the committee members) revealed that 19 per cent of the former and 32 per cent of the latter possessed a secondary or higher education.[52] At congress delegate level the proportion possessing educational qualifications beyond the elementary level was greater still (see Table 2.6).

Table 2.6   *Education of CPSU Congress delegates, 1917–22**

Congress and year	Higher education	Secondary education	Less than secondary
Sixth – 1917	32%	23%	45%
Eighth – 1919	24	25	51
Ninth – 1920	21	23	56
Tenth – 1921	16	23	61
Eleventh – 1922	13	23	64

*Sources: *VI s''ezd RSDRP(b)*, p. 295, *VIII s''ezd RKP(b)*, p. 452, *IX s''ezd RKP(b)*, p. 480, *X s''ezd RKP(b)*, p. 761, *XI s''ezd RKP(b)*, p. 716. For the proportion of delegates covered in the Congress reports see footnote to Table 2.5. The 'higher education' category includes delegates who commenced but did not complete university courses. These are not shown separately for the Sixth and Eighth Congresses, but at the Ninth, Tenth and Eleventh they numbered 11, 8 and 5 per cent respectively. Included in the 'less than secondary' category are delegates who attended the relatively superior 'urban' schools; separate figures for these were given only at the Ninth Congress, where they numbered 14 per cent. This category also includes a smaller number who commenced secondary school but did not graduate; separate figures were given for these at the Tenth Congress, where they numbered 2 per cent, and at the Eleventh, where they numbered 6 per cent.

There are two ways of looking at this evidence. On the one hand, the regime clearly enjoyed very considerable success in recruiting persons of modest formal education to the new political élite. At the top, congress delegate level, the proportion who were not secondary school or university graduates ranged from 45 to 64 per cent between 1917 and 1922.[53] On the other hand, one observes a marked correlation between educational qualifications and advancement within the élite.

In 1921 a party member who was a secondary school graduate was nearly three times as likely as a non-secondary school graduate to be an official at *uyezd* level, and six times as likely to be a *gubernia* level official or Congress delegate, while a party member with higher education was four times as likely as one who had not completed secondary school to be an *uyezd* level official, 15 times as likely to be a *gubernia* level official and 40 times as likely to be a Congress delegate.[54]

For the student of the social composition of the Soviet political élite the great importance attached to class factors in the official ideology is a mixed blessing. On the one hand, it has generated a large amount of pertinent data, especially during the pre-Stalin and Khrushchev periods. On the other hand,it has provoked at times a great deal of distortion and concealment. During the period studied in this article, official distortion was mercifully rare, and one notes on the contrary a marked frankness and honesty about such matters. However, there was sometimes a strong incentive for individuals joining the party themselves to give incorrect information about their background, and the confused conditions of the time must often have made this easy. In later years some thousands of members who joined in this period were expelled for allegedly concealing their class origin. Since by this time, however, the credibility of official sources was wearing thin, it is impossible to estimate the actual scale of such concealment: our guess is that it was quite small in numerical terms, though in the case of the highest social groups (gentry, upper bourgeoisie) it may have been proportionately great enough to produce serious errors in contemporary statistics. For our present purposes, one advantage of the social statistics published during this period was that they were based on the situation of party members at the time of the Revolution. Thus, although they provide little information about the family background of party members recruited to the élite, they tell us much about what pre-Revolutionary occupational groups these members were drawn from.

Table 2.7 represents an attempt to draw together for comparison the published data on the social composition of congress delegates from 1917 to 1922. The precision and comparability of these percentages should not be exaggerated. There were evidently some inconsistencies in the categories used by the original sources and some blurring due to incomplete coverage. More particularly, the fact that no 'no defined occupation' category was shown for Ninth and Eleventh Congress delegates suggests that the usual procedure during this period of determining social position in terms of pre-Revolutionary occupation was not followed in these cases and it is not clear what other basis was employed. It would appear, however, that at least the percentages shown for the Sixth, Eighth and Tenth Congresses are broadly comparable with each other.

The implications of Table 2.7 are best appreciated if seen

Table 2.7　　　*Social composition of Congress delegates, 1917–22**

| | Congresses | | | | |
	VI	VIII	IX	X	XI
Workers	42%	41%	59%	44%	49%
Peasants			5	3	7
Office workers	13	12	12	17	18
Intelligentsia	31	30	24	27	26
No defined occupation (largely students)	14	17		9	

*Sources: *VI s"ezd RSDRP(b)*, p. 295, *VII s"ezd RKP(b)*, p. 452, *IX s"ezd RKP(b)*, p. 481, *X s"ezd RKP(b)*, p. 760, *XI s"ezd RKP(b)*, p. 716. Percentages are given as of all delegates of whom details are available: for coverage see footnote to Table 2.5. Artisans (*remeslenniki*) have been shown as 'workers': these numbered 5 per cent at the Eighth Congress, 8 per cent at the Ninth, 4 per cent at the Tenth and 1 per cent at the Eleventh. At the Eighth and Tenth Congresses 'professional revolutionaries' were listed as a separate category (9 per cent and 2 per cent respectively); since at the Eleventh Congress these were specifically referred to as a sub-group of the 'intelligentsia', they have been so shown for these earlier Congresses as well. Details given at the Sixth and Eighth Congresses give some indication of the other 'intelligentsia' occupations. The actual numbers are as follows:

	Writers	Teachers	Medical	Lawyers	Statisticians	Technicians
Sixth	20	12	7	6	4	2
Eighth	6	19	8	8	5	16

The Eighth Congress report also listed six 'zemstvo officials' who have been included with the office workers. The 'office worker' category is variously referred to as *kantseliarskie rabotniki, sluzhashchie, kontorshchiki i drugie sluzhashchie*, etc. For a different 'official' summary for the Sixth and Eighth Congress delegates, see *IX s"ezd RKP(b)*, p. 485.

in relation to the educational data recorded in Table 2.6. The decline in the percentage with higher education corresponds with a reduced representation of the 'intelligentsia'. It is not the workers, however, that benefit from this. Despite the increased size of congresses (see note 53), the proportion of worker delegates at the end of the Civil War remained about the same as at the inception of the regime. The difference is made up, firstly, by a group of delegates of peasant background who emerged during the Civil

War, and secondly, by a substantial increase in the proportion
of delegates who worked in offices before the Revolution. The
growth in the latter category helps to explain why the percentage
of delegates with higher education dropped off. It is interesting to
note that this changed balance between the intelligentsia and office
workers appears also to have occurred in the general membership
of the party. While the proportion of non-manual workers in the
party remained remarkably steady at about 30 per cent throughout
the great expansion of 1917–21, there is substantial evidence that
far more of the non-manual recruits were office workers and far
less members of the intelligentsia than before 1917.[55]

Table 2.8   *Class composition of leading* gubernia *officials in*
              1920*

Main sphere of work	Workers	Peasants	Office workers	Intelligentsia	No data
Party	36.2%	6.9%	35.1%	12.5%	9.3%
Soviets	36.0	6.7	39.1	12.8	5.4
Trade unions	41.9	2.0	43.9	6.5	5.7
Military	25.0	3.8	46.9	9.9	14.4

*Source: *Izv Ts K,* no. 29, 7 March, 1921. The party officials category
comprised members and department heads of *gubkoms,* the soviet officials
category members, department heads, and heads of the main sub-departments of
gubispolkoms, the trade union category members of the presidia and department
heads of *gubernia* trade union committees, as well as the chairmen of the *gubernia*
committees of the principal unions. Composition of the military officials category
was not recorded.

In the *gubernia* and *uyezd* level leadership and officialdom
the advance of communists of peasant background was more
marked than at the party congress level, but otherwise no sharp
differences are apparent. Throughout the period, at all levels,
and in all fields, working-class members rarely formed a majority
and were quite often outnumbered by communists recruited from
non-manual occupations. Table 2.8, which reproduces an official
class analysis of *gubernia* level officials, as determined by their
basic pre-Revolutionary occupation, illustrates this pattern, and
also brings out the main differences between the various sectors of
the élite. By comparison with the party and soviet officials, trade
union officials included a higher proportion of manual and office

workers, and a small proportion of peasants and intelligentsia. One is struck by the low percentage of workers and the high percentage drawn from non-manual occupations among leading communists in the army. At the *uyezd* level the political élite generally included more peasants and office workers, and fewer workers and intelligentsia than at the *gubernia* level.

After 1920 the recruitment of peasant communists into the provincial élite became more rapid, and by 1922 28 per cent of *gubkom* members and 39 per cent of *ukom* members were people who had been peasants before the Revolution (ex-workers numbered 44 per cent and 38 per cent respectively).[56] This increase took place mainly at the expense of communists recruited from non-manual occupations and, while from the point of view of the 'proletarian' purist it simply meant the replacement of one lot of 'petit bourgeois' by another, it none the less involved a greater representation for strata of lower pre-Revolutionary status. It is also significant that Soviet provincial officialdom at the time the New Economic Policy was launched included so many in their ranks with personal experience of peasant problems.

OCCUPATIONAL BACKGROUND

Table 2.9 reproduces an official breakdown of a sample of *gubkom* and *ukom* members taken in May–June 1919. While some doubt attaches to the representativeness of this sample – particularly so far as the *gubkom* members are concerned – it is of interest as reporting the earliest relatively detailed data on the Soviet provincial élite. Comparison of the two levels already shows a stronger peasant representation at *uyezd* level and within the non-manual occupations a balance relatively more favourable to the intelligentsia as against the office workers at *gubernia* level.

The census of communist officials undertaken in the latter part of 1921 yielded rich information on the social composition of provincial officialdom. The fullest report available deals with nearly 15 000 officials working at *gubernia* and *uyezd* levels, and this is reproduced in Table 2.10. It includes all the principal officials in the provincial party, government and other bureaucracies, plus a group of more junior officials listed for promotion to top

Table 2.9   *Pre-Revolutionary occupation of* gubkom *and* ukom
             members – 1919*

	Gubkoms	Ukoms
Workers	31.4%	38.0%
Self-employed artisans	3.1	3.6
Farmers	3.1	8.3
Retail Trade		0.8
Teaching	9.3	7.3
Medical		1.4
Journalists	9.3	0.3
Statisticians		
Engineers	1.5	
Junior technicians		2.6
Office workers	9.3	22.0
Professional revolutionaries	1.5	
Students	9.3	15.6†
No information	22.1	

*Izv Ts K, no. 9, 20 December, 1919. The source gives both absolute numbers
and percentages, but makes some small errors in calculating the latter, which have
been corrected. The data refer to the members of 14 *gubkoms* and 146 *ukoms*.
†Source states: 'largely students'.

positions (the 'reserve'). As one would expect, the overall picture
at *gubernia* level is very similar to that obtaining in 1920 and
indicated in Table 2.8. Again, the most striking difference in occupational background as between *gubernia* and *uyezd* officials is the
far higher proportion of ex-peasants among the latter. The most
interesting aspects of these breakdowns, however, lie in the details.
It emerges, for instance, that about half the officials drawn from
the intelligentsia in the *gubernia* level élite had formerly been in
the free professions, while half had been employees of government
or private organizations.[57] Prewar occupants of administrative or
office posts made up 31 per cent of Soviet officialdom at the
gubernia level and 25 per cent at the *uyezd* level; in both cases
about one-third of those concerned had been employed in industry,
agriculture, transport or trade and two-thirds in various governmental or private bureaucracies. Former workers constituted a

Table 2.10   *Pre-war employment of 14 821 leading provincial communists in 1921**

		Gubernia officials	Uyezd officials	Reserve	Total
1. Agriculture					
(a)	Self-employed, farm labourers, petty functionaries	7.6%	19.6%	14.4%	16.3%
(b)	Administrative and office staff	1.0	0.6	0.6	0.7
2. Plants and Factories					
(a)	Workers and petty functionaries	19.4	18.6	20.8	19.0
(b)	Administrative and office staff	5.3	3.7	2.7	3.9
3. Transport					
(a)	Workers and petty functionaries	3.7	3.0	4.7	3.4
(b)	Administrative and office staff	1.6	0.9	1.8	1.2
4. Artisans					
(a)	Owners of workshops	1.6	1.7	1.5	1.6
(b)	Hired workers	5.3	5.8	6.6	5.9
5. Trade					
(a)	Administrative and office staff	2.5	2.3	2.6	2.4
(b)	Petty functionaries	2.7	2.8	3.2	2.9
6 State, public and private institutions					
(a)	Senior staff	20.3	17.5	14.9	17.7
(b)	Petty functionaries	4.0	3.4	3.2	3.5
7. Free professions		3.7	1.9	1.6	2.2
8. Others		5.0	4.4	4.8	4.5
9. Dependents		15.2	12.4	15.5	13.5
10. No data		1.1	1.4	1.1	1.4

*Izv Ts K, no. 39, March 1922.

large majority of those 1921 officials who had been employed before the War in industry, transport or trade, less than a third of whom at *gubernia* level and less than a quarter at *uyezd* level had been administrative or office workers. Altogether about one-third of all officials at both levels had been employed as wage-workers or petty functionaries in 1914, and of these a good half had been working in plants or factories. It is worth interpolating here some other relevant facts about that section of the Soviet political élite

who were former workers. The 1920 survey of *gubernia* level
officials summarized in Table 2.8 showed that nearly half the
former workers employed as party, soviet and trade union officials
and *over* half those in senior military posts had been working in the
metallurgical industries.[58] At the Ninth Congress in 1920 figures
were given of the trade unions to which delegates belonged and
again former metal-workers made up nearly half (45 per cent) of
all those in 'blue collar' unions.[59] One is tempted to relate these
facts to the image of the mighty-thewed, square-jawed ironworker
which was the party's standard symbol of the proletariat, and the
nature of this relationship might prove a fascinating study.

Perhaps the most striking fact to emerge from the 1921 census
was that almost a quarter of all senior Soviet officials in the
provinces who had acquired a definite occupational affiliation by
the outbreak of the First World War stated that they then occupied
more or less senior posts in governmental or private bureaucracies.
While it is unlikely that many of these had been in high-level jobs,
this represents significant elements of continuity between the old
élite and the new.

These data on the social composition of the new élite help to
explain the frustration and resentment among many working-
class communists at the direction being taken by the 'proletarian
revolution', which found political expression in the 'Workers'
Opposition' in 1920–1 and later in such illegal groupings as the
'Workers' Truth' and 'Workers' Group'.[60]

'ESTATES'

Although the system of social 'estates' established by Peter the
Great and his successors had lost much of its legal and practical
significance in the last decades of the Tsarist era, and exercised only limited direct influence on recruitment to the politico-
administrative élite, nevertheless the latter contained very few
persons originating in the 'peasant' estate (which included most
industrial workers as well as the farming population), and a
man's 'estate' remained the primary basis of his social identity.
Considerable interest therefore attaches to the data produced by a
question on respondents' pre-Revolutionary 'estate' included in the
1921 party census. Unfortunately, one in five of *gubernia* officials
and one in seven of *uyezd* officials left this question blank, and

it would scarcely seem too cynical to suggest that many of these came from 'higher' estates and were not anxious to advertise the fact. Although the data on this question are therefore more suspect than on most others, they appear worth recording (see Table 2.11), since they are evidently unique, and constitute the only available information on the family background as distinct from the occupational profile of the new élite. They provide further evidence of a revolutionary change in the social composition of the Russian political élite, with the formerly dominant strata being reduced to a tiny minority and representatives of the lowest stratum supplying the new majority. At the same time, this majority was scarcely an overwhelming one, and became less marked as one moved up from the *uyezd* to the *gubernia* level. A further interesting fact emerges when these data are compared with those on the pre-revolutionary occupations of the same respondents, shown on Table 2.10. They reveal a surplus of between 10 and 20 per cent in the numbers whose family background had placed them in the peasant 'estate', as compared with those who were employed as workers or peasants in 1914. In other words, the new political élite absorbed large numbers of individuals of humble origin who were already upwardly mobile before the old order collapsed.

Table 2.11   *Pre-Revolutionary estates of provincial officialdom in 1921**

Estate	Gubernia officials	Uyezd officials	Reserve	Total
Peasantry	51.5%	67.2%	58.6%	62.8%
Townsmen (*meshchane*)	19.6	13.5	16.1	15.1
Nobility	1.3	1.1	1.1	1.1
Clergy	1.0	1.1	0.9	1.0
Merchants	0.1	0.0	0.1	0.1
Raznochintsy (educated stratum of mixed non-noble origin)	5.1	2.0	1.9	2.5
Others	1.5	1.1	1.1	1.2
No data	19.5	14.0	20.2	16.2

*Izv Ts K, no. 39, March 1922.

SUMMARY AND CONCLUSIONS

The 'October Revolution' gave Russia a new political élite, manifesting very limited continuity with the élite that preceded it. This article has focused on the characteristics of this élite, not at the top leadership level but at the level of the few hundred who were most significant politically at the national stage and the few thousand who were most significant politically in the provinces. The data show that the Revolution dramatically widened access to the political élite for the following overlapping categories of the population, whose access had been limited or minimal before 1917:

(a)   members of revolutionary parties;
(b)   very young adults;
(c)   persons drawn from lower social strata, notably workers and peasants;
(d)   the poorly-educated;
(e)   non-Russians;
(f)   women.

The break in continuity was not complete. Within a very few years the new élite came to include a substantial minority who had held more or less senior administrative positions before the Revolution; since the Tsarist political élite, like the Soviet élite, was essentially administrative in character, these people can be regarded as having been at least on the fringes of the old political élite. More generally, certain salient characteristics of the old élite, notably formal educational qualifications acquired in Tsarist secondary schools and universities, became important assets in gaining access to the new élite and advancement within it.

Following through the composition of the new élite between 1917 and 1922, we find that it retained over this period its predominant youth and relatively large representation of lower social strata. On the other hand, it moved rapidly back towards pre-Revolutionary patterns with respect to the representation of women and non-Russians, although the residual gains of these groups remained significant. Furthermore, the revolutionaries who constituted the new élite in its initial phase were rapidly joined by and partly displaced by new men who adhered to the Bolshevik Party only after it gained power; by the end of our period, these 'new men' formed a substantial majority on all but the topmost echelons. These changes produced strains within the new political élite: between 'Old Bolsheviks' and 'new men', between Russians and non-Russians, and between workers and non-workers.

Persons who had previously been employed as manual workers or peasants never formed an overwhelming majority in the new political élite. At all levels former workers were matched or outnumbered by former occupants of non-manual occupations. Ex-peasants, who were very few immediately after the Revolution, increased to a substantial minority in the new élite in the course of the Civil War, especially at the lower levels. The new élite contained many persons whose family background classified them as of peasant 'estate' but who were in non-manual jobs by the time of the First World War, thus showing themselves to have already been upwardly mobile under the old order. Amongst those with a background of non-manual employment, former professionals and other members of the old intelligentsia increasingly gave way to men who had been employed in administrative or other office jobs under the old regime. The new political élite was not predominantly proletarian in origin. It was, however, predominantly plebeian, although certain characteristics associated with a privileged position under the old order constituted important assets for entering the élite and rising within it.

NOTES

1. Geraint Parry, *Political Elites* (Allen and Unwin, London, 1969) p. 13.
2. See in particular George K. Schueller, *The Politburo* (Stanford U.P., Stanford, 1951); George Fischer, *The Soviet System and Modern Society* (Atherton House, New York, 1968); and T. H. Rigby, *Communist Party Membership in the USSR, 1917-1967* (Princeton U.P., Princeton, N.J., 1968). John A. Armstrong's *The Soviet Bureaucratic Elite: A Case Study of the Ukrainian Apparatus* (Praeger, New York, 1959) deals with much the same strata as are discussed in the present article, focusing, however, on one republic in the late Stalin and early post-Stalin years.
3. See Dankwart A. Rustow, 'The Study of Elites: Who's Who, When and How', *World Politics, Vol. XVII* (July 1966) pp. 702-3. This excellent review article offers a sophisticated discussion of the problems under consideration here. See also Parry, *op. cit.;* T. B. Bottomore, *Elites and Society* (Watts, London; 1964); and Suzanne Keller, *Beyond the Ruling*

Class: Strategic Elites in Modern Society (Random House, New York, 1963).

4. Cf. Frederick W. Frey, *The Turkish Political Elite* (MIT Press, Cambridge, Mass. 1965), p. 157.

5. *Bol'shaia Sovetskaia Entsiklopediia,* lst edn, vol. II, col. 531. See also D. E. Gollan, 'Bolshevik Party Organization in Russia 1907–1912' (unpublished MA thesis, Canberra, Australian National University, 1967), pp. 68–9.

6. See Rigby, *op. cit.,* pp. 61–2.

7. *Izvestiia Tsentral'nogo Komiteta Rossiiskoi Kommunisticheskoi Partii (bol'shevikov),* nos. 7–8 (August–September 1923) p. 60 (referred to hereafter as *Izv Ts K*). Five years later, in 1927, there were still 9000 undergrounders in the party and 30 000 who joined in 1917. See *Bol'shaia Sovetskaia Entsiklopediia,* lst edn., vol. II, col. 537.

8. *Izv Ts K,* no. 9 (December 1919).

9. *XI s''ezd RKP (b),* pp. 50, 555, 659.

10. *Izv Ts K,* no. 42, (June 1922).

11. *Izv Ts K,* no. 43, July 1922.

12. *IX s''ezd RKP(b),* p. 483.

13. *X s''ezd RKP(b),* p. 762.

14. *IX s''ezd RKP(b),* pp. 482–3.

15. *IX s''ezd RKP(b),* p. 485.

16. *Izv Ts K,* no. 15, 24 March, 1920.

17. With the emergence of the 'Democratic Centralists' and 'Workers' Opposition' in 1920–1 ex-members of other parties began to attract attention as sources of disaffection and 'petit-bourgeois' ideas. Officials conducting the 1921 purge were instructed to scrutinize this category of party members with particular care (see *Izv Ts. K,* no. 33, October 1921), and they constituted nearly 5 per cent of all expelled or dropping out voluntarily during the purge (see *Izv Ts. K,* no. 4 (40) 1922).

18. *Izv Ts K,* no. 39, March 1922.

19. *Vos'moi s''ezd RKP(b) Mart 1919 goda: Protokoly* (Moscow, 1959), p. 452 (referred to hereafter as *VIII s''ezd RKP(b)*).

20. *IX s''ezd RKP(b),* p. 482.

21. *X s''ezd RKP(b),* p. 762.

22. *Izv Ts K,* no. 29, 7 March 1921. The connection, if any, between this influx of ex-Mensheviks and such developments as the emergence of the Workers' Opposition and the difficulties encountered by the regime in the trade union movement at the end of the Civil War is a question requiring further investigation.

23. See Rigby, *op. cit., ch. 11.*

24. On the Politburo, see Schueller, *op. cit.,* pp. 15, 45; on the Central Committee, see *Bol'shaia Sovetskaia Entsiklopediia,* 1st edn., vol. II, col. 539–40.

25. *VIIIs''ezd RKP(b),* p. 452. This percentage is based on incomplete data and includes delegates aged 40, whereas the percentages given for the Ninth and Tenth Congresses refer to delegates aged 41 and over.

26. *IX s''ezd RKP(b),* p. 480.

27. *X s''ezd RKP(b),* p. 760.

28. See *IX s''ezd RKP(b),* p. 486. No average age was published for Tenth Congress delegates but the detailed breakdowns into age-groups referred to in notes 26 and 27 indicate that the averages for these two congresses must have been very close.

29. Cf. *X s''ezd RKP(b)*, p. 760 and *XI s''ezd RKP(b)*, p. 367.
30. *Izv Ts K,* no. 39, March 1922.
31. *Izv Ts K,* no. 29, 7 March 1921.
32. Based on analysis of lists of Central Committee members.
33. *Izv Ts K,* no. 1, January 1923, gave the figure of 7.8 per cent for January 1922.
34. *Izv Ts K,* no. 39, March 1922.
35. *X s''ezd RKP(b)*, p. 760.
36. *Izv Ts K,* no. 29, 7 March 1921.
37. *IX s''ezd RKP(b)*, p. 480.
38. *X s''ezd RKP(b)*, p. 760.
39. *XI s''ezd RKP(b)*, p. 367.
40. *Izv Ts K,* no. 39, March 1922.
41. On the Politburo, see Schueller, *op. cit.,* pp. 9–12. On the relative over-representation of Great Russians among the pre-revolutionary Bolsheviks, see David Lane. *The Roots of Russian Communism* (Royal Van Gorcum, Assen, Netherlands, 1969) pp. 44–6.
42. See Rigby, *op. cit.,* p. 366.
43. *Izv Ts K,* no. 39, March 1922.
44. See Leonard Schapiro, *The Communist Party of the Soviet Union* (Random House, New York, 1960), pp. 220-7.
45. *Izv Ts K,* no. 37, January 1922.
46. See *Bol'shaia Sovetskaia Entsiklopediia*, 1st edn, vol. 11, col. 539-40.
47. See Schueller, *op.cit.,* pp. 23, 70.
48. *Izv Ts K.* no. 1, January 1923. Analysis of a substantial sample of party members in 1919 gave the proportion with secondary and higher education as 13 per cent. While some uncertainty attaches to these figures, the implication of a significant decline in educational levels in the party after 1919 seems plausible. See Rigby, *op.cit.,* p. 401.
49. In 1913 only 290 000 of the Russian Empire's population of 159 million (i.e., 0.2 per cent) possessed a secondary or higher education. (See *Itogi vsesoiuznoi perepisi naseleniia 1959 goda: SSSR,* (Moscow, 1962) p. 80.) The proportion cannot have been much higher in the early 1920s.
50. Rigby, *op.cit.,* pp. 401-3.
51. *Izv Ts K,* no. 9, 20 December, 1919.
52. *Izv Ts K,* no. 39, March 1922.
53. Table 2.6 suggests a steady decline in educational levels among Congress delegates. However, the number of delegates increased substantially with every Congress till those attending the Tenth were about three times as numerous as those at the Sixth. Thus the later Congresses clearly represented wider circles of the party élite than did the earlier ones, and since educational levels rose at successively higher echelons, some decline in average educational qualifications was to be expected. This steady expansion in Congress size (though with some reduction between the Tenth and Eleventh) is also relevant to interpreting the data in Tables 2.1 and 2.5, but the possibility of its having seriously disturbing effects on the comparison is considerably greater in the case of Tables 2.6 and 2.7. Nevertheless, one can say that, as the Bolshevik élite at national level expanded and entrenched itself after the Revolution, it recruited increasing numbers with modest educational attainments.
54. Based on data in *Izv Ts K,* no. 39, March 1922, and *X s''ezd RKP(b)*, p. 761.
55. See Rigby, *op.cit.,* pp. 67, 74-5, 85.

56.　*Izv Ts K,* no. 42, June 1922. There was a similar growth in peasant representation in the party at large, from 8 per cent in 1917 to 15 per cent in 1918 to 28 per cent in 1921. See Rigby, *op.cit.,* pp. 79, 85.

57.　On the reasonable assumption that the proportion of *gubernia* officials classified as 'intelligentsia' remained, as in the previous year, about 7 per cent (*Izv Ts. K,* no. 29, 7 March, 1921). An official attempt to collapse the 1921 figures reported in Table 2.10 into broad class categories did not separate intelligentsia and office workers. It gave the following breakdown of officials:

	Gubernia	Uyezd
Workers	35.1%	33.6%
Peasants	7.6	19.6
Office workers and intelligentsia	36.0	28.6
Dependants, etc.	21.3	18.2

　　(Izv Ts K, no. 39, March 1922)

58.　*Izv Ts K,* no. 29, 7 March 1921.

59.　*IX s''ezd RKP(b),* p. 485. The best represented 'blue collar' unions were the Metal-workers (87 delegates), Railways (22), Printers (17), and Textile-workers (11). 'White collar' unions included 'Responsible Workers' (113), Education and Culture (39), and Journalists (19). All but 160 of the 530 delegates covered were enrolled in some union or other.

60.　See Schapiro, *op.cit.,* pp. 209, 276–7, and Rigby, *op.cit.,* pp. 74–5, 104–8.

3. Early provincial cliques and the rise of Stalin*

Few scholars would disagree that Stalin's use of his power over appointments to build up a personal following or clientèle in the party apparatus was a major factor in his rise to dominance in the 1920's and 1930's. True, there are differences of emphasis on the significance of this factor. While some would accord it overwhelming importance in explaining Stalin's victory over his rivals and the consolidation of his dictatorship, others would place equal or even greater stress on such factors as his tactical skill in the power game at the top leadership level and his capacity to project policies attuned to the interests or psychology of wide circles in the party or the bureaucracy.[1] Single-cause explanations of important historical events are rarely convincing, and in this case too we would be wise to think in terms of the interplay between several factors, of which those mentioned are probably the major ones, operating in different mixes at different levels and at different times. In such a view Stalin's success in building up a clientèle within party officialdom would figure as a necessary but not a sufficient condition of his rise to dominance, and such indeed is how it appears in the best and most influential accounts of this matter.[2]

That it *was* a necessary condition remains true even if we take Trotsky's view that Stalin was more a tool of his followers ('the bureaucracy') than the other way round. For he could not have served their purpose unless he had both the motivation and the capacity to advance them and their interests against those of other party and government officials who supported his rivals, including Trotsky himself. However, while we may prefer the conventional wisdom as to who was rider and who was horse in this alliance,

*Soviet Studies, vol. XXXIII, no. 1 (January 1981) pp. 3–28.

Trotsky's view has the great merit of highlighting the *reciprocal* benefits involved. At the same time it should be apparent that assumptions of reciprocity are built into what I have called the 'conventional wisdom' as well, that is, an exchange of protection and advancement on the one hand against compliance and support on the other.

There is of course nothing unusual about one or more patron-client networks assuming key importance in a country's political system, whatever significance we place on the fact – usually evaded by Marxists – that perhaps the most egregious modern example is found in the country pioneering 'socialism'. Indeed recent years have seen the emergence of a considerable descriptive, comparative and theoretical literature on political clientelism, largely stimulated by its salience in the politics of 'modernizing' countries.[3] Students of Soviet politics have begun to take note of this literature, finding in it conceptual legitimation for what had become for many an academically suspect line of research.[4] Some very large questions remain unanswered, however, and indeed largely unasked. What were the origins of political clientelism in the USSR? How does it relate to the socio-political system generally? Has its character and importance changed over time? If we wish better to understand the dynamics and developmental tendencies of the Soviet political system, such questions will need to be seriously examined.

But are we making problems where none exist? Is not the clientelist network a universal human phenomenon? Why should its existence in the Russia of the 1920's require special explanation? As for its salience, is it not sufficiently explained by the pressures and temptations of 'democratic centralism' and the ambitions and cunning of Stalin? Alas, this will not do. Well-nigh universal it may be, but political clientelism varies enormously over time and place as to its importance and its role in the political system as a whole, and such differences are usually found to depend not only on specificities of political structure but on prevalent norms and practices in the wider society. This will be apparent if one enquiries why eighteenth-century political parties in Britain were dominated by patronage but twentieth-century parties are not, why political clientelism is salient in Italy but far less so in France, or why it is salient in *both* contemporary China *and* contemporary Japan.[5] If it flourished so luxuriantly in the Russia of the 1920s, then it may have found particularly favourable soil there. Perhaps this is where we should start looking.

Before broaching the question of origins, however, it may be worth recalling some relevant characteristics of the 'developed socialist society' of the Soviet Union today. We are all familiar with the importance for Soviet citizens of *svyazi* (connections) and *protektsiya* (patronage, protection) in managing their everyday lives. One's success in building up networks of reciprocal favour can be vital for everything from obtaining food and other consumer items in short supply to organizing repairs to one's apartment or dacha, from obtaining theatre tickets to securing inclusion in a 'delegation' to the West. Within the workplace *protektsiya* can be helpful or even essential in securing advancement or in diverting with impunity official resources for personal benefit. For the achievement of production plans administrators often depend heavily on their *svyazi* to overcome hold-ups in supply of materials or components or to cope with other difficulties. The scale and pervasiveness of such reciprocal services has led some scholars to speak of a 'second economy' of which they constitute the major component.[6]

Now students of political clientelism in other settings have often drawn attention to the prevalence in societies in which it flourishes of norms and practices akin to those just described,[7] and there is indeed an obvious congruence between the two: both rely on personalized, informal relationships of reciprocal favour rather than on the impersonal, formal rules of a 'modern' capitalist market or bureaucracy. Of course it is not argued that 'connections' and 'protection' play *no* part in the private or public organizations of 'modern' capitalist societies, but simply that they appear to be of marginal significance there rather than of central importance as in certain other countries. The nature of the linkages between clientelism in the political sphere and the reliance on connections and protection in everyday life will naturally depend on the institutional structure of the country concerned as well as on its cultural specificities. Against this background, can we view the 'second economy' of the Soviet Union as being matched by a 'second polity', centring on clientelist relationships?

Certainly there is some well-known *prima facie* evidence of such a clientelist 'second polity'. At the summit of power the recent elevation to key party and government posts of former subordinates of Brezhnev from his days in Zaporozh'e, Dnepropetrovsk and Moldavia parallels Khrushchev's earlier 'packing'of the leadership with his old Ukrainian and Moscow oblast 'cadres', and before that again the fluctuating fortunes of long-time protégés of Zhdanov, Malenkov and others of Stalin's lieutenants. At lower echelons accusations levelled against various oblast, republican and district party secretaries over the last two decades of having filled senior posts in their bailiwicks with their cronies echo similar accusations made during the 1950s, 1940s and earlier. Indeed political clientelism appears to be one of the most durable features of the power system bequeathed by Stalin to his successors. In this context it is ironical that perhaps the most frequently quoted 'exposure' of clientelist practice was made by Stalin himself, in the course of his speech to the February–March 1937 plenum of the Central Committee, when he taxed certain party leaders transferred from one region to another with having dragged along large numbers of their protégés to serve under them in their new posts.[8] The irony is a double one, since in the immediate aftermath Stalin was to kill off most of his own prominent followers, including the particular leaders attacked.

The question therefore arises: does clientelist politics in the USSR owe its origins to the Stalinist system, with Stalin filling top provincial posts with his protégés and these 'little Stalins' proceeding to do the same in the districts under their command, and so on down the line? Or did clientelist practices arise spontaneously on the basis of informal social norms and relationships prevailing in the early Soviet period, Stalin simply having the wit to make use of them and to weave them into a system of personal dominance? A single paper can scarcely attempt a definitive answer to this question. However, it can bring together some of the relevant evidence and perhaps suggest some tentative conclusions.

One question which should be simply noted at the outset, only to be set aside out of considerations of space, is the extent to which the citizens of early Soviet Russia had been disposed by their social formation and experiences in the pre-Revolutionary past to rely heavily on informal reciprocal relationships in the conduct of their lives.Certain it is that such relationships and specifically clientelist behaviour were far from unknown in the bureaucracies of imperialist Russia, though their extent and contours have never been systematically studied.[9] However emphatically Bolshevik officials may have rejected such elements of the traditional 'political culture', many may have become unconsciously infected by them in the process of working in and through offices largely staffed by functionaries inherited from the old regime. It would be too facile, however, to rely on such speculations in explaining the early emergence of clientelist behaviour in the Soviet regime, and we would do better to ask ourselves whether there were not aspects of the actual situation in which Bolshevik officials found themselves which encouraged such behaviour.

At the time of the seizure of power the key positions in the new organs of government, both at the centre and locally, were allocated by the corresponding Bolshevik party committee and by and large filled from their own number with the addition of some other local Bolsheviks of high standing in the party. Recruitment to secondary posts, however, was far more spontaneous and personalized, and it is not surprising that top officials, faced with exercising totally new responsibilities for which they possessed little or no relevant experience or training, tended to seek out assistants whom they knew from earlier association to be loyal, effective and reliable. Lenin set an immediate example, making V. D. Bonch-Bruevich his Head of Chancery in *Sovnarkom* and L. A. Fotieva his principal secretary (and later Secretary of *Sovnarkom*); these had been his closest assistants (apart from his wife) when he was seeking to direct the infant Bolshevik movement from Geneva in the early years of the century. Other leaders followed suit. For example, Sheila Fitzpatrick reports that the first officers recruited by Lunacharsky to his Education Commissariat were drawn from former associates on the cultural-educational sectors of the Petrograd Duma and Party Committee.[10] These trusted associates were often found very close to hand, in the shape of wives or other near relatives. Again, the example was set at the highest level. Party secretary Sverdlov had his wife K. T. Novgorodtseva as one of his principal assistants in the embryo Central Committee apparatus. Looking around those assembled at a *Sovnarkom* meeting in 1918, Lenin was liable to encounter the cherished faces of his wife Nadezhda Krupskaya (there as Deputy People's Commissar of Education), his sister Anna (likewise representing the Education Commissariat) and his brother-in-law M. T. Elizarov (as Acting People's Commissar of Railways and later head of the Insurance Administration). As this example indicates, close relatives of top Bolsheviks might well be placed not only on the latter's personal staffs but in leading posts in other organs of the regime. As Fitzpatrick reports, the Education Commissariat became, 'like the *Zhenskii otdel* [Department for Work among Women] of the Central Committee and, in later years, Ryazanov's Marx–Engels Institute – a place of employment for wives and sisters of Bolshevik politicians: its members included the wives of Lenin, Trotsky, Zinoviev, Kamenev, Dzerzhinsky, Krzhizhanovsky and Bonch-Bruevich, Lenin's sister Anna Elizarova and the two sisters of Menzhinsky'.[11]

It would be misleading to characterize such appointments of former associates or close relatives simply as patronage or nepotism as these terms are commonly understood. For the most part these people were valued first and foremost as trusted and readily *available* fellow revolutionaries eager to give loyal service to the infant regime in a situation where reliable and devoted lieutenants were at a premium and had to be found without delay. Nevertheless, it would be unrealistic to suppose that motives of personal attachment and mutual commitment played no part; certainly it would have been difficult to convince Bolshevik officials at lower echelons that they were entirely absent.

It is provincial officialdom that commands particular attention for the purposes of this paper, since it is generally agreed that it was from their number that Stalin's clientèle was to be mainly drawn. And it can be shown, I believe, that, however influential the example of the top leadership may have been in undermining inhibitions to clientelist behaviour in the provinces, the conditions under which provincial officials functioned tended independently to generate such behaviour. The grounds for this view warrant consideration in some detail.

The twenty thousand or so members of the Bolshevik underground on the eve of the downfall of the monarchy were distributed through several dozen regional organizations, based mainly on the provincial (*gubernia*) divisions of the empire, and enjoying a considerable degree of local autonomy and democratic participation both in making decisions and choosing their leaders. The central leadership could exercise only the most general guidance and control, and for the most part had little information as to what was going on in the local organizations. When a directive or organizer arrived from the centre the embattled local committees usually welcomed this as assistance rather than resenting it as interference. Not surprisingly, these regional organizations often developed something of a distinct 'culture' of their own, particularly the largest ones in Petrograd, Moscow, the Urals and the Donbass, and this persisted into the early post-revolutionary period despite the vast influx of new members.

Following the Bolshevik seizure of power in Petrograd, the local Bolshevik committees organized similar takeovers in the provincial centres and began to establish a new Soviet administration led by their key members. The transformation of the core of the party into a salaried officialdom had begun, though it is important to note that at this stage there was virtually no full-time *party* apparatus as such. The Soviet state apparatus proliferated vastly in 1918 and 1919, staffed partly by party members but perforce largely by former officials and other middle-class people who then frequently sought and were granted party membership. It would be unjustified to make bland assumptions about the reasons why people, both workers and non-workers, joined the party during these years of extreme danger and deprivation, but it is a fact that possession of a party card could give a vital advantage in the competition for jobs, housing, improved rations and security.[12] An official analysis of a large sample of party members in October 1919 showed that 60 per cent were officials of governmental or other official organizations, a quarter in the Red Army – very few of whom could have been ordinary soldiers – and 11 per cent worked in factories.[13] Another contemporary sample, taken from the central provinces of Russia proper and excluding the military organizations, showed that only 4 per cent were workers or peasants holding no administrative position; 57 per cent were in government jobs and the rest in other positions of authority, mostly in industrial and commercial organizations.[14]

Meanwhile important changes were transforming the character and position of the local party committees. First there was the extension of centralized control, direction and discipline over provincial officialdom which began early in 1918 and was greatly accelerated as the Civil War got under way. The executive committees of the provincial and local soviets lost most of their original autonomy (the soviets themselves atrophied) and were largely thrust aside by the local agents of the Cheka, the Food Supplies Commissariat and the Military Councils, armed with 'exceptional powers' and accountable only to their superiors in Moscow. In this situation, the party committees were at first unable to exert much administrative authority and were little more than a propaganda appendix to the state bureaucracy. Concern over this tendency was voiced as early as the Seventh Party Congress in March 1918, but it was not till the next Congress a year later that serious steps were taken to reassert the authority of the party committees by (1) making them responsible for the allocation of local party members to posts in all fields, including formally elective posts; (2) strengthening their guiding and disciplinary powers over party members working in government and other organizations exercised through the party caucuses (*fraktsii*) in these bodies; and (3) making their key members full-time, salaried officials backed up by their own administrative apparatus.[15] Although it took them some time to get organized and their control over the locally deployed officials of powerful central agencies remained limited till the latter were curbed at the end of the Civil War, by 1921 the hierarchy of party committees was well on the way to exercising that key role in the Soviet political system which it has retained ever since. Ironically, while intended in part to counter the bureaucratization of the regime by separating the party from state officialdom and giving it power to control the latter, these measures had the effect of further entrenching bureaucratization by extending it to the party itself.

These developments have attracted much attention from Western historians who have read various lessons into them depending on their preconceptions. Most accounts have focused on the confrontations between successive opposition groups and the group in power concerning the former's accusations of overcentralization, bureaucratization, the elimination of 'worker's control', of growing inequalities, the employment of 'bourgeois' officials and army officers, and so on. However, our interest here is directed at what was happening in the provincial organizations, and although fights over these large issues sometimes erupted here as well, it would be a great mistake to imagine that they dominated the political life of many of these organizations for much of the time. Fights there certainly were in these organizations, but to understand what they were about we must look a little more closely at their circumstances.

First, the membership of party committees had changed much since the seizure of power. Some established members became totally absorbed into the government machine. Many others went into the Red Army (sometimes as volunteers, sometimes under mobilization orders) and of these some perished, some returned to take other senior positions, and some, as befits old soldiers, simply faded away. Their place was taken by young men (and a handful of women) who for the most part were astonishingly recent recruits to the party. As early as 1919 less than a third of the members of provincial (*gubernia*) committees and a sixth of those of county (*uyezd*) committees had been in the party before the February Revolution.[16] The majority of those called upon to exercise the powers of the new party machine, therefore, whatever might have been their motives for throwing in their lot with the Bolsheviks, could claim neither much political experience nor the kind of revolutionary commitment which leads men to enter an illegal organization. Nor were most of them former workers,[17] so they could scarcely join unreservedly in Opposition condemnation of those other Johnny-come-latelys of middle-class background who were now staffing government offices in such large numbers.

Next, the conditions of work. Since communists running the party committee, the executive committee of the soviet, the Cheka, the local military command, the economic council and so on were all under unrelenting pressure from their respective superiors in Moscow to perform the impossible with pitifully inadequate means, and their formal powers and mutual relationships were extremely weakly defined, they were inevitably brought into constant conflict or else arrived at informal accommodations usually involving the violation of instructions and mutual cover-up. The party leadership was quick to see the pathological side of this – and there were always plenty of critics to draw it to their attention – but they never did seem to perceive the necessity of the 'informal organization' if provincial officials were to do their job at all. Their 'solution', first resolved on at the Eighth Congress in 1919, was to shift officials around constantly. At the Ninth Congress the following year the Central Committee secretary Krestinsky, explaining that he and his staff had so far lacked the resources to undertake systematic reassignments, stated that they had limited themselves to cases where conflicts between rival groupings had reached the point where total paralysis of the local administration threatened, and then they had simply taken the members of one group (usually the weaker – very occasionally both groups) and transferred them to new jobs outside the province, sending in 'reinforcements' from elsewhere.[18] The latter were sometimes placed in the key positions, whereupon fresh conflicts might arise between these 'appointees' (*naznachentsy*) and the previously dominant group, in which the former tended to prevail with the backing of the Central Committee.

Nor must we ignore more purely personal factors. The conditions of chaos and deprivation which made the fact of party membership a vital resource in ensuring the necessities of life placed an even greater premium on responsible office. Money wages were relatively equal, but during the Civil War most payment was in kind,[19] supplies were more often than not insufficient, and distribution was in the hands of political and administrative authorities. While it is difficult to estimate the incidence of gross corruption, a certain level of 'abuse of position for personal ends' seems to have been fairly general, at least to the extent of ensuring that you did get your rations even if others went short, that you got a little extra, and that you had priority access to the occasional 'luxuries'. For this reason and in order to benefit from the innumerable services and immunities which officials were able to grant or withhold, it was essential to establish good connections with your fellow communists staffing the various official agencies in your province.

By 1920 this had generated such intense dissatisfaction among those excluded from these advantages and such agonized heart-searching among a section of the leadership that it became the central issue of a party conference held in September of that year, under the revealing rubric of 'On returning the party to health' (*ob ozdorovlenii partii*).[20] The two major opposition groups which had recently emerged and were strongly represented at the conference, the 'Democratic Centralists' and the 'Workers' Opposition', blamed the 'disease' on the methods of 'bureaucratic centralism' which had become entrenched during the Civil War, but while the former saw the problem mainly in decision-making terms (hierarchy versus democracy) the latter saw it in sociological terms (centralized administrative methods excluded the workers from influence over affairs and put power and privilege in the hands of 'bourgeois specialists', whose mores set the tone for party officialdom – all too often of bourgeois origin themselves).[21] There was something in both these judgements and, although nobody – and least of all the official rapporteur

Zinoviev – offered a penetrating analysis of what was going on in the local organizations, the transcript of this conference is a rich source of illustrations and revealing sidelights on the developments outlined above. A few brief extracts must suffice:

> It is no secret to anyone that in many places the word 'communist' has become a term of abuse simply because some communist, be it at the centre or locally, allows himself such a level of luxury that a worker or peasant cannot fail to form the attitude towards him that his behaviour is not in the slightest degree better than the behaviour of the old time bourgeois [Sapronov].[22]
>
> We should achieve the situation where the communist party, its members, not only do not have privileges, but where every communist knows that we will make him answerable for his abuses by the same standards (*po tomu zhe sudu*), and even more so, as the *spetsy*. . . This is where the main problem lies: in the localities they are afraid to arrest a man if he has power, the man may be a public scandal but they are afraid to touch him [Rykov].[23]
>
> As you know, there is a decree about the distribution of gold, which lays down that private individuals are not allowed to have more than 20 grains (*zolotniki*). However, one can observe that in our soviet [government] agencies our soviet ladies have put on a whole shop-window of gold, wherever they've dug it up from. We're told that we are just pointing to trifles. But when we meet the same phenomenon in the party, when we meet the same *grandes dames* with a jeweller's shop-window round their necks, we can't help reacting . . . there are some members of our party, including those in positions of responsibility, who for two years now have been holding forth at all the meetings and assemblies and talking about genuine socialism, and they can't even talk their own wives around (*sagitirovat' odnoi svoei zheny*) [Kotlyar].[24]

Some of the illustrations offered went beyond the level of frankness considered politically expedient, and were omitted from the official transcript. For instance, the report of Kutuzov's speech was cut off at the point where 'Comrade Kutuzov gave a number of examples to show how easily the psychology of a man can change when he moves from a worker milieu to a responsible post. The change can occur thanks to the ease of transgressing the limits of the permitted'.[25]

But for our topic perhaps the most pertinent comment was made by Khodorovsky who, as chairman of a provincial executive committee, was in a position to know:

People who have been settled for a long time in [jobs in] the provinces get their family and personal lives arranged, set themselves up with connections, and when you want to interrupt this peaceful existence they start claiming that the local organization will suffer.[26]

Khodorovsky was unreservedly for central intervention to break up this pattern, but some of his fellow local officials viewed the holier-than-thou posture of central luminaries with more than a touch of cynicism. Mitrofanov, recalling the attacks of Zinoviev and others on the party leaders in Rostov, who allegedly joined forces with the bourgeoisie against the workers, observed that

Rostov lies on the route between Moscow and [the North Caucasus health resort of] Mineral'nye Vody, and stars of various magnitudes tend to stop off on the way there, regarding it as their duty to collect a round of applause from the Rostov workers.[27]

It is worth noting here that while the bad example and influence of the 'bourgeois specialists' was commonly blamed for the privileged life-style arranged for themselves by provincial communist bosses, the latter were also of course aware that their superiors in Moscow rarely went short and many probably entertained extravagant notions of the delights of the famous 'Kremlin ration'. This was clearly a touchy issue, and in the wake of the Ninth Party Conference the Central Committee set up a three-man enquiry (popularly known as the 'Kremlin Control Commission') which was claimed to have reduced the privileges of senior Moscow officials 'within limits which would be understandable to any party comrade, and which would at the same time refute rumours and talk about conditions in the Kremlin, which are unfounded'.[28]

The pressures, then, for local officials to form themselves into mutually supportive groups and côteries derived from the interests both of their work and their personal lives – and the two were often difficult to separate. Such groupings might be based on particular formal organizations, but more usually they cut across organizational lines. There might be two or more operating in a particular locality, giving rise to sharp conflicts for influence and dominance. The growing authority of the party committee within the circle of local organizations and agencies and the fact that there were still real elections in the party (even if key officials might already be 'recommended' from above) meant that conflicts between such groupings often focussed on efforts to keep or win control over the committee. While, as we shall see, groupings were sometimes based on some common affiliation and at times were identified with particular party-wide oppositions, they were undoubtedly for the most part, in David Hume's terms, cliques of 'interest and affection' rather than cliques of 'principle'.

The remedies prescribed by the Ninth Party Conference were twofold: to pursue the policy of reassigning local officials with greater system and vigour, and to set up 'control commissions' at the centre and in the provinces entrusted with looking into the discipline, honesty and efficiency of party organizations. Both produced results very different from what was expected of them. The control commissions, if their members did not get drawn into the dominant local network themselves, tended to become aligned with the local 'outs' engaged in feuding with the party committee.[29] On the other hand, when provincial bosses were transferred and new ones sent in from Moscow, what then tended to happen was pithily described by Lutovinov at the Ninth Party Conference. Contesting the picture presented by the rapporteur Zinoviev, Lutovinov stated:

> He said that we send a comrade out from the Central Committee to the provinces with a recommendation and say, 'we are recommending this [party] worker to you, check him out and assign him to some job or other.' But you know if that were the case there could be no objections. In practice what happens is quite different. These people, who are sent out to the provinces by appointment of the Central Committee with the broadest mandate, make short work of the [local] people, just like a cook with the potatoes.[30]

Lutovinov went on to give a number of examples, but these were cut out of the official record (we shall be examining one such case below). And of course as the 'appointees' got rid of the formerly dominant officials, they were able to promote new ones in their places who were personally dependent on them and ultimately on support from the centre.

In the three months following the Ninth Party Conference the *Orgburo* posted 105 leading officials to take over control of no less than 25 provincial party organizations:[31] in some cases, as we shall see, they had quite a fight on their hands before bringing the local in-group to heel. But meanwhile the party was entering a period of internal crisis which briefly left a distinctive mark on the character of inter-group struggle in the provinces.

As the Civil War drew to a close leading Bolsheviks found themselves deeply divided over what changes were now needed in the political, administrative and economic arrangements which had gone to make up the system of 'War Communism'. Hesitation and divisions at the top combined with profound dissatisfaction among lower-level officials and the party rank-and-file to boost support for the major opposition groups in the party, particularly the Workers' Opposition. These issues, moreover, were fought out against a background of extreme material deprivation, economic breakdown, and smouldering resentment among the workers and peasants over their powerlessness at the hands of the agents of the regime, which found expression in a rash of strikes, disturbances and local peasant risings. Matters took a new twist in December 1920 over the question of the role of the trade unions, on which the leading oligarchy itself was sharply divided. It was decided to allow an open party discussion on the issue and permit the protagonists of different 'platforms' to canvas support in the local organizations for the election of delegates at the Tenth Party Congress, due in March 1921, at which the question would be resolved. The three main 'platforms' were those of the Workers' Opposition, a group led by Trotsky and Bukharin, and the 'Platform of the Ten', which included Lenin. The 'trade union discussion' was the high point of intra-party democracy and freedom of expression in the history of the Soviet communist party. In the local organizations, although oppositionists had previously been active in a number of them, it was only during this period that alignments of principle became a major factor in local cleavages, since officials were forced willy-nilly to take a stand. It was the 'Ten' who won a majority among the Tenth Congress delegates, but then the whole matter of internal party divisions took on a new light with the outbreak of the Kronstadt revolt, which the delegates interrupted their deliberations to help suppress. Internal opposition was now seen by most party leaders as too dangerous a luxury, the congress resolved to ban party factions, and henceforth divisions of principle resumed their former minor role in local party politics, while the power of the Central Committee (in practice the *Orgburo* and Secretariat) to appoint and remove formally elective local leaders was reinforced. Sufficient vestiges of local autonomy and democracy remained for some years to come to provide rich soil for clique formation and inter-clique feuding, but the right and capacity of the party bosses in Moscow to intervene where expedient was now less and less in question.

To illustrate these developments I propose to take the case of the Nizhny-Novgorod (now Gor'ky) party organization, relying mainly on the memoirs of Anastas Mikoyan, who was sent there by the Central Committee in the wake of the Ninth Party Conference, and later went on to greater things.[32] Mikoyan's predecessor as Moscow's man in Nizhny was none other than Vyacheslav Molotov, who, according to Mikoyan, had enjoyed the co-operation of local leaders in the fight to restore the province's economy but never succeeded in breaking the grip of 'the close-knit localist clique' which 'ran everything'. Though this group consisted mainly of pre-revolutionary bolsheviks of working-class origin, they had allegedly reached a *modus vivendi* with the remnants of the local bourgeoisie and several of them, in fact, having requisitioned merchants' houses, had proceeded to marry their daughters – which is indeed a classical *modus vivendi* between defeated and victorious élites.

Mikoyan was confronted with the power of this clique immediately on his arrival. He had been posted by the *Orgburo* as chairman of the presidium of the provincial party committee, but by the time he got there a conference had been held which abolished the post by replacing the presidium with a five-man bureau, all positions in which, he was told, were already filled. When he nevertheless insisted on staying (probably against their expectations), he was co-opted to the provincial committee – but not its dominant bureau – and made a deputy chairman of the soviet executive committee. He was given the very demanding and unrewarding task of running the province's economic administration, no doubt to distract his energies from politicking.

A few weeks later an event occurred which presented him with his first opportunity. There was great unrest among the 40 000 soldiers of the reserve army garrison in Nizhny over the terrible material conditions and the harsh discipline to which they were subjected, and this surfaced at a meeting of soldiers sponsored (but badly prepared) by one of the district party committees; the organizers lost control of the meeting, which passed a resolution demanding demobilization and an end to military operations. Anti-Bolshevik slogans were openly and generally voiced in the garrison and authority broke down (the situation looked so threatening that Dzerzhinsky, alerted to it by a district party secretary who had formerly worked under him in the Cheka, offered to send a brigade of reliable troops and an armoured train to restore order, but the offer was declined). In the midst of the crisis the clique leaders and Mikoyan and his two or three local adherents all pulled together to organize the support and carry out the measures which allowed them after a week to bring the situation under control without bloodshed. Mikoyan's claim to have taken the lead in dealing with the crisis seems credible: at least it was he who was threatened with prosecution for arresting the hated commander of the Nizhny garrison without the sanction of the Commander-in-Chief of the Reserve Army Goldberg (a commission of enquiry sent from Moscow vindicated him, and Mikoyan suggests that Lenin's approval of his actions had been crucial). In any case, the established leadership was discredited for allowing the crisis to develop in the first place, and their two top members, the secretary of the provincial party committee and the chairman of the soviet executive committee, were transferred to other provinces. But despite this, although Mikoyan was now elected to the bureau, he was passed over for both the latter positions, other leading members of the clique being elected.

The next round was fought during the 'trade union discussion'. There was a good deal of sympathy for the Workers' Opposition in Nizhny, apparently due in part to the strong connections between some local Bolsheviks and the Workers' Opposition leader Shlyapnikov, who had worked in the giant Sormovo plant there many years previously (the director of the Sormovo plant Chernov was himself an ardent Workers' Oppositionist). Mikoyan and his small group of supporters were the main protagonists of the 'Platform of the Ten'. The dominant clique did not take a solid position, but some of its main leaders opted for the Workers' Opposition and the others tended to fall in line. Later, as the tide began to turn against the Workers' Opposition, several changed their positions. The relative unimportance of issues of political principle in the motivation of the local bosses is indicated by the contribution to the trade union debate of the provincial party secretary Popov, which Mikoyan quotes from the party archives:

I have not expressed a definite point of view because of lack of the spare time to devote to acquainting myself with the platforms proposed, but to the extent that I have been able to examine the latter I sympathize most of all with the 'Workers' Opposition' . . . but possibly after closer study I will have to change and settle on some other platform.[33]

In the midst of the 'trade union discussion' the clique focused their attacks on 'the Ikonnikov-Mikoyan group' (Ikonnikov, a young district party secretary, was Mikoyan's most active supporter), and there were moves to appeal to Moscow to have them removed as disturbers of the peace. Later, at the provincial party conference, Mikoyan commented as follows:

Some people have made out that the whole fault lies with two people sitting in the provincial committee; if it were not for them everything would be all right . . . Yes, on questions of principle we [two] have shared the same opinions but, for example, one might imagine that the majority of the provincial committee, who support Lenin's viewpoint, should often be arguing against the 'Workers' Opposition', but in fact there have been no fights in the provincial committee against the Opposition, there have only been fights against Ikonnikov and me, although we do not belong to the 'Workers' Opposition'. The provincial committee does not share the opinions of the 'Workers' Opposition', but nevertheless appoints representatives of the 'Workers' Opposition' to the counties, and this in the majority of cases. What is this – is it a personal clique or is it not? When principles hamper the interest of the personal clique, they are pushed into the background.[34]

While the clique was divided and vacillating in the 'trade union discussion' Mikoyan and his supporters were working strenuously and wholeheartedly for the 'Platform of the Ten', constantly pushing the simplistic line that it was a question of support for Lenin or support for Trotsky or Shlyapnikov. In the event they won a narrow victory for the 'Ten' at the provincial party conference. However, there was almost an embarrassing dénouement. Mikoyan and Ikonnikov allowed themselves to be outmanoeuvred at the meeting of the 'slate committee' whose job it was to prepare a list of candidates for the provincial party committee, and a list consisting predominantly of the old clique members was adopted. In the few hours separating the meeting of the 'slate committee' from the final sitting of the conference, at which the election was to take place, Mikoyan and his supporters feverishly canvassed the delegates, allegedly arguing that if the conference supported Lenin, it must elect a leadership committed to carrying out Lenin's policies. An 'unofficial' slate was drawn up, with the assistance of the local Cheka chief Busarev, who was another of Mikoyan's supporters, and this defeated the 'official' list on the floor of the conference. Mikoyan's adherents and other 'Leninists' now had a majority in the provincial committee, and they also secured the election of delegates to the Tenth Party Congress who were declared supporters of 'The Platform of the Ten'. When the provincial committee convened it elected a new bureau in which the Mikoyan group had a majority of four to one, with Mikoyan as secretary. 'Only now', comments Mikoyan, 'after five months packed with struggles against the local clique, against the "Workers' Opposition" and the Trotskyites, was I able to set about the task for which I had been sent to Nizhny by decision of the *Orgburo* of the party's Central Committee in the autumn of 1920.'[35]

Nevertheless, though the decisive battle was won, the war was not yet over. The clique had been defeated in the provincial party committee, but it was still strongly entrenched in other local organizations, particularly the soviet executive committee and the trade union council. The chairman of the former, Khanov, tried to whip up support for an appeal to the Central Committee against the 'demagogic' activities of Mikoyan and his supporters. Shortly before the provincial party conference the Central Committee had sent in a second 'appointee', Ter-Elizaryan (another Armenian) intended as new soviet executive committee chairman. In the communist party caucus at the provincial congress of soviets, however, Khanov and other clique members at first defeated the executive committee slate recommended by the provincial party committee, and it was only through the threat of party disciplinary action against caucus members that Mikoyan was able to have his way (even then 71 out of 161 members voted against the party committee's list). The new executive committee duly elected Ter-Elizaryan as chairman. However, fights continued over the staff of the executive committee. At one point Mikoyan's opponents succeeded in removing one of his closest supporters from the position of head of the education department. Again the imposition of party discipline, supported from Moscow, was necessary to remove the clique's adherents from the key administrative posts in the soviet.

Mikoyan had no less trouble bringing to heel the local trade unions, in which Workers' Opposition influences remained strong – partly sustained, according to Mikoyan, by the efforts of Chelyshev, one of the stalwarts of the old Nizhny clique and now a member of the party's Central Control Commission, who had been an active Workers' Oppositionist and now acted as a channel of influence between the dogged Shlyapnikov and his old friends in Nizhny. Again there was a prolonged row in the party caucus of the provincial trade union congress over the slate of committee members, the delegates finally submitting to party discipline and accepting the provincial party committee's slate only on the understanding that Mikoyan would acquiesce in a complaint being sent to the Central Committee. Shortly afterwards an emissary arrived from Moscow, and spent ten days looking into this matter, as well as into complaints that members of the 'former' Workers' Opposition were being victimized, and into other issues on which the provincial party committee had been at loggerheads with the trade unions. At a special party meeting in Nizhny and in his written report presented to the Politbureau on his return the emissary stated his conclusion that 'the struggle of the provincial party committee with the remnants of factional groups has been conducted in accordance with the decision of the Tenth Party Congress'. Again Mikoyan was vindicated.

Thus, armed with the sharp blade of party discipline and his hand strengthened at crucial junctures by the ruling oligarchy in Moscow, the 'appointee' Mikoyan contrived – although it took him nearly a year to complete the job – to finish off the clique formerly running the Nizhny province, 'like a cook with the potatoes'. And it was he, moreover, who saw to the filling of the vacancies so created. As he puts it, 'the promotion to leading work on the provincial level of more and more workers and also officials from the counties and urban districts was carried out by us very actively in those years'.[36] A new team was being installed in the province of Nizhny-Novgorod, formed by young communists who had demonstrated their suitability by their support for Mikoyan in his struggles with their predecessors.

Between the Tenth Party Congress and Lenin's death in January 1924 there was a steady increase in both the control of the central party machine over provincial party officialdom and the authority of the latter over governmental and other organizations in their areas.[37] Nevertheless, as mentioned earlier, local cliques and inter-clique feuds remained a prominent feature of the Soviet political scene. Indeed, while in retrospect the decisions of the Tenth Party Congress banning factions and strengthening the centralized, hierarchical principle can be seen as marking a watershed, to contemporaries it must often have seemed as if provincial political life was continuing much as before. Here there is space to note only a few of its more interesting manifestations.

First, although we have so far talked mainly about the provincial level, it should be realized that cliques also formed among officials at the subordinate county and urban district levels, and these might or might not be tied in closely with the dominant provincial clique. On the other hand, the Central Committee had set up at this period a number of oblast bureaux, their members at first directly appointed by the *Orgburo*, and responsible for groups of provinces or national republics, chiefly in the more outlying areas. Sometimes relations between these bureaux and the dominant groups in the provinces became strained. For instance, in 1922 the Omsk Provincial Committee was feuding for some months with the Siberian Regional Bureau, mainly over personnel appointments in the province. When Moscow intervened to back up the Regional Bureau, the Central Committee was flooded with letters threatening resignation. Thereupon the Regional Bureau was authorized to undertake a 're-registration of the whole Omsk organization with the object of cleansing it', and to expel from the party even district leaders if necessary. At this point most of the district officials deserted their provincial bosses, 'claiming that they had been misinformed about the true state of affairs by a few leaders'. Only the core members of the provincial clique held out, the provincial secretary being expelled from the party and his chief supporters receiving lesser punishments.[38] As this case indicates, hierarchial inter-echelon relationships could be as important as horizontal inter-organizational relationships in the pattern of local clique formation and conflict.

Secondly, both from contemporary sources and memoir accounts one has the impression that it was by now taken for granted that good working relationships among local officials would be reinforced by personal bonds of friendship and mutual assistance.

When, however, Moscow felt obliged to intervene because of conspicuously bad economic or political performance or severe inter-group conflict (or for reasons of top-level political interest), then the additional charge of groupist behaviour was liable to be laid. Such intervention could also be provoked by particularly scandalous manifestations of the intra-group bond, of which criminal conspiracy was the most obvious example. Alcohol was a common cement of group solidarity – and had been even during the prohibition era of the Civil War – and repeated drunken orgies could lead to disciplinary action from above.[39] The Central Committee's written pre-congress report in 1923, criticizing the increased concern of provincial officials to collect personal property and lead a privileged life-style, referred to 'the growth of all sorts of banquets and the celebration of holidays and "jubilees" of their organization, accompanied by copious drinking'.[40] Reports of more unusual forms of cement include 'the case of the members of the Lipovets [County] organization, who met in a group and discussed the question of sex life, approaching the question from a vulgar Philistine point of view, where petit-bourgeois pornography occurred' (alas, no details). Several men and women, including the county party secretary and the chairman of the county executive committee, were disciplined over this by the Central Control Commission.[41]

Thirdly, although spokesmen for the central party machine were constantly claiming that local inter-clique feuds had been reduced there is ample evidence that they were still rife. In fact a special conference of regional, provincial and county party secretaries at the end of 1921 focused on this as one of the major problems facing the party,[42] and at the Eleventh Congress a few months later Zinoviev said that while at local levels groupings on a policy basis had been virtually eliminated, personal cliques were now no less a challenge since their conflicts could totally paralyse the administration of whole areas, and he listed 28 provinces where such conflicts had recently been engaging the attention of the Central Committee.[43] There does seem to have been some decline over the following year, although perhaps the leaders (or some of them) were simply becoming reconciled to the phenomenon; indeed Stalin told the Twelfth Congress that such inter-group conflicts had their good side, since they arose from efforts of local officials to form themselves into a close-knit effective working team.[44]

There were two new factors contributing to this turbulence. One was the discharge from the army of a large number of senior communists, who had to be found jobs. Some were taken into the central offices of the party, government, trade unions and so on, and others were sent out to the provinces, sometimes to their original organizations, sometimes not. The incumbent local bosses had no wish to move aside, and friction was often intense.[45] In a feud lasting several months in the Vologda province, for instance, ex-army communists, posted at first to more junior posts, eventually gathered the numbers to topple the established leadership.[46] Whoever won, however, and very frequently there was no such direct confrontation, the return of the old soldiers exacerbated the competition for office and tended to disturb existing patterns of mutual accommodation.

The second new factor encouraging inter-group conflict was the increased likelihood of Central Committee intervention, which tempted minority cliques in the provinces to blow up issues on which the dominant clique was on weak ground in the hope that Moscow might launch a reshuffle from which they could benefit. Events in Tula province in 1922–33 provide an example. For some time there had been tension between a more powerful group centred on the provincial party secretary Meerzon and a weaker group led by a certain Teplov. Then at the Tenth Congress of Soviets there occurred an unsuccessful challenge to Meerzon's candidature for membership of the Central Executive Committee (*VTsIK*), on the grounds of his political past: he had been a member of the Bund till 1919 and had even been under Bolshevik arrest for a time in 1918. The Teplov group now seized on this issue in a bid to overthrow Meerzon and his friends, claiming that the latter's methods violated party principles, and they succeeded in provoking an investigation by a Central Committee commission headed by Dzerzhinsky. This challenge failed, however, as the latter's report stated that there were no issues of principle involved, simply an inter-group feud, and the Central Committee confirmed Meerzon in charge, although it obliged him to reach an accommodation with the Teplov group. That was not the end of the story. One or both of the contenders evidently scented blood, for the feud was kept on the boil. A further commission was sent from Moscow, this time headed by Rykov, and threatened re-postings if things did not settle down.

Shortly afterwards Meerzon was in fact given a new job, in the central party apparatus, where he remained for nine years, which suggests that he enjoyed the confidence of Stalin and his friends. How the Teplov group fared we have been unable to establish.[47] Another illustration may be taken from the Vologda province, where in February 1923 the local control commission accused the provincial party secretary and the chairman of the soviet executive committee of 'non-party conduct', and 'certain local comrades' then got up a move to remove the two leading officials from their jobs. The move failed, since the representative of the Central Control Commission vindicated the accused officials and rebuked their accusers for 'artificially exaggerating [their] errors'.[48]

At the Eleventh Party Congress Zinoviev gave the following rough typology of local clique conflicts: 'the younger people against the older, county-based people against the city-based, the party-based against the soviet-based, those working in the economic councils against those working in the trade unions, and finally those based in the food supply committees against those working in the economic councils'.[49] Stalin's analysis, offered a year later at the Twelfth Congress, placed less emphasis on the institutional basis of local cliques. The main cleavages, as he saw them, were between 'the locals and recent arrivals, proletarians and intellectuals, young and old, people from the centre and people from the provinces [*okrainnye*], and people of different nationalities'. And he continued, 'all these heterogeneous elements which go up to make the provincial committees bring with them different attitudes [*nravy*], traditions and tastes and on this basis brawls and feuds erupt.'[50] Both agreed that real issues of principle or policy were hardly ever involved.

There is ample documentary evidence of both institutionally-based and what one might call sociologically-based cliques, and of their conflicts. Regarding the former, however, it should be pointed out that there were often genuine institutional jealousies involved as well as the personal interests of the officials concerned. Many of these were provoked by the continued efforts of the party machine to expand its authority over other bureaucracies. Locally deployed officials of the latter could sometimes find themselves caught between pressures from the provincial party committee and their superiors in Moscow. For instance, in 1922 the plenipotentiary of the food supplies commissariat in the south-east region was

disciplined by People's Commissar Smirnov for following regional
party directives rather than his own; whereupon the secretary
of the regional committee, none other than Mikoyan, recently
transferred from Nizhny-Novgorod, telegraphed an objection to
the Central Committee, which 'helped', and the official concerned
henceforth served as a loyal member of Mikoyan's team.[51]

Inter-clique conflicts based on different ethnic affiliations were
quite widespread at this period, and perhaps deserve a special
glance. In the Volga-German Autonomous Republic there was a
feud between the 'Marxstadt people' and the 'Pokrovsk people',
that is, Germans versus Russians.[52] In the Votyak (now Udmurt)
region the Votyaks claimed the right to a majority of places on
county party committees and all places on the regional committee,
and when they could not achieve this (they secured only four of
the fifteen seats on the regional committee) sought unsuccessfully
to shift the balance in their favour by having the Russian industrial
city of Izhevsk taken out of the region.[53] In the Mari region
the 'natives' got the upper hand and voted all the Russians
off the regional committee. Similar ethnically aligned groups
of officials contended in Baku, the Kirgiz (now Kazakh) and
Kalmyk Regions, Turkestan, and the Tatar, Bashkir and Crimean
Autonomous Republics.[54] In Pskov Province, a large group of
Latvian communists, who had settled there after the Bolshevik
defeat in their homeland and were mostly unable to obtain official
jobs, formed 'virtually a separate Latvian organization within the
party organization as a whole', and feuded with the provincial
committee (the Central Committee intervened to insist on some
of them being given senior posts and transferred the rest to other
provinces).[55]

Two general trends may be noted in the character of local
clique formation over the early Soviet period to 1923. The first
was structural: the progressive strengthening of vertical, leader-
oriented relationships. In the earlier period inter-personal bonds
were predominantly horizontal, not dependent on the patronage of a particular leader occupying some key office. There
were exceptions: in some regions even at this period cliques
had something of the character of a personal following. An
example was Zinoviev's dominant clique in Petrograd province.
Zinoviev was chairman of the soviet, but was effective boss of
the party organization as well, and an attempt by party secretary

Uglanov to assert control over the party machine in 1921–2 was defeated, and Uglanov had to be shifted out. But Zinoviev was of course a member of the Politbureau, and exceptional circumstances of some kind were usually present where clique leadership was strongly personalized in this early period. More typical was the pattern we encountered in Nizhny-Novgorod, where the dominant clique retained its cohesion and viability while its successively most prominent members (Kremnitsky, Chelyshev, Khanov, Khramov, Kozin, Vorob'ev, Popov) were switched from job to job or even moved out of the organization. However, as the authority of the local party machine over the other bureaucracies grew, while at the same time the provincial secretary became steadily more dominant within the party organization, so inter-clique conflict came more and more to focus on capture of the provincial party bureau and especially the post of secretary. In the process office-holding came to depend primarily on the patronage of the provincial secretary, rather than the mutual support of a horizontally-linked group. Again, the Nizhny-Novgorod case has given us an illustration of this transformation: the people who took over there after the old clique was eventually ousted were clearly first and foremost Mikoyan's men. Here, too, one can point to exceptions, most commonly involving groups which reflected and exploited some strong pre-existing factor of social identity and solidarity, as in the case of the ethnically-based cliques just noted. Such factors may, indeed, still play a part in political clique formation down to our own day. However, by 1922–3 the dominant cliques in many, if not most provinces, were essentially clientèles of the provincial party secretary, who was himself more likely than not an 'appointee' sent in by the *Orgburo*.

And this brings us to the second main trend: whereas in the early period the ramifications of provincial cliques and of inter-clique conflicts were as a rule strictly local, by the early twenties they were being tied in with national-level networks of top leaders in Moscow; and in the majority of cases this meant Stalin. It is usual to date Stalin's dominance of the party machine to 1922, when he became General Secretary. But in fact he was effectively in charge from the time of the Tenth Congress when his adherent Molotov was made Responsible Secretary of the Central Committee and he himself the only member of the Politbureau also serving on the Organizational Bureau, to which the Secretariat was responsible and which normally had the last word on party personnel matters. There is no doubt that by 1921 Stalin already exercised the predominant influence over senior appointments in the provinces. In 1922 another close supporter, Lazar Kaganovich, was put in charge of the Central Committee's Personnel (*Uchetnoraspredelitel'nyi*) Department. As Robert V. Daniels has put it, beginning in 1921

> there ensued a complex process whereby the Party Secretariat, pursuing its function of rooting out dissension and building the Party into an efficient instrument of political control and supervision, became more and more a power unto itself. The trend toward a military mode of organization and operation did not cease until the entire political life of the country came under the domination of a hierarchy of individual Party secretaries, all under the supreme command of one man, the General Secretary Stalin. Decisive in this process was the establishment of control by the central Secretariat over the local organizations, which gave Stalin the foundation for controlling the Party congresses and through them, in time, dominating the entire policy-making summit of the Party and the State.[56]

If the new cohort of provincial party secretaries nominated by Stalin were to exercise effective control and to ensure the election of party congress delegates who would be loyal to Stalin, one essential was to purge the local bureaucracies of officials belonging to the formerly dominant clique, with their independent bases of solidarity, replacing them with a clientèle recruited largely from persons formerly at odds with the previous bosses. This process was already being vigorously pursued in 1921–3, and not surprisingly some of Stalin's critics were quick to see dangers in it. For instance, this is how Preobrazhensky characterized it at the Twelfth Congress in 1923:

> Comrades who have come to the locality and do not meet with sufficient support . . . group around themselves certain comrades who disagree with the local people, and as a result we get a state within a state.[57]

Against this background, Stalin's 'discovery' of the good points of local inter-clique feuds takes on a new light. For the 'tight-knit, cohesive core-group capable of exercising leadership as one man', the 'healthy aspiration' to build which was responsible for 'nine-tenths' of current local feuds,[58] was now to be a constituent part of his nationwide network.

The main conclusion to be drawn from this analysis will by now be apparent. Political clientelism in the USSR did not spring 'fully armed' from the head of Stalin, but instead developed over a considerable period 'within the womb' of early Soviet society, Stalin's role in its birth being more that of midwife than of parent. The early domination of provincial officialdom by cliques bound by informal personal bonds of reciprocity was due both to the specific politico-administrative circumstances in which they functioned and the general conditions of life which encouraged everyone to rely heavily on personal connections and mutual favours for their daily bread, security, and any luxuries that were going. Since control and allocation of goods and services were largely in the hands of local officials, both 'official' and 'personal' strands of reciprocal favour between these officials became intertwined and constituted powerful bonds of solidarity, although rival cliques formed in this way often operated in the same area. As the authority of the party apparatus over other official agencies grew and the party secretary became the key official in the local committee, himself increasingly dependent on the confidence of the central party machine for obtaining and retaining office, these local cliques took on more and more of a clientelist character with the provincial party secretary as patron. As we have seen, this process was well advanced by the time Stalin secured control of the Central Committee apparatus, and plainly it required no exceptional perspicacity or wiliness on his part to discern the possibility and advantage of progressively converting the corps of provincial party secretaries into a personal following and encouraging the latter to do the same with local officials coming under their authority. This, however, is not to say that if some Politbureau member other than Stalin had become General Secretary in his stead he would necessarily have had the wit and will to exploit these opportunities as Stalin did.

One final question. Once the transformation of provincial cliques into clientelist followings under the patronage of Moscow-chosen party secretaries was completed, did the politico-administrative and social conditions which originally gave rise to these cliques disappear or cease to be relevant? We would argue that they neither ceased nor became irrelevant, a proposition which would probably command fairly general agreement but which it lies beyond the scope of this paper to attempt to demonstrate. The value of informal connections and protection for the effective exercise of politico-administrative roles and for satisfying personal needs and wants did not disappear when the Civil War came to a close, and consequently the same pattern of pressures and opportunities which originally gave rise to provincial cliques continued to characterize them after their *Gleichschaltung* and incorporation into Stalin's political machine. This becomes very apparent, for example, when one examines the material in the Smolensk Archive on the 1926 and 1928 purges in that province.[59] Indeed, as suggested earlier in this paper, these conditions persist down to our own day and help to explain the persistence of clientelist politics in the USSR a quarter of a century after Stalin's death. This suggests that any discussion of perceived or anticipated changes in the importance or character of political clientelism in the USSR should range beyond the narrowly political sphere and take account of persistence and change in the broader administrative and socio-economic environment in which Soviet officials operate.

NOTES

1. See Jerry F. Hough and Merle Fainsod, *How the Soviet Union is Governed* (Cambridge, Mass. and London, 1979) pp. 143-6.
2. Cf. Boris Souvarine, *Stalin: A Critical Survey of Bolshevism* (Sydney and London, 1940), chs VI–IX, and Leonard Schapiro, *The Communist Party of the Soviet Union*, 2nd edn., London and New York, 1970).
3. Keith R. Legg has recently provided a valuable review of this literature in his *Patrons, Clients and Politicians. New Perspectives on Political Clientelism* (Berkeley, Calif., n.d.), while Steffen W. Schmitt *et al.* have published a useful reader, *Friends, Followers and Factions. A Reader in Political Clientelism* (Berkeley, Calif., 1977). See also Ernest Gellner and John Waterbury (eds), *Patrons and Clients in Mediterranean Societies* (London, 1977), especially the chapters by Gellner, Weingrod and Waterbury.
4. See especially the symposium on this topic in *Comparative Communism*, vol. *XIII*, nos 2 and 3 (Summer–Autumn 1979) pp. 159-211.
5. See Alan Zuckerman, *Political Clienteles in Power. Party Factions and Cabinet Coalitions in Italy* (Beverley Hills and London, 1975); Joseph La Palombara, *Interest Groups in Italian Politics* (Princeton, N. J., 1964); Nobutaka Ike, *Japanese Politics: Patron–Client Democracy* (New York, 1972); Chie Nakane, *Japanese Society* (London, 1970); Albert M. Craig, 'Functional and Dysfunctional Aspects of Government Bureaucracy', in Ezra Vogel (ed.), *Modern Japanese Organization and Decision-Making* (Berkeley, Calif., 1975); and Andrew J. Nathan, 'A Factionalism Model for CCP Politics', *China Quarterly*, no. 53 (Jan.-March 1973) pp. 34-67. More generally see Jeremy Boissevain, *Friends of Friends. Networks, Manipulators and Coalitions* (Oxford, 1974).

6. See Gregory Grossman, 'The "Second Economy" of the USSR', *Problems of Communism*, vol. *XXVI*, no. 5 (Sept.-Oct. 1977) pp. 25-40.
7. See notes 3 and 5.
8. See I. V. Stalin, *Sochineniya*, ed. Robert H. McNeal (Stanford, Conn. 1967) vol. I (XIV) pp. 230-1.
9. Although the topic is attracting increasing attention. See, e.g. Daniel Orlovsky, 'High Officials in the Ministry of Internal Affairs', in Walter Pinter and Don Rowney (eds), *Russian Officialdom: The Bureaucratization of Russian Society from the Seventeenth to the Twentieth Century* (Chapel Hill, 1980); Daniel L. Ransel, *The Politics of Catherinian Russia. The Panin Party* (New Haven Conn. and London, 1975). Cf. Alexander Ular, *Russia from Within* (London, 1905) pp. 106-23.
10. Sheila Fitzpatrick, *The Commissariat of Enlightenment. Soviet Organization of Education and the Arts under Lunacharsky* (Cambridge, 1970) p. 10.
11. Ibid., p. 19.
12. On the character of the party membership during the revolutionary and Civil War period, see T. H. Rigby, *Communist Party Membership in the USSR 1917-1967* (Princeton, N. J., 1968) ch. 1.
13. Ibid., p. 79.
14. *Devyatyi s"ezd RKP(b). Protokoly* (Moscow, 1960) p. 573.
15. See Schapiro, op. cit., pp. 247-9.
16. See *Izvestiya Tsentral'nogo Komiteta*, no. 9, 20 December 1919. A few more had been members of other socialist parties.
17. Ibid.
18. *Devyatyi s"ezd RKP(b)*, pp. 43-4.
19. See Mervyn Matthews, *Privilege in the Soviet Union. A Study of Elite Life-Styles under Communism* (London, 1978) p. 60.
20. See *Pravda*, 27 September 1920.
21. See *Devyataya konferentsiya RKP(b). Protokoly* (Moscow, 1972) *passim*.
22. Ibid., p. 161.
23. Ibid., pp. 177-8.
24. Ibid., pp. 168-9.
25. Ibid., p. 187.
26. Ibid., p. 167.
27. Ibid., p. 202.
28. Ibid., p. 322.
29. A feud in the Astrakhan province early in 1922 reached the point where the provincial control commission expelled the provincial party secretary from the party, whereupon the Central Committee disbanded the control commission. See *Izvestiya TsK*, no. 4, April 1923.
30. *Devyataya konferentsiya RKP(b)*, p. 164.
31. *Izvestiya TsK*, no. 26, 20 December 1920.
32. A. I. Mikoyan, *V nachale dvadtsatykh* (Moscow, 1975) ch. 2. There are obvious problems presented by the use of such sources, and I have sought to avoid reliance on those parts of his account which seem improbable in the light of other available evidence.
33. Ibid., p. 64.
34. Ibid., p. 76.
35. Ibid., p. 85.
36. Ibid., p. 127. He goes on to quote from his report to the provincial party conference in August 1921: 'Of the five members of the presidium of the provincial [soviet] executive committee we took four in the period directly

from urban and rural district jobs. [The fifth was the Moscow 'appointee' Ter-Elizaryan.] The leadership of the provincial women's department has been fully restaffed with district officials. Two new workers have been brought into the provincial food supplies committee. The same job has been carried out in the provincial department of social security, the urban services and other departments of the provincial executive committee' (Ibid.).

37.   The best account of this is Robert V. Daniels, 'The Secretariat and the Local Organizations in the Russian Communist Party, 1921-1923', *American Slavic and East European Review*, vol. XVI, no. 1 (March 1967) pp. 32-49.
38.   *Izvestiya TsK,* no. 42, June 1922, and no. 44, August 1922. The following year the Siberian bureau had similar trouble with the Enisei Provincial Committee. See, ibid., no. 4 (52) April 1923.
39.   Of the 815 disciplinary cases dealt with by the Conflicts Sub-Department of the Central Committee in the five months to February 1921, 69 involved charges of drunkenness. See *Izvestiya TsK,* no. 28, March 1921.
40.   *Dvenadtsatyi s''ezd RKP(b). Stenograficheskii otchet* (Moscow, 1968) p. 792.
41.   *Izvestiya TsK,* no. 1 (49) January 1923.
42.   See *Odinnadtsatyi s''ezd RKP(b). Stenograficheskii otchet* (Moscow, 1961) p. 559.
43.   Ibid., pp. 402-3.
44.   *Dvenadtsatyi s''ezd RKP(b). Stenograficheskii otchet,* p. 66.
45.   See T. H. Rigby, 'The Soviet Political Elite 1917-1922'. *British Journal of Political Science,* vol. 1 (1971) pp. 418-19 (this volume, Chapter 2). Largely in response to the resentment of Old Bolsheviks who had spent the Civil War years at the front, and now returned to find the good jobs occupied by young stay-at-homes, it was resolved that provincial party secretaries should be members of pre-October Revolution standing and county secretaries of at least three years standing, but his rule was only gradually and incompletely enforced (ibid.). One effect of the soldiers' return was a sharp reduction in the already modest percentage of women in senior party and government posts in the provinces (ibid.). p. 424).
46.   *Izvestiya TsK,* no. 40, March 1922.
47.   See *Izvestiya TsK,* no. 1 (49) January 1923, and no. 4 (52) April 1923; *Dvenadtsatyi s''ezd RKP(b),* pp. 799-800, and *Odinnadtsatyi s''ezd RKP(b),* p. 835 (biography of Meerzon).
48.   *Izvestiya TsK,* no. 4 (52) April 1923.
49.   *Odinnadtsatyi s''ezd RKP(b),* p. 402.
50.   *Dvenadtsatyi s''ezd RKP(b),* p. 66.
51.   Mikoyan, op. cit., pp. 178-9.
52.   *Izvestiya TsK,* no. 4 (52) April 1923.
53.   Ibid., no. 37, January 1922, and no. 42, June 1922.
54.   Ibid., no. 37, January 1922.
55.   Ibid., no. 4 (52), April 1923.
56.   Daniels, 'The Secretariat and the Local Organizations in the Russian Communist Party', pp. 32-3.
57.   *Dvenadtsatyi s''ezd RKP(b),* p. 145.
58.   Ibid., p. 66.
59.   See the Smolensk Archive WKP 33 and WKP 291. The relevant facts are summarized in Merle Fainsod, *Smolensk under Soviet Rule* (Cambridge, Mass., 1958) pp. 48 ff.

4. The origins of the nomenklatura system*

The nomenklatura system, under which the Communist Party apparatus controls the choice of personnel for hundreds of thousands of posts, a large proportion of them formally elective, in every sphere of national life, and at all levels from the central government down to the village soviets, is generally agreed to be one of the basic constitutent elements of the Soviet socio-political order. The essence of this order has been the attempt consciously to manage every area of socially relevant activity, outside a closely circumscribed private sphere, through an array of hierarchically structured formal organisations, all coordinated and directed at the centre and at successively lower levels by the apparatus of the Communist Party. Although some subsidiary use is made of market mechanisms, and mass participation and initiative in support of official programmes are encouraged, both chance and opposition have been seen as abhorrent to such an order, and for very good reason. For both chance and opposition are disruptive not only of the specific purposes of those managing the society, but of the very pattern of assumptions and relationships on which their capacity to manage it depends, and therewith both their legitimating goal of 'communism' and their own safety, power and privileges. It is not surprising, therefore, that such apparently inoffensive terms as *stikhiinost* (spontaneity), *samotek* (undirected movement) and *liberalizm*(tolerance) have been imbued with such deprecatory force in the Soviet lexicon.

This abhorrence of chance and opposition has always been

*'Staffing USSR Incorporated: The Origins of the Nomenklatura System', in Inge Auerbach, Andreas Hillgruber and Gottfried Schramm, (eds), *Felder and Vorfelder russischer Geschichte: Studien zu Ehren von Peter Scheibert,* (Rombach, Freiburg, (1985) pp. 241–54, and (slightly revised as in the present version) *Soviet Studies*, vol. XL, no. 4 (Oct. 1988) pp. 523–37.

particularly obvious in the sphere of leadership and personnel policy. As Lenin remarked at the Eleventh Congress in 1922, 'if the Central Committee is deprived of the right to direct [*rasporyazhat'sya*] the allocation of personnel, it will be unable to direct [*napravlyat'*] policy'.[1] That Lenin should have taken such a position was completely consistent with his prescriptions for the party as a centralised, disciplined organization of professional revolutionaries, and its hegemonic, 'vanguard' role *vis-à-vis* the working class and its organizations, prescriptions which had long marked him and his Bolshevik followers off from the rest of Russian Marxism, however imperfectly they may have been achieved in practice prior to the Revolution. Nevertheless, while these prescriptions do lie at the root of the nomenklatura system, it is important to realise that Lenin took no direct part in the creation of that system, which in fact was only beginning to take shape at the time of his death.

An essential condition for any effective system of personnel management is a clear allocation of jurisdiction among the various authorities involved. This is all that was meant by the Soviet term 'nomenklatura system' (*nomenklaturnaya sistema*) when it was originally introduced and there is nothing intrinsically sinister or peculiar in the fact that all official bodies in the Soviet Union involved in personnel administration operate according to a listing or schedule (Russian: *nomenklatura*) of the posts they are responsible for staffing. There are three aspects, however, which make of the nomenklatura system in the USSR and other communist countries something qualitatively new and unique among modern societies: first, the concentration of important positions in all official and 'voluntary' organisations in the *nomenklatury* of *party* committees; secondly, the inclusion of *elective* positions (and most of the more important ones are in form elective); and third, the *comprehensiveness* of the system, which omits no position of any significance in the society, and thereby incidentally converts the occupants of nomenklatura positions into a distinct *social* category.[2]

As with many other aspects of Soviet politics and society, it is only since the early 1950s that the nomenklatura system has attracted serious scholarly attention. Its main outlines are now clear, even if many important details of its operation remain unknown or obscure.[3] Its origins back in the 1920s, however,

have received little attention,[4] yet arguably these have proved
of more fundamental and lasting significance than all the great
struggles and debates among leadership factions on which scholars
of the period have poured out oceans of ink. Study of these origins
can be very rewarding, both for what they can tell us about the
political and social history of the period itself, and also (owing to
the comparative openness of party official sources at that time) for
the clues they can give us about obscure aspects of the operation
of the system down to our own day. We seek here to redress the
balance in some small measure.

Why, as noted earlier, did the nomenklatura system take several
years from the time of the Revolution to establish, despite its
evident congruence with Lenin's prescriptions? The answer lies in
the difficulties encountered in meeting certain basic preconditions
for the operation of such a system, namely:

1. the subordination of soviets, the state apparatus, business
    firms, the trade unions, and all other 'voluntary' organiza-
    tions, not merely to the *political* leadership of the party, but
    to the *administrative* authority of its apparatus;
2. the total subjection of the party membership to the appa-
    ratus, and therewith the effective conversion of elective
    processes into appointive ones; and
3. the assembling of necessary administrative resources; staffs,
    data banks, procedural rules, etc.

The existing literature has much to say about the first two
of these preconditions, but we should nevertheless dwell briefly
on how their creation enmeshed with the building of a unified
personnel management system centred on the party apparatus. We
might first remind ourselves that up to 1919 there was virtually no
party apparatus, in the sense of an organization of full-time, paid
officials. It was certainly the Communist Party that exercised the
'dictatorship of the proletariat', but it exercised it by capturing
control of the soviets and through them the state machine, the
key positions in which were promptly filled by its leading members
both at the centre and in the provinces and localities. The building
of a full-time party officialdom, initiated at the Eighth Congress,
was aimed primarily at achieving more effective central direction

and co-ordination of the party's cadres, dispersed as they were through various often competing organizations (commissariats, soviet executive committees, army, Cheka, etc.) each with its own hierarchy of command and local interest base.[5] The Eighth Congress decreed that the party members in these multifarious state bodies around the country should be grouped into 'fractions' 'strictly subordinate to party discipline', that is, obliged to carry out the directives of the local party committee, which should 'lead' them, but not 'supplant' them.[6] And demonstrating how closely the issue of party authority and unity was seen to be bound up with that of centralized personnel management, it was further resolved that:

> The correct allocation of party forces is at present the chief guarantee of success and one of the most important tasks. The whole matter of assignment of party functionaries [*rabotniki*] is in the hands of the Central Committee of the party. Its decision is obligatory upon all. In every *gubernia* [province] the *gubernia* forces are allocated by the *gubernia* committees of the party, and in the capitals by the city committees under the general guidance of the Central Committee.[7]

And to enable the party committees to carry out this work of directing and staffing the various official and 'mass' organizations, their key members were now freed of other duties and given the backing of a burgeoning corps of organizers and office assistants. The staff of the Central Committee itself rose from 30 in March 1919 to 80 in December, to 150 in March 1920 and to 602 a year later.[8] While there was some early resistance by leading communists based in the soviets, by 1921 the hierarchy of party secretaries and their staffs, directed by the Central Committee Secretariat, had become the principal instrument through which the ruling party oligarchy controlled the country. The party now exercised *administrative* as well as political authority in the emergent new society. And because nearly everything had meanwhile been nationalized, this administrative authority of the party extended to most industrial, financial, transport, educational, cultural and media institutions. It also extended to the country's most important voluntary organizations which, like the soviets, had been turned into 'transmission belts' of the party by first eliminating all contending political influences working in them and then obliging the party members in charge of them to submit unreservedly to direction by the corresponding party committee. The attempt by the Worker's Opposition to restore the autonomy of the trade unions early in 1921 was soundly defeated, and such aspirations were henceforth made punishable as an 'anarcho-syndicalist deviation'.[9]

The second precondition for the *nomenklatura* system, the total subjection of the party membership to the apparatus, took longer to achieve, the basic reason being that the Bolshevik tradition was far from being as completely undemocratic as some of its critics have made out. It may have been the most authoritarian, conspiratorial, centralized and 'militarily' disciplined wing of the Russian Social-Democratic movement, but as in the rest of that movement many of its members had absorbed something of the democratic ethos valued by their fellow social democrats further west, and especially in Germany. Thus while one must broadly agree with the *Pravda* editorial writer who stated in 1952 that 'in the period of the illegal existence of our party, when party organizations were obliged to have a purely conspiratorial character, party committees were composed from top to bottom by the way of appointment or cooptation',[10] lip service was always paid to the principles of election and decision making by free discussion and majority vote which were supposed to be observed to the extent that circumstances permitted,[11] and a democratic element was indeed often present in the actual operation of local party organizations.[12]

Against this background, one can understand the widespread disappointment and bitterness that surfaced when the upsurge of internal party democracy during the Revolution soon gave way to the old pattern of appointment of nominally elective officials, to restrictions on freedom of discussion and to the limitation of effective participation in policy making to a tiny oligarchy in Moscow. It would be naïve and misleading to explain the various party opposition movements between 1919 and 1921 solely in these terms, for other issues and cleavages also played a big part: policy disputes within the oligarchy itself, the selfish interests of local cliques and rival bureaucracies, 'ins' versus 'outs', and so on. But the common element in all these movements was struggle between the authoritarian and democratic elements in the party tradition and party behaviour, a struggle that came to a head in the 'trade union dispute' of early 1921, and was then definitively resolved, as we have seen, in favour of authoritianism. The Tenth Congress in March of that year, along with its resolution condemning the Workers' Opposition and their ideas of trade union autonomy, approved another resolution moved by Lenin 'On Party Unity', the burden of which was to render subject to expulsion any party members who criticized the leadership in public or who got together to promote policies or candidates at variance with those of the leadership.[13] These were accompanied by other statements reaffirming the traditional lip service to freedom of discussion and the elective principle,[14] the first blast of a hypocritical and demagogic smokescreen under which the party apparatus was empowered to 'put the lid on the opposition', in Lenin's words, and was provided in the process with the powers enabling it to consolidate its authority over the party membership. This outcome of the confrontation between the party's democratic and authoritarian strands cannot be explained purely by the personal authority of Lenin, the panic engendered by the Kronstadt revolt, which coincided with the Tenth Congress, or the weakness of democratic values and experience in Russia, significant though these facts were. It could not have happened had the arguments and means used to suppress opposition to the leadership not had such firm roots in the party's doctrines and past practices. In fact it was now the party's apparatus and not its rank and file members who were the most authentic heirs to that centralized, disciplined organization of 'professional revolutionaries' which was Lenin's pre-Revolutionary ideal, a point which understandably was not often publicly made by its apologists.[15]

After the Tenth Congress the Central Committee Secretariat rarely faced major obstacles in getting its nominees elected as provincial leaders, or the latter in having *their* nominees elected as district or city leaders, obstacles which could still be encountered at the beginning of 1921.[16] Nevertheless, the death throes of 'intra-party democracy' were to exhibit some impressive contortions before they came to an end. What kept them going was the series of splits within the ruling oligarchy itself, splits which continued till Stalin established his unchallenged personal dominance at the beginning of the 1930s. Successive defeated leaders like Trotsky and Zinoviev, despite their impeccable authoritarian records, now attempted to use the forms and language of democracy, kept alive by the very hypocrisy of the oligarchy's own propaganda, to rally their supporters and strive for a comeback. Their successes were always localized and temporary, for the apparatus, since 1921 firmly in Stalin's hands, always won the second and final round, albeit with difficultly at times.[17] While they lasted, however, they provided a vivid if pathetic demonstration of the fact that the proclaimed principles of free discussion and elections were also not without genuine roots in the party tradition. Nevertheless, with each successive year, as more and more independent-minded communists dropped out, were expelled, bought off or intimidated into silence, and the residue were swamped by hordes of pliable and career-minded new members, such challenges to apparatus direction became less and less thinkable. The forms of election were still usually observed. The reality, however, was an increasingly centralized, comprehensive and depoliticized system of personnel administration.[18]

For meanwhile the party's managers had also been hard at work creating the third of our preconditions for such a system, namely its *administrative* requirements in the form of staffs, procedures and information. It is to these we must now turn. Up to 1919 the party did not possess even the rudiments of such administrative requirements. Key appointments at the centre were decided without any particular system, mostly by Lenin, Yakov Sverdlov (who acted as CC Secretary in the time left over from his onerous work as Chairman of the Central Executive Committee of the Congress of Soviets) and whoever else was most closely concerned.[19] So far as the provinces were concerned, since the CC had only intermittent written contact with most of their party committees[20] there is little reason to contest Osinsky's remark that 'comrade Sverdlov stores information about all the party workers of Russia, wherever they might be, in his head. At any moment he could say where each of them was located, and it was he who transferred them'.[21] The trouble was that Sverdlov had just died, and the party's personnel 'files' perished with him. In practice, the local party committees, themselves formed primarily by co-optation, had been largely left to allocate the jobs in the new Soviet administration as it suited them.

The Eighth Congress in March 1919 approved the establishment in the CC of a Political Bureau (Politburo), an Organisational Bureau (Orgburo) and a Secretariat, the last-named to set up and work through a number of departments.[22] The Records and

Assignment Department (*Uchetnoraspredelitel'nyi otdel*, known as *Uchraspred*) was set up a month later, and was to be the main instrument of the CC in the task described by the congress as 'systematically reallocating party workers from one field of work to another and one district to another with the aim of putting them to most productive use'.[23] Lack of personnel records, however, combined with the disorganized conditions of the Civil War to rule out much 'system' for the first couple of years of the department's operation. Much of the time of its tiny staff was at first taken up with displaced party members who simply turned up on its doorstep (100–150 a day at times) and were dispatched to organizations and regions known to be short-staffed. In the period April–November 1919 inclusive, the department posted 2182 party workers, while the Orgburo, 'which itself assigns the most responsible comrades', posted 544. But the bulk of *Uchraspred*'s early postings were made not on an individual basis but as 'mobilizations', in which a quota of members was levied from local organizations and sent off to areas of grave staff shortage – mostly at this stage the military. Nearly 20 000 'mobilized' communists were assigned by *Uchraspred* in 1919.[24]

The following year the scale of Central Committee personnel work expanded enormously. Between April 1920 and March 1921, when the staff of *Uchraspred* rose from nine to thirty, there were no less than 16 000 individual postings, as well as 26 000 transferred under a total of fourteen mobilizations (these were largely for the military, but included 6000 for the railways, mobilizations of Polish, Lithuanian, Armenian, Tatar and Galician communists to work in their home territories, and even one of 130 women communists to work in the Astrakhan fisheries). Postings during this period included nearly 6000 to party work in the provinces and 1800 to party work in Moscow, 1700 to jobs in the central government and 200 to central trade union bodies. The CC also found jobs for 851 graduates of its Communist University,[25] forerunner of the Higher Party School which was to prove such an important channel of promotion within the CC nomenklatura.[26]

In 1921–2 improvization began to give way to system. Mobilizations, increasingly resented now the Civil War was over, were scaled down and were rare after 1922,[27] while the CC began to limit its involvement in low-level appointments in order to concentrate on more senior personnel, mainly in central and *gubernia* posts.[28] The *gubernia* staffing records essential to any effective system of personnel management began at last to be established. By March 1921 all *gubkomy* (*gubernia* committees) and most central government bodies had provided the lists of their officials requested some months earlier and on this basis *Uchraspred* set up its main card index.[29] By November this comprised 23 500 'responsible workers' in all major fields of activity. However, its accuracy was impaired by the frequent neglect by *gubkomy* of their obligation to report all transfers made locally.[30] Personal files based on questionnaires and other information were also compiled on more important categories of officials.[31] The questionnaires filled in by all half a million or more communists during the 1922 party census were lodged in the Central Committee and similar questionnaires were to be forwarded on all new members.[32]

A further prerequisite for any *nomenklatura* system which allocated jurisdiction over appointments to specific posts is a specification of the posts themselves, that is an 'establishment'. Of course, the government bodies taken over by the Bolsheviks each had their establishment (Russian: *shtat*) and this essential element in any rational administrative system soon gained acceptance by the new rulers, and was later extended to the party itself and to other 'voluntary' bodies, starting with the Komsomol (Young Communist League) and the trade unions. By January 1922 the CC had laid down a comprehensive set of establishments comprising all 'party workers' from the provincial (*gubernia*) level down to the basic cells (*yacheiki*), and budgeting and staffing were to be brought into conformity with these. Under this every official was classified according to a complex system of categories, for example, the head of an *ukom* (*uyezd* committee) organization department was a category III group 2b official, and the secretary of a *gubkom* was a category IV group 1a official.[33] Despite appearances, this was *not* a revival of the pre-Revolutionary 'Table of Ranks', telling though it might be as evidence of the bureaucratization of the party's internal processes. Something a bit closer to the 'Table of Ranks' did emerge, however, during this period, in the form of a ranking of 'party workers' in official positions as being of central, *oblast, gubernia, uyezd*, or rank-and-file (*ryadovoi*) 'scale' (*masshtab*). It is quite clear from the way these terms were employed that they represented an individual seniority classification and *not* a reference to the location (administration level) of their employment.[34] The use of this classfication system seems to have been discontinued later in the decade, and indeed as the hierarachy of *nomenklatury* emerged it rendered this and other indices of the seniority of officials redundant.

It would be naïve to see in the changes in party personnel practices in this period simply a process of rationalization, genuine and important though that was. For this was just the time when Stalin was taking the party apparatus into his hands, and beginning to use it to consolidate his authority. Power over appointments, the capacity to 'reward his friends and punish his enemies', was his key weapon. Stalin was already the dominant force in the central party machine by 1921, when he was the only Politburo member also serving on the Orgburo, and his ally Vyacheslav Molotov was in charge of the CC Secretariat. The following year he became General Secretary. His chief power resources were *Uchraspred* and the Organization and Instruction Department (*Orgotdel*), now headed by another protege, Lazar Kaganovich. The two departments began to co-operate in stocktaking and planned reassignments of provincial personnel.[35] In this way entrenched local cliques were broken up and the odd nest of oppositionists dispersed, and leaders installed on whom Stalin could rely, who set about turning the local organization into a 'bulwark of the CC' and of its chief.[36] With Stalin presiding at meetings of the Orgburo and Secretariat, these bodies now took over from *Uchraspred* a far larger proportion of senior appointments: at least a thousand in the year April 1922–March 1923, including no less than 42 *gubkom* secretaries.[37]

Space permits only a brief glance at the early evolution of personnel procedures in the provinces. *Uchraspred* departments were set up in the *gubkomy*, but merely to provide information to the bureau (inner executive) of the *gubkom*, which was supposed to make all appointments. In practice some bureaux left many personnel decisions to their *Uchraspred* department, while others totally ignored or even abolished it. Staff assigned to the departments were of low quality and constantly changed.[38] In mid-1921 Stalin's friends in the CC Secretariat began to take this situation in hand. The *gubkom Uchraspred* departments were replaced by records and statistics sub-departments coming under Kaganovich's *Orgotdel*, and headed by officials of senior rank who were not to be changed for at least six months, and were to observe uniform, centrally-prescribed procedures.[39] Following a census of provincial and local officials, a conference of *gubkom* secretaries was convened in December 1921 on further changes and improvements in personnel work at the *gubkom* and *ukom* (*uyezd* committee) levels. The emphasis was on changing the 'abnormal' (although usual) situation 'in which the leading comrades of responsible officials constitute a closed group', extremely difficult for any official promoted from *uyezd*, *volost* or factory level or from another locality to penetrate.[40] All this undoubtedly helped the new *gubkom* secretaries sent in by the CC Secretariat to re-staff the local apparatus with politically reliable cadres. Although, as can be seen from CC circulars issued in 1922 and 1923, the efficiency of personnel administration in the provinces remained well below Moscow's expectations,[41] the local party committees were now clearly exercising *administrative* control over senior appointments in all spheres of activity. For example, reports supplied by the district party committees (*ukomy*) to the Central Committee showed that they allocated all told 3806 personnel in the month of June 1922, including 247 to their own staffs, 652 to work in local soviet and governmental agencies, 136 to trade union posts, 492 to managerial jobs, 129 to educational institutions and 50 to medical institutions.[42]

The gestation of the nomenklatura system was now well advanced. The midwifery arrangements were put in train by the Twelfth Congress in April 1923, which instructed the CC 'to take all measures for the expansion and strengthening of the [personnel] records and assignment organs of the party at the centre and in the localities with the aim of embracing the totality of communist and communist-sympathising functionaries' so as to achieve 'a correct and comprehensive system of keeping records on and selecting the leading and responsible officials of soviet, managerial [*khozyaistvennykh*], co-operative and trade union organizations', along with party officials at all levels.[43] The birth itself can be firmly dated to 12 June 1923. On that day the Orgburo issued a resolution (*postanovlenie*) prescribing new procedures for the appointment and transfer of senior offical, which were to be based on two lists (*nomenklatury*), the first comprising posts which could change hands only by a decision (*postanovlenie*) of the CC (which in practice turned out to mean the Secretariat, Orgburo or Politburo), and the second comprising posts which had to be cleared (*soglasovany*) with the *Orgburo*.[44] Just four months later, on 12 October, the baby cut its first tooth; a draft nomenklatura for the CC was presented to the Orgburo and duly approved.[45] Well-nursed and nourished by Stalin's faithful assistants and despite the inevitable childhood complaints and tumbles, it soon grew into a sturdy and formidable infant.

Implementation of the new system presented the least difficulties with respect to those party officials, mostly at provincial (*oblast* and *gubernia*) level, coming under the CC nomenklatura, although the frequent failure of local committees to report changes or to respond to CC proposals for transfers was to exasperate *Uchraspred* for some time to come. Extending the system to embrace government officialdom, however, was to be a more complex and lengthy process. Of course, party bodies had been placing communists in government positions at all levels from the first days of the regime, but this had been on a totally haphazard basis. Moreover, as the commissariats and other agencies of the regime got established, their leaders, senior party members though they were, tended to resent undue party intrusion into their staffing prerogatives. It was probably no coincidence that it was only when Lenin, till recently a very dominating 'Head of the Soviet Government', lay paralyzed from his penultimate stroke, that the CC apparatus began to prepare the ground to assume systematic control over the appointment of government officials. In mid-1923 *Uchraspred* moved to establish working relationships with the personnel sections in the various government agencies, and the chiefs of these sections were made subject to approval by the CC.[46] By November it claimed to have 'succeeded to a considerable extent in taking within its grasp the allocation of party forces within the state apparatus'. The establishments of some 100 central agencies had been studied and *nomenklatury* for them drawn up, resulting in 5562 of their posts being placed on the records of the CC.[47] As can be inferred from the CC's written report to the Thirteenth Congress in May 1924, about 3500 government officials had by then been included in the CC's nomenklatura No. 1 and 1500 in its nomenklatura No. 2 (or in some cases on those of lower-level party committees), while a further category of posts on the CC's records remained under the jurisdiction of the government bodies concerned, which, however, had to inform the CC of any changes. Meanwhile, at the end of 1923 *Uchraspred* had set up a number of commissions to review the senior officials of government agencies, and of the 1102 reviewed up to the time of the Congress 278 had been recommended for dismissal or transfer.[48]

In 1924, after three years of ever-closer co-operation, the CC's *Orgotdel* and *Uchraspred* were combined into a single enormously powerful *Ograspred*, or Organization and Assignment Department, which took responsibility for the entrenchment, extension and refinement of the nomenklatura system in the following years. It pushed on with the effort to limit CC personnel work to senior officials (85 per cent of those assigned in 1924 were of '*uyezd* scale' or higher compared with 75 per cent in 1923),[49] and concentrated more and more on the occupants of CC nomenklatura posts.[50]

Important new instructions were issued at the beginning of 1926. These substantially trimmed the CC's nomenklaturas Nos. 1 and 2, to 1870 and 1640 posts respectively, but at the same time added to nomenklatura No. 1 a 'supplementary' list of 1590 elective posts, for which *ad hoc* special commissions were to be entrusted with ensuring the election of the CC's candidates by the conferences or other bodies concerned. A further group of some hundreds of mostly provincial posts were added as a second 'supplementary' category to nomenklatura No. 1, bringing the total number of posts requiring CC decision to over 5500. An additional 'departmental [*vedomstvennaya*] nomenklatura No. 3', consisting of important officials of central bodies not included in nomenklaturas Nos 1 and 2, was to be compiled by *Ograspred* in consultation with the bodies concerned. The latter were authorized to make appointments to these positions without prior CC approval, presumably notifying *Ograspred* of their decisions, although this is not specifically stated in the instruction.

The accompanying commentary specifies that decisions on nomenklatura No. 1 appointments were taken by the Politburo, Orgburo or Secretariat, while those on nomenklatura No. 2 required the 'agreement and sanction' of one of the CC Secretaries. An additional instruction prescribed rules for consultation between the CC, central governmental and other bodies concerned, and provincial party committees, on the election of senior local officials on the CC's nomenklaturas. And perhaps most importantly of all, provincial and republican party committees were now instructed to compile their own nomenklaturas modelled on those of the CC.[51]

A few weeks later new arrangements were approved regarding jurisdiction over posts in the CC's nomenklatura No. 1. The Politburo was to have direct control over 272 positions (*dolzhnosti*) staffed by 657 officials working in 117 agencies (*vedomstva*) and organizations, the Orgburo over 513 positions (713 officials) in 436 agencies and organizations, and the Secretariat over 389 positions (542 officials) in 287 agencies and organizations.[52] Unfortunately, no further details were provided and so far as the author is aware no subsequent information is available on the identity or even the number of official appointments which the party's topmost bodies reserve to themselves. Although the nomenklatura system quickly assumed key importance it did not immediately supplant all other forms of party involvement in the appointment of officials. For example, *Orgraspred*'s report for the last quarter of 1926 showed that even then, of the 1753 officials posted by the CC in this period only 235 were on the CC's Assignment (i.e., No. 1) Nomenklatura; 99 were 'mobilized' for special assignments, 319 posted on graduation from higher educational institutions, and the remaining 1100 were simply officials individually reassigned although not on the CC nomenklatura.[53] However, in the first quarter of 1927 the number of non-nomenklatura appointments was reduced to 279 and in the second quarter to a mere 79.[54] *Orgraspred* also carried out constant reviews of the personnel work of various agencies and organizations, often resulting in specific instructions on retraining or transfer of personnel. For example, in one week of July 1927 it issued decisions based on consideration of reports on the personnel work of local party committees, of credit institutions, of the consumers' co-operative organization, and of state trading institutions, and began reviewing reports on industrial managers and trade union officials.[55]

Some major regional and republican party committees had begun to switch their personnel work over to the nomenklatura system well before the CC instruction of January 1926 made the system generally obligatory. Both the Moscow Committee and the Ukrainian Central Committee were operating on the basis of nomenklaturas of 5000 each in 1924.[56] The North Caucasus *krai* (territorial) committee was another of those already working to a nomenklatura by 1924, and it was even sending back officials dispatched to it by subordinate committees for reassignment without its authorization before this practice was adopted by the Central Committee itself.[57] However, it was only in 1926 that most provincial and lower committees began the changeover to the new system, and a review by *Orgraspred* towards the end of the year revealed considerable confusion. There were enormous discrepancies in the range of posts placed on nomenklaturas: those compiled by *gubkomy*, for example, ranging from 332 to 1117. There was no consistency in allocating posts between nomenklatura No. 1 and No. 2, and some provincial committees failed to set up a departmental (No. 3) nomenklatura altogether. In many cases nomenklaturas existed only 'formally', i.e., personnel administration was not yet geared to them, and in others nomenklaturas had not yet even been compiled at local levels, especially in the *raikomy* (district committees). The most widespread errors noted were the inclusion of too many posts and the location of them too high up the party hierarchy. The Belorussian Central Committee even placed the heads of local health clinics on its nomenklatura No. 2. *Orgraspred* revealed that it was belatedly preparing model nomenklaturas which provincial and local committees should use as a basis for revising their lists.[58]

Fortunately we possess the full text of the nomenklaturas of the Smolensk *gubkom* for 1928 and the Western (*Zapadnyi*) *obkom* for 1929 (the Smolensk *gubernia* having meanwhile been incorporated into the newly-formed Western *oblast*.)[59] Since presumably a measure of standardization had by now been achieved these can be regarded as reasonably representative. Space does not permit a detailed analysis, but some general points should be noted. First, while the 1928 listing consists of the three nomenklaturas defined as in the 1928 instructions, the 1929 one is limited to two, nomenklatura No. 1 now being defined as 'posts for which the selection and appointment (*podbor i naznachenie*) of officials is executed by resolution of the bureau of the Western *obkom*', and No. 2 as 'posts for which the selection and appointment of officials is executed by resolution of the secretariat of the *obkom*'. Secondly, in both cases the majority of posts are listed as coming under the nomenklatura of more than one body. For instance, senior officials of the Western *obkom* were on the nomenklatura of the CC as well as that of the *obkom* itself, the editors of *okrug* (large district) newspapers were on those

of the CC, the *obkom*, and the *okrug* committee, the chairmen
of *oblast* trade union branches were on the nomenklaturas of the
obkom, the central committee of their union and the people's
commissariat (ministry) for the field concerned. Altogether in
1929 there were 279 posts on nomenklatura No. 1 and 349 on
nomenklatura No. 2, a total of 628. Of those on the *obkom*
nomenklatura No. 1, 88 were also on the CC nomenklatura,
comprising fifty party officials, fourteen soviet officials, ten newspaper editors, three bank directors, three trade union officials,
the *oblast* Komsomol secretary, co-operatives' board chairman,
Economic Council (*sovnarkhoz*) chairman, procurator, OGPU
chief, and chairman of the *oblast* court, and finally the rectors
of two higher educational institutions; forty were *oblast*-level and
forty-eight *okrug*-level officials.

The fact that most posts figured on the nomenklaturas of more
than one body leads us to our final point: while the formal
regulations, instructions and nomenklaturas themselves set the
parameters within which personnel decisions were made, they
tell us very little about the political realities of actual decisions.
Which of the bodies involved initiates the decision? How real is
the prescribed consultation (*soglasovanie*)? When does the right
of approval become an effective power of appointment, and
when is it reduced to a mere formality? What role can the
individual concerned play in securing desired appointments and
shaping his or her career? And behind such questions lie others
related to the informal structure of power: to inter-agency and
inter-echelon jurisdictional rivalries, local networks, patronage
followings, and so on. It is possible to find out a good deal
about such matters,[60] but this lies beyond the scope of the present
chapter.

Since the developments outlined here, the Soviet Union has suffered the traumas of forced industrialization and collectivization,
the purges of the 1930s, and the Second World War; Stalin's
dictatorship has come and gone, and the country has become
one of the world's two superpowers. Meanwhile the machinery
and procedures of personnel administration have not remained
unchanged. In 1930 *Orgraspred* was divided again into its two
original components, in 1934 personnel work was shared out
between a new Department of Leading Party Organs and various
'branch' departments (agriculture, transport, etc.), in 1939 it was

reconcentrated in a Cadres Directorate (*upravlenie kadrov*) and in the late 1940s again split between a Department of Party, Trade Union and Komsomol Organs and a number of branch departments, a situation that broadly persists today, although there is no doubt that the present Department of Organizational -Party Work is the dominant instrument of personnel control. These successive reorganizations were paralleled at lower levels of the party hierarchy.[61] Meanwhile, in the early 1930s personnel work was largely focused on staffing the new industrial bureaucracy, in the later 1930s on replacing the hundreds of thousands purged from all official organizations by men (and a few women) drawn from the new Soviet-trained 'intelligentsia'; during the war, party committees greatly extended their direct involvement in personnel decisions, often even undertaking the transfer of ordinary workers,[62] and this was followed by a campaign to trim *nomenklatury*, concentrate on more senior personnel, and reduce turnover.[63] Nevertheless, throughout all these changes and right down to our own day the nomenklatura system of *Herrschaft durch Kader*, in Glaessner's apt phrase, has retained the essential features evolved during the 1920s and has continued to lie at the core of the Soviet socio-political order.

Clearly, there are important implications here for the student of current changes in the USSR. The oft-stated intention of the Gorbachev regime to move away from excessive reliance on '*komandno-administrativnye metody*' in all areas of social life cannot go far before meeting obstacles in the assumptions and entrenched practices of the nomenklatura system and the interests that are anchored in it. This they obviously understand, and indeed the highlighting of *demokratizatsiya* in 1987, especially the move to contested elections of party committee secretaries and factory managers, may indicate a determination to tackle these formidable obstacles head-on. But are they really ready to give up that centralized, administrative allocation of the nation's 'cadres' on which the existing social order and not least their own power within it have substantially rested, or are they rather seeking to preserve it in a more effective form less obviously at variance with those democratic claims through which they seek to draw legitimacy? If the latter, the *perestroika* under way will scarcely amount to a 'revolution'.

NOTES

1. V.I.Lenin., *Polnoe sobranie sochinenii*, (hereafter *PSS*) 5th edn., (Moscow, 1964) vol 45, p. 123.
2. See Michael Voslenksy, *Nomenklatura. Die herrschende Klasse der Sowjetunion* (Vienna, 1980); A. Ivanov, Nomenklaturnyi klass', *Posev*, March 1973. pp. 34–6; Alec Nove, 'Is There a Ruling Class in the USSR?', *Soviet Studies*, vol. XXVII, no. 4 (October 1975) pp. 615–38. The perception and resentment of the nomenklatura system as bound up with the exclusive power and privileges of a ruling class or élite is reflected in dissident *samizdat* writings, but it appears to be only in Poland in the Solidarity era that it emerged as a public issue. See Takayuki Ito. *Controversy over Nomenklatura in Poland. Twilight of a Monopolistic Instrument for Social Control* (Sapporo, 1982).
3. Descriptions in Soviet official sources are understandably reticent. A more helpful than usual account is given by E. Z. Razumov, First Deputy Head of the Central Committee's Department of Organisational-Party Work, in his *Problemy kadrovoi politiki KPSS* (Moscow, 1983) pp. 53–65. On the system's operation in the late Stalin period see T. H. Rigby, *The Selection of Leading Personnel in the Soviet State and Communist Party* (Ph.D. Thesis, University of London, 1954) chs 7 and 8. See further Borys Lewytzkyj, 'Die Nomenklatur – ein wichtiges Instrument sowjetischer Kaderpolitik', *Osteuropa*, 1961, pp. 408–12; Jerry F. Hough, *The Soviet Prefects* (Cambridge, Mass., 1969) pp. 114–16, 150–70; Bohdan Harasymiw, 'Die sowjetische Nomenklatur. I. Organisation und Mechanismen' and 'II. Soziale Determanenten der Kaderpolitik', *Osteuropa*, 1977, pp. 583–98 and 665–81; Bohdan Harasymiw, '*Nomenklatura*: The Soviet Communist Party's Leadership Recruitment System', *Canadian Journal of Political Science*, vol. II (1969) pp. 493–512; Thomas Lowit, 'Y a-t-il des Etats en Europe de l'Est?', *Revue francaise de sociologie*, vol. XX (1979) pp. 431–47; John Löwenhardt, 'Nomenklatoera en corruptie in de Sovjetunie', *Internationale Spectator*, vol. XXXVII (1983) pp. 429–39; T. H. Rigby and Bohdan Haraymiw (eds), *Leadership Selection and Patron-Client Relations in the USSR and Yugoslavia* (London, 1983), especially the Introduction by T. H. Rigby and ch. 2, '*Nomenklatura*: Check on Localism', by John Miller. See also Gert-Joachim Glaessner's valuable study of personnel administration in the GDR, *Herrschaft durch Kader. Leitung der Gesellschaft und Kaderpolitik in der DDR* (Opladen, 1977) especially Teil IV and Exkurs I.
4. There is a brief outline in Leonard Schapiro. *The Communist Party of the Soviet Union,* 2nd edn. (London, 1970) p. 319f.
5. On the matters discussed in this section see Walter Pietsch. *Revolution und Staat. Institutionen als Träger der Macht in Sowjetrussland 1917-1922,* (Cologne, 1969), Schapiro, op. cit., chs XIII–XIV, and E. H. Carr, *The Bolshevik Revolution 1917–1923* (Pelican edn., London, 1966), vol. I, chs 8–9.
6. *Vos'moi s''ezd RKP(b). Mart 1919 goda. Protokoly* (Moscow, 1959) p. 428.
7. *Vos'moi s''ezd RKP(b), p. 426.*
8. See *Desyatyi s''ezd RKP(b). Mart 1921 goda* (Moscow, 1963) p. 56, *Izvestiya Tsentral'nogo Komiteta* (hereafter *Izv. TsK*) no. 8, 2 December 1919, no. 28, 5 March 1921, and no. 3(51), March 1923.

9. See Carr, op. cit., vol. I, pp. 203-7, and Schapiro, op. cit. ch II.
10. *Pravda*, 7 December 1952, Cf. B. N. Ponomarev *et al.* 'The Local Party Committee was Appointed by the Central or Regional Committee', *Istoriya KPSS* (Moscow, 1960) p. 115.
11. Even by Lenin. See, e.g., his 'Svoboda kritiki i edinstvo deistvii', *PSS*, vol. 13 (Moscow, 1960) pp. 128-30. See also the decision during the 1905 Revolution calling for a consistent application of elective principles within the party in keeping with the country's new-won political liberties, *KPSS v rezolyutsiyakh* (Moscow, 1953) vol. 1, pp. 99-100.
12. For examples, see articles by I. Koganitsky and A. Shlyapnikov in *Revolyutsiya i VKP (b) v materialakh i dokumentakh*, vol. VII (Moscow, 1928) pp. 240-2, and *Partiya Bol'shevikov v gody novogo revolyutsionnogo pod''ema 1910-1914 gody. Dokumenty i materialy* (Moscow, 1962) pp. 292-3.
13. See *Desyatyi S''ezd RKP(b)*, pp. 571-6.
14. The resolution '*Po voprosam partiinogo stroitel'stva' (Desyatyi S''ezd RKP (b)*, pp. 559-71) is wholly in this spirit.
15. The identification, however, was made quite explicitly by Andrei Bubnov in his article '*Ob apparate*', in *Pravda*, 18 December 1923.
16. See T. H. Rigby, 'Early Provincial Cliques and the Rise of Stalin', *Soviet Studies* vol. XXXIII, no. 1 (January 1981) pp. 15-19 (this volume, ch. 3).
17. The Smolensk party archives contain an unusually well-documented example of temporarily successful 'opposition' activity, in this case in the Bely *uyezd* (district) during 1926, and of how it was dealt with by the provincial apparatus. See Smolensk Archive. WKP 25, Report of *gubkom* members Zimenkov and Kuchinsky to the *gubkom*. For a note on the 'Trotskyite' and 'Zinovievite' oppositions in Kaluga *gubernia* and their repression, see WKP 44, Outline Report on the work of the Kaluga *gubkom* of the VKP (b), p. 10.
18. For more detail, see T. H. Rigby, 'Party Elections in the CPSU', *Political Quarterly,* vol. 35 (1964) pp. 422-9.
19. On the selection of People's Commissars, see T. H. Rigby, *Lenin's Government. Sovnarkom 1917-1923* (Cambridge, 1978) ch. 10.
20. *Vos'moi s''ezd RKP (b)*, pp. 504-13.
21. Ibid., pp. 165.
22. Ibid., pp. 424.
23. Ibid., pp. 426.
24. *Izv. TsK.* no. 8, 2 December 1919.
25. These figures appear in *Izv. TsK*, no. 28, March 1921.
26. The future General Secretary Konstantin Chernenko was a full-time student there in 1943-5.
27. Already in 1921 most mobilizations were seriously underfulfilled and provoked many resignations from the party. See *Izv. TsK*, no. 39, March 1922. In 1922 there was a small mobilization for work at the *uyezd* level, and an ambitious one aimed at getting a thousand 'bureaucratized' party functionaries out of Moscow, which caused enormous administrative difficulties and was never completed. See *Izv. TsK*, no. 3 (51) March 1923. Then in 1924 there was a mobilization of 3000 to reinforce the party, government and trade union apparatuses in the rural areas. See *Spravochnik partiinogo rabotnika*, vypusk 4 (Moscow, 1924) pp. 149-50 and *Izv. TsK*, no. 4 (62) April 1924, pp. 75-6.
28. *Izv. TsK*, no. 39, March 1922. The number of CC assignments was halved in 1921 and halved again in 1922. But 4738 of the 10 321 postings made

in the period April 1922–March 1923 were of 'responsible' (i.e. senior) officials, an *increase* on the previous year. See ibid. no. 3 (51) March 1923.

29. *Izv. TsK,* no. 28, 5 March 1921.
30. Ibid., no. 36, 15 December 1921.
31. Ibid., no. 43, July 1922 and no. 2 (50) February 1923.
32. *Spravochnik partiinogo rabotnika,* vypusk 3 (Moscow, 1923) pp. 128–30.
33. See *Izv. TsK,* no. 1 (37) January 1922, pp. 40–1.
34. Compare, for example, the figures given for the 'scale' of officials appointed by *ukomy* in June 1922 with the figures given for the administrative levels from which they were posted, in *Izv. TsK,* no. 9 (45) September 1922. Similarly the 1970 officials posted by the CC to positions in *central* institutions between April 1924 and February 1925 were said to comprise thirteen of central, 99 of *oblast,* 877 of *gubernia,* and 971 of *uyezd* 'scale'. See ibid., no. 22-3 (97–8), 22 June 1925.
35. See Report of *Orgotdel, Izv. TsK,* no. 33, October 1921.
36. See Rigby, 'Early Provincial Cliques', and Robert V. Daniels, 'The Secretariat and the Local Organisations in the Russian Communist Party, 1921–1923', *American Slavic and East European Review,* vol. XVI (1967) pp. 32–49.
37. See *Izv. TsK,* no. 42, June 1922, no. 43, July 1922, no. 9 (45) September 1922, no. 11–12 (47–8) Nov.–Dec. 1922, and no. 3 (51) March 1923.
38. Ibid., no. 37, January 1922.
39. Ibid., nos 27 and 32, 1921; *Spravochnik partiinogo rabotnika,* vypusk 2 (Moscow, 1922) pp. 69–70.
40. Ibid., pp. 46–7.
41. See *Spravochnik partiinogo rabotnika,* vypusk 3, pp. 141–2.
42. Nearly a thousand were transferred to work in other *uyezdy* or placed at the disposal of their *gubkom.* See *Izv. TsK,* no. 9 (45) September 1922.
43. *Dvenadtsatyi s''ezd RKP (b). 17-25 aprelya 1923 goda. Stenograficheskii otchet* (Moscow, 1968) pp. 704–5.
44. *Izv. TsK,* no. 1 (122) 18 January 1926. The happy event does not appear to have been reported publicly at the time, and the text of the resolution has not been traced.
45. *Izv. TsK.* no. 1 (59) January 1924. A CC plenum held on 8 November 1923 authorized *Uchraspred* to use the new nomenklatura as a basis for 'a systematic review of the leading staff of all agencies and organizations'.
46. *Izv. TsK,* no. 5 (53) June 1923 and no. 7-8 (55–6) Aug.–Sept. 1923.
47. Ibid., no. 9-10 (57–8) Oct.–Nov. 1923. At that time 2783 of these posts were occupied by party members. It would seem that the bulk of this work had been carried out by the middle of the year. See ibid., no. 5 (53) July 1923.
48. *Trinadtsatyi s''ezd RKP (b). Mai 1924 goda. Stenograficheskii otchet* (Moscow, 1963) p. 805. For further details on the review of officials, see *Izv. TsK,* no. 3 (61) March 1924, and no. 4 (62) April 1924.
49. See *Izv. TsK* no. 22-3 (97–8) 22 June 1925.
50. Some organizations, however, continued to send junior officials to the CC for reassignment without authorization, and in 1926 *Orgraspred* announced that it would simply send such officials back to where they came from. See *Izv. TsK,* no. 45-6 (166–7) 22 November 1926.
51. For summaries of the instructions and official commentary see *Izv. TsK,* no. 1 (122) 1926.

52. *Izv. Tsk,* no. 9 (130) 8 March 1926. This amended a previous allocation of jurisdiction over CC nomenklatura no. 1 posts adopted late in 1924.
53. *Izv. TsK,* no. 9 (182) 7 March 1927. Most of these 1100 had probably been sent to the CC for reassignment by lower party committees. Some of them presumably entered the CC's Nomenklatura No. 2. Only 98 of them (9 per cent) lacked at least *'uyezd* scale' seniority.
54. *Izv. TsK.* no. 19 (192) 23 May 1927 and no. 39 (212) 22 October 1927. The former reported that some 700 communists sent for reassignment to the CC by local committees had been redirected by *Orgraspred* to the Moscow Committee or back to other committees. Evidently it took a year before the threat to do this made in January 1926 began to be strictly carried out.
55. *Izv. TsK,* no. 30–1 (203–4) 18 August 1927.
56. Ibid., no. 45–6 (166–7) 22 November 1926.
57. Ibid., no. 19–20 (140–1) 24 May 1926.
58. Ibid., no. 45–6 (166–7) 22 November 1926.
59. See Smolensk Archive, files No. WPK 33 and 40 respectively.
60. There is some valuable material relating to the 1930s in Merle Fainsod, *Smolensk under Soviet Rule* (New York, 1958), especially chs. 3, 4 and 11, and the present author discusses these matters mostly in relation to the late Stalin perod in 'The Selection of Leading Personnel', ch. 8.
61. The standard account of these changes is in M. Fainsod, *How Russia is Ruled,* rev. edn. (Cambridge, Mass., 1963) ch. 6.
62. For two authoritative articles on personnel policies during the War period, see N. Shatalin, 'O rabote s kadrami', *Partiinoe stroitel'stvo,* no. 20 (Oct. 1943) pp. 11–19, and N. Semin, 'Iz praktiki otdela kadrov obkoma partii', ibid., no. 24, (Dec. 1943) pp. 26–31.
63. Turnover of officials on the nomenklatura of the Ukrainian CC went down from 31% in 1946 to 11% in 1948. However, the size of the *nomenklatura* remained about 15 000. See V. I. Yurchuk, 'Vosstanovlenie i ukreplenie partiinykh organizatsii na Ukraine v 1945–1953 godakh', *Voprosy istorii KPSS,* no. 6 (1962) p. 80.

5. The nomenklatura and patronage under Stalin*

Each Communist Party committee has its nomenklatura or detailed list of the posts under its jurisdiction. The nomenklatura defines those party, government and other posts to which individuals may not be appointed without personal interview and prior approval by the offices of the party committee concerned. Responsibility for the selection of officials is to a large extent vested in the party committees into whose nomenklatura they enter.[1] However, as will be seen later, the actual recommendation of officials emanates in a certain proportion of cases from the subordinate body concerned and the party committee's role is reduced to one of ratification. In other cases the main responsibility for the appointment of a class of officials may be vested in a particular committee, although they are also placed on the nomenklatura of a higher party committee for approval. Many of the posts on the committee's nomenklatura are assigned to it by decisions of higher party committees, but they appear to exercise a considerable degree of discretion in the posts they add to these. Thus, the Sverdlovsk Regional Committee subjected its nomenklatura to a review in 1943, as the result of which it was cut by 25 per cent, the posts eliminated being devolved upon the subordinate district and city committees.[2] Consequently, considerable differences may be found in the size of the nomenklatura of various party committees at the same level.

In 1952 the nomenklatura of the regional committees in Kirgizia averaged about 800, and those of the city and district committees about 220.[3] At the same period the nomenklatura of the Bobruisk City Committee in Belorussia was fixed at 513,[4] while in 1947 the

*From *The Selection of Leading Personnel in the Soviet State and Communist Party* (Ph.D. Thesis, University of London, 1954) chs 7 and 8, with minor editorial changes.

Molotov City Committee, containing a much larger party organization and with subordinate ward (*raion*) committees, had about
800 posts on its nomenklatura.[5] Some time before this, however,
the North Kazahkstan Regional Committee, although it had a
comparatively small party organization to deal with, had 2600
on its nomenklatura, while one of the district committees of the
Yaroslavl Region had as many as 700.[6] In the larger industrial and
administrative cities, the nomenklatura is probably much greater
as a rule than in the examples mentioned, although precise data
are not available. In the years 1946–8, the Tbilisi City Committee
made over 1000 appointments to posts on its nomenklatura, which
probably greatly exceeded this number.[7]

In the two years ending March 1951 the Moscow City Committee and its ward committees between them filled about 3000
nomenklatura posts.[8] The nomenklatura of the republican central
committees would seem usually to number several thousands. That
of the Kirgiz Central Committee, which contained approximately
2700 posts in 1952, must be amongst the smallest.[9] In Georgia, that
proportion of the Central Committee's nomenklatura to which
wartime appointments were made alone totalled 7947.[10]

These figures give some idea of the scope of party committees'
direct jurisdiction over appointments. Their cadre responsibilities,
however, are not confined to nomenklatura officials. If the need
for personnel, however junior, arises in any field, and the body
concerned is unable to meet this need from its own resources,
it is up to the local party committee to come to its assistance.
N. Shatalin, who served briefly after Stalin's death as Central
Committee Secretary responsible for cadres, gave the following
example: suppose that a regional party committee, on checking
the work of a machine-tractor station (MTS), finds that it is being
hindered by the shortage of a mechanic, the regional committee
should require its agriculture department to select a person for this
post even though it does not come into its nomenklatura, and if
necessary should have a suitable mechanic transferred from some
other organization.[11] Nor is the party's control over appointments
confined to party members. Where suitable non-party candidates
are available they also may be placed by party committees in posts
on their nomenklatura.[12]

Before examining the main categories of posts entering the
nomenklatura of party committees at the various levels we should

look a little more closely at the sources of relevant information. In a very few cases, the party decision allocating a class of officials to a particular level in the party apparatus is printed in publications available to foreigners. Thus in 1950 the daily organ of the Belorussian Central Committee and Government published a decision of the Belorussian Central Committee on book-publishing and marketing in the republic, which included articles placing the managers of bookshops on the nomenklatura of city committees, and the heads of local outlets of the Belorussian Book-selling Trust on the nomenklatura of district committees.[13] A decision of the All-Union Central Committee published in March 1954 contained the following provision:

> With the aim of heightening the responsibility of local party organs for the correct allocation and training of leading *kolkhoz* cadres, it is acknowledged as necessary that the chairmen of collective farms should be placed upon the nomenklatura of the regional and territorial committees and the central committees of the national communist parties, and the vice-chairmen of collective farms, leaders of production brigades and heads of livestock farms upon the nomenklatura of the district committees.[14]

In other cases such decisions, although not actually printed, are referred to explicitly by party authorities. For example, the Ukrainian Second Secretary, A. I. Kirichenko, wrote in 1952: 'With the aim of strengthening control over the selection of propaganda cadres the Ukrainian Central Committee has placed upon its nomenklatura the heads of departments of propaganda and agitation of the city and district committees'.[15] Before this, these posts in the Ukraine had been on the nomenklatura of the regional party committees.[16]

Apart from statements referring to changes in the nomenklatura, there are occasional direct references to such and such a class of officials figuring on a certain nomenklatura. Thus an inspector of the Belorussian Central Committee wrote in 1952: 'The secretaries of the primary party organizations constitute the most numerous and important category of officials on the nomenklatura of the City Committee.[17] Another example is a 1946 statement that over the previous eighteen months 48.3 per cent of the officials on the nomenklatura of the Kiev Regional Committee had been changed, including 26 per cent of the first secretaries and 38.6 per cent of the second secretaries of the district committees, 45 per cent of the chairmen of the executive committee of district soviets, and 94 per cent of the heads of the trade departments of district executive committees.[18]

More often one must fall back on statements ascribing the responsibility for *particular appointments* to various party committees. For example, in 1946 the First Secretary of the Kazakh Central Committee wrote as follows:

> In many instances, as a result of the lack of a serious approach, the business of changing a particular official triggers a mass reshuffle of cadres from one post to another. Here is a characteristic example. In order to fill the vacant post of Chairman of the Galkinsky District Executive Committee the Pavlodar Regional Party Committee set about shifting four officials: to the post of chairman of the Galkinsky District Executive Committee the Regional Committee planned to transfer the Chairman of the Mikhailovsky District Executive Committee, to the post of the latter the Chairman of the Regional Planning Commission, and to the Regional Planning Commission, the Head of the Statistical Administration.[19]

The clear implication of this statement is that the prime responsibility for the choice of chairmen of district executive committees and certain regional government officials – chairman of the regional planning commission and head of the statistical administration – lies with the regional party committee (and not with, for example, the district party committee or the republican central committee). Such a statement, however, is not in itself enough to show that these posts are on the nomenklatura of the regional committee alone, since the context does not exclude the possibility that in deciding on these changes the regional committee was acting on the basis of powers devolved upon it by the Kazakh Central Committee, which retained for itself the right of approving them. Nevertheless, if we encounter a number of such cases, and find that responsibility for such appointments seems always to be attributed entirely to the regional committee, it would seem reasonable to ascribe them to the latter's nomenklatura.

How comprehensively do these various sources reveal the locus of responsibility within the party apparatus for appointments to the main categories of official positions?

Let us first consider posts in the party apparatus itself. The most

senior category of party officials outside the Central Committee's Politburo and Secretariat are the secretaries of the regional
(*oblast'*) and territorial (*krai*) committees of the RSFSR and the
central committees of the other fifteen union republics.[20] As we
have already observed, these are placed fairly and squarely in
the nomenklatura of the All-Union Committee by the Party
Statutes themselves, article 42 of which states: 'The regional
and territorial committees and the central committees of the
communist parties of the union republics elect corresponding
executive organs comprising not more than 11 persons, including
three secretaries subject to the approval of the Central Committee of the Party.' However, it is not clear from this who
is responsible for the secretaries of those regional committees
which are formed within several of the union republics other
than the RSFSR (which has no republic party bodies).[21] Is it
the All-Union Central Committee or the Central Committee of
the republic concerned? It is certainly the latter which has the task
of choosing and recommending these officials, and they appear
to be able to remove them at will.[22] However, except possibly in
the case of the regional secretaries of the smaller Central Asian
republics, it seems likely that this class of officials would normally
have to be cleared in Moscow.[23] It would be strange if this were
not so at least in respect of the Ukraine, whose regions average
scarcely less in population and economic importance than those
of the RSFSR. Nevertheless, even there the initiative and primary
responsibility for the choice of regional committee secretaries falls
to the republic central committee. The Ukrainian First Secretary
stated in May 1952 that 'the Ukrainian Central Committee committed mistakes in promoting certain immature and incompetent
officials – Comrade Kostenko to the post of Secretary of the Lvov
City Committee and Comrade Babichuk to the post of the (First)
Secretary of the Zhitomir Regional Committee – who did not cope
with the business entrusted them and were recently relieved of their
duties'.[24]

The party secretaries at the next level down, the city and district
committees, are stated in the party rules to be subject to the approval of the regional and territorial committees and the republic
central committees (art. 50). Here there was a reversion after the
Second World War to the position prevailing until towards the
end of the Great Purges. It is not certain when the decision of

August 1938[25] placing the first, second and third secretaries of these committees upon the nomenklatura of the All-Union Central Committee lost its force.

In the RSFSR there were numerous cases in the postwar years confirming the responsibility of the regional and territorial party committees for the choice of district secretaries.[26] In those republics without regional units this class of appointments may similarly be identified as coming under jurisdiction of the republican committees.[27] In the republics which are subdivided into regions the relevant clause of the party rules is again ambiguous. It seems clear from press reports, however, that in the Ukraine, Belorussia, Uzbekistan and Kazakhstan it is the regional committees which pick out and recommend the candidates for district party secretaries' posts, though it is possible that they need to be cleared by the republican Central Committee.[28] In Tadjikistan, on the other hand, the selection of district secretaries is in the hands not of the regional committees but of the Tadjik Central Committee,[29] and this would appear to apply also in Turkmenia.[30] In Kirgizia the evidence is contradictory, but suggests that the Kirgiz Central Committee took over from the regional committees the choice of district secretaries in the latter half of 1953.[31] The selection of secretaries for the majority of city committees is the responsibility of the regional committee,[32] but as Kirichenko's statement quoted above shows, the party secretaries of the most important cities in the non-Russian republics come under the jurisdiction of the republican central committees. On this analogy it is probable that the secretaries of the major cities of the RSFSR are on the nomenklatura of the All-Union Central Committee. In the republics without regional divisions, the city secretaries, like the district secretaries, are chosen by the republican central committees, and this appears also to be the position in the smaller republics of Central Asia.[33] It would seem reasonable to assume that the superior party committee to whose nomenklatura the secretaries of a particular city committee are assigned lies at the same administrative level as that to which the government organs of the city are answerable,[34] though it has not been possible to gather enough evidence to establish this. The city committees are charged with the choice of secretaries for their subordinate ward (city *raion*) committees.[35]

The majority of secretaries of primary party organizations are included in the nomenklatura of the city and district committees, and in the larger cities, of their ward (*raion*) committees.[36] However, as has been mentioned, article 58 of the party rules assigns the secretaries of the primary party organizations of the ministries to the nomenklatura of the Central Committee, and those of the republican ministries are probably subject to approval by the republican central committees. The secretaries of the party organizations of the regional organs of central agencies likewise appear to come under the direct jurisdiction of the regional party committee.[37] It would seem likely that in major production enterprises, whose party organizations may number several hundreds, the secretary would require the approval of committees above the city or district level, but the data is lacking to verify this.

With respect to the officials of party committees below secretarial rank, the general rule appears to be that the heads of departments come under the jurisdiction of the next higher party committee, while the more junior staff members are on the nomenklatura of the committee employing them.[38] This pattern, however, is not universal. For example, regional committees seem to be responsible for the choice of directors for their own party schools,[39] while in the smaller republics the district and city department chiefs appear to be the responsibility of the republic Central Committee itself.[40] On the other hand, as was mentioned earlier, the heads of the district and city departments of propaganda and agitation in the Ukraine were transferred from the nomenklatura of the regional committees to that of the republic's Central Committee, and this change may also have been made in other republics. It is possible also that the heads of other departments of the city and district committees, notably their departments of Party, Trade Union and Komsomol Organs, have also been made subject to approval by the republic Central Committees. At the same time, it would seem likely that the responsibility for choosing and recommending candidates for these posts remains in the hands of the regional committees.

The allocation of local government posts to the nomenklatura of this or that party committee follows fairly closely that of their opposite numbers in the party apparatus. The choice of chairmen of the executive committees of local soviets up to regional and territorial level is vested in the next higher party committee.[41] The smaller Central Asian republics again appear to be an exception to this, as the chairmen of executive committees of the city and district soviets in these areas, like the secretaries of the corresponding party committees, have apparently been transferred from the jurisdiction of the regional committees to that of the republican central committees.[42] The deputy chairmen and department heads of local executive committees, as well as the heads of local organs of public offices outside the jurisdiction of the local soviets (with the apparent exception of the Ministries of Internal Affairs and State Security–MVD and MGB), and possibly also the Ministry of State Control, are approved by the next higher party committee on the recommendation of the corresponding party committee. The choice of chairmen of village soviets appears to be the sole responsibility of the district party committees.[43]

At higher levels in the government apparatus less information is available. On the analogy of the procedure followed at the regional, city and district levels, one would expect the selection of the chairmen of republic councils of ministers to be vested in the All-Union Central Committee, while the deputy chairmen and ministers would be approved by the latter on the recommendation of the republican party committees. This can be verified only partly from Soviet press statements. There is no doubt as to the responsibility of republic party committees for the nomination of republic ministers.

Statements like the following suggest, in fact, a high degree of local autonomy in the appointment and removal of republic ministers:

> In July 1952 the Bureau of the Georgian Central Committee discussed the question of the activity of the Ministry of Social Security of Georgia. By decision of the Bureau the Minister Comrade Chkhetiani, who had not provided the Ministry with proper leadership, was relieved of his duties.[44]

Although it seems likely that new republic ministers would need to be confirmed by the All-Union Central Committee, no direct evidence of this has been obtained. No mention of republic party committees' participating in the choice of republic MVD and MGB Ministries has been found, and it would seem that the All-Union leadership retains full control over appointments to these posts. The republic party authorities, however, are apparently held responsible for the appointment of ministers of justice as well as of the heads of the republic branches of at least some all-union agencies.[45] They appear to have sole authority over the appointment of deputy ministers and the heads of chief administrations in the republic governments,[46] and of more junior officials of the ministries.[47]

Most of the information upon the basis of which the above generalisations have been formulated appeared in the course of statements condemning from above actual choices of officials made by republic and local party authorities. This source of evidence is naturally lacking in respect of classes of appointment coming under the direct jurisdiction of the All-Union Central Committee. In general, it would seem reasonable to suspect that wherever criticisms are conspicuously absent in respect to appointments to some category of senior posts, this category is in the hands of the All-Union Central Committee. This is borne out when applied to party appointments, where we find that criticisms are met with in respect of all classes of posts except those which are stated by the rules themselves to require the approval of the All-Union Central Committee – the secretaries of the republic central committees and of the regional and territorial party committees. If this principle is invoked in an attempt to discover which appointments in the state apparatus are vested in the All-Union Central Committee, the resulting list conforms to what would be expected on the analogy of how responsibility for lower level government appointments is distributed: federal ministers and other senior personnel of the central organs of federal ministries and agencies, the chairmen of republic councils of ministers, and of the executive committees of regional and territorial soviets in the RSFSR.

In organizing the selection of the leading personnel of trusts and enterprises, two courses would appear to be open to the Soviet authorities. Having secured party control over the appointment of senior officials of the industrial ministries, they might devolve upon the latter the entire responsibility for operative industrial appointments; or they might retain substantial direct control over these appointments also within the party apparatus itself. The second course has so far been followed. There is ample evidence of the dominant role played by party committees in the choice of many senior industrial executives. Statements like the following are common in the Soviet press: 'Recently the (Leninabad) City Committee issued a decision to transfer Comrade A. from the post of Director of the Conserves Cannery to that of Director of the Meat Cannery.'[48] The Secretary of the primary party organization of a Moscow factory complained at his ward party conference:

> Over the last four years we have had four directors. This is all explained by the fact that the Raion Committee and the Moscow City Committee pay little attention to the qualifications of officials in advancing them to posts. Last year Shchegolev was appointed director of our factory. We warned the Raion Committee and the City Committee of the party that the candidature of Shchegolev was not suitable for the post of director. The previous year he had been removed from another leading post for not coping with the work entrusted to him. However the Raion Committee and the City Committee would take no notice of the opinion of (us) subordinate officials. As a result Shchegolev, after working for three months with us, had to be removed from his position.[49]

The choice of the leaders for industrial organizations may be vested in the district, city, regional or republic party authorities, depending upon the importance of the organization.[50] It is probable that the Secretariat and relevant departments of the All-Union Central Committee are consulted over appointments of heads of enterprises classified as being of All-Union importance, although the rarity of press criticism of appointments at this level suggests that the involvement of Politburo members supervizing the ministries concerned usually reduced the role of the CC apparatus to a minor one.

The participation of party committees in the choice of industrial executives is not confined to trust and factory managers, but extends to the second-rank leaders of enterprises.[51] The following are a few examples of posts stated to be on the nomenklatura of various city committees:

1. head of the planning department of a weaving mill;
2. chief accountant of a timber combine;
3. chief engineer of a meat cannery;
4. head of the supplies department of a brewery; and
5. vice-director of a city industrial trading trust.[52]

In agriculture the most important category of officials, the collective farm chairmen, formally elected by the general meeting of collective farmers, were until 1954 chosen by the district party committee, under the general supervision of the regional committee.[53] The latter, however, seems usually to have taken little interest. For example, in 1952 the chairmen of a hundred of the collective farms in the Ternopol Region had been working for some time without the Agriculture Department of the Regional Committee bothering to submit their candidatures for approval by the Bureau of the Regional Committee.[54] The heads of livestock farms, brigade leaders and other subordinate executives of the collective farms, usually appointed by the formally elective board of management, were also subject to some general supervision by the district party committee. For example, *Pravda* wrote with approval in May 1952 of the work of a party instructor sent by a district committee to a collective farm to overcome shortfalls in output, who secured the election of a new primary party organization secretary, the latter then helping him to reallocate the leading personnel of the collective farm.[55] Such intervention, however, does not appear to have been typical, and the choice of junior leaders in the collective farms seems normally to have been left to the farm chairman and the secretary of the primary party organization. The Central Committee decision of March 1954 placing collective farm chairmen on the nomenklatura of the regional and territorial committees and the republic central committees, and deputy chairmen, heads of livestock farms, and brigade leaders on those of the district party committees,[56] was clearly aimed at tightening party control over the choice of collective farm cadres, although actual nominations of persons for these posts may often have remained at the levels formerly making these appointments.

Appointments of directors of MTSs have always been under the control not of the district committees but of the regional committees, and in republics without regional divisions by the republic central committees.[57] These are also responsible for the appointment of deputy directors and chief mechanics of MTSs.[58]

It is probable that state farm directors also come under the direct jurisdiction of the regional and republic committees, but the data is lacking to establish this.

So far, we have been considering how the party's responsibilities for personnel assignment are distributed between different levels in the hierarchy of party committees. Let us now turn to the internal structures and procedures involved. The basic, if often violated, principle is that persons chosen for posts on the nomenklatura of a party committee should not be formally installed until approved at a sitting of the bureau of the party committee,[59] normally, after personal interview by the bureau. The work of finding candidates for nomenklatura posts, however, is normally entrusted to officers of the appropriate departments of the party committee. The departmental structure of the party apparatus has undergone almost constant change,[60] and it will be sufficient here to outline the way it operated from the 1930s to the aftermath of Stalin's death.

Over the decades of Soviet power the party leadership has fluctuated between preferring an apparatus articulated according to the various functions assigned to it (selecting personnel, verifying fulfilment of decisions, propaganda and agitation, and so on) and one articulated in terms of the various fields of activity under its control (for example, agriculture, industry, the arts, trade and finance, state administration). Until 1934 the former approach predominated,[61] but at the Seventeenth Party Congress 'functionalism' was condemned and the apparatus reorganized on a 'production-branch' basis.[62] The redistribution of responsibilities, however, seems to have met with a good deal of passive resistance, based partly on the force of inertia and partly on reasoned opposition to the new arrangements, and in many areas the new Departments of Leading Party Organs merely took over the functions of the former Assignment Departments and concentrated in their hands the choice of personnel for all fields of activity, with the blessing of the local party secretaries.[63] Such tendencies were for a time strongly deprecated, but by 1937, as is clear from Zhdanov's speech to the Eighteenth Congress,[64] the Central Committee itself had begun to take the same line. By the time of the Eighteenth Congress in early 1939, the Leading Party Organs Departments had effective responsibility for all classes of appointments, and they were then formally designated Cadres Departments, placed under special cadres secretaries of the party committees, and their duties of checking fulfilment transferred to other departments.[65] This was part of a reorganization of the party apparatus as a whole, which went far towards reviving the previously condemned functionalism.

From 1939 until about the end of 1948, each committee's cadres department was responsible for recommending to the committee's bureau candidates for all posts on the committee's nomenklatura. Its activities were not confined to this, however, as it was charged with supervizing the work of government and production organizations in its area with junior personnel for whose appointment these were directly responsible.[66] This latter obligation often led the cadres departments into a position where the heads of public offices and enterprises came to depend upon them to decide all questions of appointment and transfer, no matter how junior the employee concerned.

> In a number of party organizations the cadres departments do not concentrate on the choice of officials for decisive posts, but squander their efforts on trifles, trying to select cadres for everyone and everything. Not infrequently, instead of setting to rights the work of the cadres departments of the appropriate offices, they are engaged entirely in themselves meeting 'orders' for personnel.[67]

There were cases where factory executives even invoked the aid of the cadres departments of local party committees in taking on rank and file workers.[68] Such tendencies were naturally exaggerated during the War, when there was an extreme shortage of qualified personnel, but they seem to have persisted throughout the life of the cadres departments.[69]

At the end of 1948 and the beginning of 1949 the party apparatus was again reorganized, and there was a virtual return to the 'production-branch' structure of the years 1934–9. This involved the abolition of the cadres departments, the distribution of their functions among the various branch departments, and the liquidation of the post of cadres secretary. Although a number of statements were made by party leaders to the effect that this reorganization would improve the selection of personnel, no reasons were given why this should be so.[70] As Merle Fainsod, and others after him, have suggested, it may have been precipitated by the changed balance of power within the Central Committee Secretariat which resulted from Zhdanov's death in August 1948.[71] It seems probable, however, that the role of the branch departments in the selection of personnel had been growing for a number of years. As early as 1943 the Cadres Secretary of the Sverdlovsk Regional Committee wrote that:

At the present time the Cadres Department has begun much less to select cadres for industrial enterprises. The branch departments are taking an active part in this work, the Cadres Department establishing control over their proposals and checking from general party positions the line along which this or that official should most expediently be employed.[72]

Under the post-1948 arrangements the branch departments became responsible for recommending personnel both for the 'objects of administration' in their field (enterprises, schools, stores, and so on) and for the government offices directly administering these.[73] The jurisdiction of the Department of Administrative, Finance and Trade Organs extended to officials of the judiciary and the procuracy. The scope of the various sectors of the Department of Party, Trade-Union and Komsomol Organs is sufficiently obvious from the department's name. Selection of personnel for branch departments of subordinate party committees appears, however, to involve consultation between the branch department concerned and the Department of Party, Trade and Union and Komsomol Organs, and the secretaries of party committees responsible for propaganda are chosen by the departments of party, trade union and komsomol organs and of propaganda and agitation in collaboration.[74]

The party apparatus underwent a further reorganization in the immediate aftermath of Stalin's death, involving the merging of some departments, without, however, modifying the 'production-branch' basis. Some republics diverged somewhat from the basic pattern of branch departments, in keeping with their particular economic profile.[75]

The apparatus of party committees at lower levels, which parallels that in the republic central committees, was similarly consolidated.[76] Between September 1953 and March 1954 the apparatus of the rural district committee was completely reorganized. Instead of the three secretaries each being responsible for a related group of departments which supervized through their instructors the relevant fields of activity for the whole district, the districts were now divided up into zones, one for each MTS,[77] and a secretary assigned to each zone. The secretary was required to make his headquarters in the MTS, and became responsible for all aspects of party activity, including the choice of cadres within his zone. He had a staff of instructors, each responsible for one, or at the most two, collective farms.[78] The departments of party, trade union and komsomol organs of the district committees were replaced by organization departments, entrusted with cadres work and checking on fulfilment of decisions by primary party organizations in government offices and production enterprises, both industrial and agricultural. The post of third secretary was abolished, and the second secretary was made responsible for both the new organization department and the department of propaganda and agitation,[79] while the first secretary had the task of overall co-ordination.[80] These changes were a by-product of Khrushchev's massive drive to heal the ills of Soviet agriculture, and were the harbingers of more radical reorganizations that followed the consolidation of his dominance.

This outline of the departmental structure of the party apparatus tells us much about how responsibility was distributed within party committees for the selection and recommendation of leading personnel. We should now note two further elements of party personnel administration before passing to a closer examination of how this enormous and complex state and party machinery operated in practice. First,the importance ascribed to the keeping of extensive personal files of officials entering the *nomenklatura*. These files, formerly kept in the records section of the cadres departments, are required to contain:

1. a record of posts previously held by the official with an assessment of the results achieved in each and the reasons for transfer;
2. testimonials of primary party organizations;
3. indices, if possible statistical, of performance in his present post;
4. data gathered in the course of investigations into the work of his organization;
5. notes on the reactions of persons with whom he has had dealings;
6. impressions formed by officers of the party committee itself.[81]

When the cadres departments were abolished, the personal files were handed over to the various branch departments.[82] Although such documentation is supposed to play only a subordinate role in the selection and promotion of officials, in certain circumstances it could assume primary importance. Nevertheless, in many party committees personal files appear to be kept rather haphazardly. Towards the end of 1952, *Pravda* complained that:

> The formal bureaucratic approach to the study of cadres is reflected in the way personal files are maintained. In the personal file of this or that official, one may find, side by side, a pro forma listing data on transfers of employment, but saying nothing about the reasons for such transfers, some old references or other, and a few empty, standardized testimonals. But on the other hand, it is hard to find documents in the file which give a complete picture of the political and professional qualities of the official.[83]

The other practice to be noted is the keeping by party committees, in addition to records on nomenklatura officials, of lists of individuals suitable for promotion to nomenklatura posts: a 'reserve of cadres'. The establishment of such reserves was called for by Stalin in 1937, at the height of the Great Purges when he laid down the principle that every party member occupying a responsible post should pick out two persons capable of replacing him.[84] Such reserves were subsequently set up not only for party appointments but for those in government offices and enterprises, and persons placed on the reserve of cadres were to be prepared for advancement by being given ever more testing assignments.[85] During the War party committees apparently tended to let their cadre reserves go by the board, but considerable concern was shown by the Central Committee in the early postwar years that they should be properly reconstituted.[86] Nevertheless, the party press continued to report cases where failure to fill vacancies for party, government and industrial officials was ascribed to the slackness of party committees in selecting and training a proper reserve.[87]

If personnel administration is one of the central preoccupations of the party apparatus, and its role in this field is clearly pre-eminent, does this mean that the vast body of constitutional, legislative and regulatory provisions assigning specific personnel responsibilities to a whole range of government agencies[88] and officials is purely formal and lacking in practical significance? There is ample evidence that this is not the case. The leaders and cadres departments of government offices and enterprises, it seems, play a part in the selection not only of junior officials, but also of personnel for posts of sufficient importance to enter the nomenklatura of party committees. Many indications of this fact might be mentioned. Thus we find the USSR Minister of Agriculture warning the Head of the Agriculture Department of the Sverdlovsk Regional Executive Committee and his deputy in charge of stockraising, that he would have them dismissed if their work did not improve.[89] The party organization of a ministry is rebuked for its slackness in checking people recommended for promotion by officials of the ministry, and so failing to prevent unsuitable appointments.[90] It is stated that 'the ministries enjoy a large role in the selection and training of managerial personnel'.[91] Government officials are taken to task for mistakes in the selection not only of technicians and specialists,[92] but even senior administrators in local executive committees.[93]

There may thus be four active participants in the selection of a government official or industrial executive: the government office legally entrusted with appointing or approving him, the party committee to which this office is responsible (in practice usually its appropriate department), the head of the organization to which the appointment is being made, and the party committee to which it is responsible. In the case of the head of the agricultural department of a regional executive committee, for example, the bodies involved would be the Ministry of Agriculture, the Central Committee (through its agriculture department), the Regional Executive Committee (i.e., its Chairman), and the Regional Party Committee. In appointments to productive organizations, the party organization of the enterprise may also play a part.

The possibilities these arrangements offer for conflicts of will and purpose will be appreciated. Nevertheless, it would seem that appointments are often arranged without any special complications, and this is probably because both the party and government bodies responsible for approving appointments tend to leave the effective say to the bodies recommending them, while the latter, being in continuous day-to-day collaboration, can usually reach a decision on a personal basis, often by a telephone conversation. Thus there was a vacancy for an MTS director in Gorky region. An applicant appeared at the offices of the regional executive committee, and was directed to the deputy head of the agriculture department responsible for MTSs. The latter got in touch with the head of the appropriate sector in the agricultural department of the regional party committee, and agreement was reached to appoint the applicant to the post, apparently in full confidence that no obstacle would be raised by the party and government bodies responsible for approving the appointment.[94]

However, the approving organization is not invariably satisfied with a passive role, nor is the nominating organization always ready to avail itself of its powers. These facts may be illustrated by two examples. In the first, a party district committee resolved to promote a very successful collective farm chairman to be vice chairman of the district executive committee, and the regional authorities approved this. However, it soon became apparent to the regional party committee that he was not coping with this work, whereupon they intervened and directed the district committee to return him to his former post.[95] The second case shows a regional committee refusing to collaborate in a district committee's attempt to escape from the responsibility of finding a candidate for a post subject to its recommendation.

> The secretary of the Belogory district committee Comrade Yachkrinsky kept on urging the regional committee to send a specialist for the post of head of the district agricultural department. We did not send such an official, but instead obliged the district committee to pick someone out from among the young specialists in the district. And indeed very little time was needed to settle the question on the spot – the district committee promoted to the post the senior MTS agronomist Comrade Gumenyuk, who is coping well with this work.[96]

Not all regional committees appear to show such exemplary firmness in insisting that subordinate bodies play their proper part in selecting personnel. As mentioned earlier, this was especially the case during the War, when the organs responsible for recommending candidates had the standing excuse of the extreme shortage of qualified personnel. Shatalin has given an example of the kind of relationship that might emerge between government and party bodies.

> The cadres department of the Chkalov regional committee began seeking out officials for practically all the organizations of the region, completely relieving the economic leaders of responsibility for choosing cadres. When an MTS director was needed, the regional agriculture department, without taking the trouble to look for a

suitable employee itself, applied to the regional committee. If the candidate fixed on in the cadres department of the regional committee did not suit, there came a telephone call from the regional agriculture department: 'No, this is not a suitable candidate, pick us another.'[97]

The answer found to this problem by one regional committee was to dismiss the head of the agriculture department of the executive committee and his deputy in charge of cadres, and to insist that their successors find their own candidates for vacant posts, producing firm recommendations for the regional committee's consideration.[98]

At the same time party committees may go to the other extreme and fail to provide assistance when subordinate bodies are genuinely unable to find suitable candidates for important vacancies. The Uzbek Central Committee was charged with this at the republic's 1954 party congress. The first secretary of the Tashkent region stated:

> For about two years the Tashkent regional irrigation administration has been without a leader. The agriculture department of the Central Committee (Comrades Babkov and Shamsutdinov) are quite aware of this. Every time the question of a leader for the regional irrigation administration is raised, they make promises, but in practice they do nothing whatever about it.[99]

Slowness on the part of party committees in considering persons recommended by subordinate bodies may also produce delays in appointments. At the beginning of 1954 there was a vacancy for a head of the building materials administration in the Vinnitsa region of the Ukraine. The regional committee of the party proposed a comrade Bagry for the post; Bagry was sent up to republic capital Kiev, but had to wait for nearly a month before he could get an interview in the department of construction and municipal economy of the Ukrainian Central Committee.[100]

We have now seen party committees allowing themselves to be pushed into the role of wholesale suppliers of cadres to subordinate bodies, and on the other hand, of showing reluctance to expedite even the most urgent appointments. We must now observe them in another guise: voluntarily taking on all responsibility for selecting personnel, and refusing to allow subordinate organizations any say in this. For example, the secretary of a ward party committee in Kiev claimed that of the eight persons approved in recent years by the Kiev city committee as director of the ward market, seven of them were sent without first obtaining the agreement of the ward committee.[101]

The director of a Moscow factory complained that after he dismissed an employee who had been 'disorganizing production', the ward party committee telephoned to have him reinstated.[102] In another case a city party committee issued a decision to transfer a factory director from one factory to another. Neither the responsible ministry nor the director himself agreed to this, but the city committee insisted, and they were obliged to fall in line.[103]

What is even more interesting is that the heads of higher-level government offices are also found going over the heads of party committees in making appointments and dismissals. This appears to happen where they are given a free hand by the superior party committees to which they are answerable. The following criticism levelled at a certain Comrade Vernikovsky, head of the Chernovtsy regional department of light industry, provides a typical example:

> Over the last eighteen months he had changed the majority of factory directors. And even when the city party committee came out decisively on behalf of the young and capable shoe factory director Comrade Shinkarenko, opposing his unwarranted removal from his work, Vernikovsky, with the tacit agreement of the regional party committee, did not change his decision.[104]

In the cases so far referred to, differences of opinion over appointments led to no real conflict, to one side or the other giving way to the stronger or more determined contender. But matters do not always end so simply. At times disagreements over an appointment lead to sharp conflicts which may have far-reaching consequences. On the simplest level such conflicts may merely involve passive resistance by one of the parties disagreeing with the decision made but not strong enough to reverse it.

> The district poultry industry office was headed by a certain Nemtsov, an untrustworthy person. The district party committee raised the question of dismissing him and nominated a suitable replacement. The cadres department of the regional committee gave its agreement. However, the chief administration of the poultry industry dragged the matter out for months. As a result Nemtsov embezzled several tons of state produce.[105]

At times one party, acquiescing unwillingly in an appointment or removal, may take reprisals by attempting to make things difficult for the new appointee, and this may also affect the course of subordinate appointments. This happened in 1952–3 in the case of a disagreement between the Belorussian livestock procurement office and the Grodno regional authorities. The Grodno regional party committee, claiming that the regional livestock procurement office was 'riddled with crooks and rogues', dismissed its head, and promoted a 'young, energetic and honest comrade' in his place. This did not suit the head of the republic livestock procurement office Akhmatov, who set about undermining the position of the new appointee in every possible way. For example, the new regional head attempted to get rid of the head of one of the region's district livestock procurement offices, who had already had three dismissals for embezzlement, and the regional party committee secured Akhmatov's agreement for this. Akhmatov issued an order authorizing the changes recommended by the regional authorities, but the very same day signed a further order revoking the first. The regional authorities could get no explanation of this action from him, and in the end the first secretary of the regional committee had to take up the matter with the republic party authorities.[106]

A similar but more complex case began with nothing more than a letter to a railway newspaper written by a train driver who claimed that the head of his depot had been victimizing him on account of criticisms he had made. The vice-head of the political department of the local railway sector took exception to this letter, asserting that it had been inspired by a third party and demanding that the train driver reveal who had really written it. The driver objected that there was no one else whatsoever involved. The vice-head of the political department then declared that the charges contained in the letter were without foundation, and he called a sitting of the bureau of the depot party organization, followed by an extraordinary plenary meeting of the party organization. This was attended by two locally powerful officials: the head of the political department of the railway sector and the secretary of the district party committee. At the plenary meeting the secretary of the party organization of the depot, Anokhin, came out in defence of the train driver, claiming that his charges that the head of the depot suppressed criticism were correct. The head and vice-head of the railway's political department and the secretary of the district party committee thereupon directed their fire at Anokhin. They made the telling point that Anokhin had once had the temerity to criticize the first secretary of the regional party committee, Comrade Markov. This attack secured the desired result, and the meeting voted that the train driver's letter be withdrawn. Previously, at the meeting of the bureau of the depot's party organization, the head of the depot had declared that he could no longer work with Anokhin, and the latter had been removed from the post of secretary of the party organization. When this was put to the general meeting, however, the rank and file rallied to Anokhin's support, and the decision to remove him was reversed. At this stage the matter was taken up by the Ukrainian republic-level newspapers. The political department of the south-western railway district, in which the railway sector involved was situated, then intervened, investigated, found that suppression of criticism had in fact occurred, and requested the bureau of the regional party committee to dismiss the head of the depot and the head and vice-head of the political department of the railway sector from their posts. The regional committee, still under the leadership of the same Markov whom Anokhin had once criticised, declined to take this action. The head of the depot was in fact removed, but was soon given a better appointment. The head and vice-head of the political department were reprimanded, but left in their posts. They allegedly continued to suppress criticism in the party organization of the depot, fully supported by the secretary of the district committee, presumably another protege of Markov. Meanwhile, the communists in the depot continued to stand by Anokhin, whose support, it would appear, lay in the higher levels of the railway's political department.[107]

This case is a good illustration of how the fate of lower level officials may be decided by the balance of power between different systems of 'protection'. It is also useful as an introduction to the four other themes requiring treatment in order to complete this discussion of the main factors operating in the selection of cadres: the tendency of officials on the nomenklatura of a party committee to develop into a closed circle; victimization of critics who threaten the stability of such a closed circle; nepotism; and the role of rank-and-file recalcitrance in upsetting higher level assignments to elective posts.

Nepotism in the narrow sense of seeking special advantages for relatives in securing attractive posts is a big enough problem in the Soviet Union to have earned a specific condemnation by Central Committee Secretary Malenkov in his report to the Nineteenth Party Congress in 1952.[108] Cases of nepotism are often reported in the press. Thus a collective farm chairman, who makes a mess of his work and has to be dismissed, seeks the help of the chairman of the district executive committee, who is a close relative of his, to secure the post of chairman of an industrial co-operative (*artel*); there he engages in extortion and has to be removed again, but his relative arranges with the regional authorities to have him posted as chairman of another collective farm.[109] Most such cases refer to fairly low-level appointments, and a disproportionate number of them are reported from Central Asia and other relatively traditional areas.[110] However, the number of close relatives of top leaders who turn up in prominent posts gives rise to the suspicion that nepotism may operate at higher levels also. At the Nineteenth Congress, however, Malenkov seemed to be far more concerned about a related, though quite distinct, problem.

> Not infrequently, people who are honest and competent, but peremptory in their intolerance of shortcomings, and therefore a cause of annoyance to executives, are shouldered out on various pretexts and replaced by people of dubious value, or even entirely unfit for their jobs, but compliant and subservient enough to suit the tastes of certain executives. Owing to such distortions of the party line in the matter of selection and promotion of personnel, we get in some organizations close coteries who constitute themselves into a sort of mutual insurance society and set their group interests higher than the interests of party and state.[111]

The existence of such 'coteries' and 'mutual protection societies' is nothing new. Stalin referred to them at the time of the Great Purges.[112] In 1946 a Central Committee journal pointed to the prevalence of conditions:

> where instead of a leading group of responsible officials, one gets a family-group of closely-bound individuals, an *artel*, whose members receive their jobs on fief, as it were, and try to live harmoniously, without offending each other, and not washing their dirty linen in public when shortcomings are discovered in their work, try to protect each other from criticism, from whatever quarter it comes. It is understandable that no 'voice from below' complaining about faults in work is capable of penetrating such a coterie.[113]

As reports of such 'mutual insurance societies' became no less frequent over the years, despite continuous and violent denunciation, they should perhaps be regarded as a natural product of the existing system of government in the Soviet Union. Their existence presupposes first of all the ability of local leaders to protect favoured subordinates from criticism or the results of criticism. We have already met with some evidence of this. Many further illustrations might be cited. Party leaders hush up scandals involving members of their circle.[114] Where this is impossible, they arrange counter-propaganda to protect them. For example, when *Pravda Ukrainy* criticized the head of the Ukrainian Chief Administration for Hunting and Trapping as a dishonest and worthless official, powerful supporters, in particular the head of the Agriculture Department of the Ukrainian Central Committee, organized his defence in the form of 'spontaneous' letters from the public.[115] If despite such efforts proteges are dismissed, local leaders may intervene to reinstate them. Thus we find the head of the political department of a railway sector complaining that:

> There have been no few cases where we have removed leaders who have compromised themselves, and the head of the Transport Department of the regional Party Committee Comrade Karyukov has insisted that they be given other responsible posts.[116]

To give an example from another field, the Rector of the Kiev State University removed the professor of French in 1952, on the grounds that he had revealed himself not properly qualified for the post; but in no time he was back in the chair again, by decision of the regional party authorities.[117]

The second precondition for the entrenchment of patronage groupings is the ability of the leaders to place their supporters in other positions of trust when superior authorities insist on their replacement. The saying was reportedly current in the Nikolaev region of the Ukraine, that 'If you get into the nomenklatura of the regional committee, even the devil can't hurt you; if you make a mess of things in one organization, you'll be transferred to another, and won't even have to suffer reduction in status.'[118] Many examples were given, including the case of a district agent of the Ministry of Procurement, who was taken to court for serious violations of the law; under pressure by certain officials of the regional party committee, the district court let him off lightly, and soon afterwards the district party committee and the regional agent of the Ministry of Procurement found another leading post for him, with the approval of the regional party committee.[119] This occurred more than a year after the Ukrainian Central Committee had gone to the lengths of issuing a resolution

> To regard it as impermissible that certain party organs limit themselves in the advancement of cadres to a narrow circle of people, of officials who have not coped with their work or have compromised themselves, and these people not only fail to be demoted, but they are sent to equivalent or even more senior posts.[120]

Scarcely a week goes by without the Soviet press producing its crop of incidents of this kind, the persons enjoying protection in this manner ranging in status from collective farm chairmen and factory directors to district, city and regional party secretaries and republic ministers.[121] Over a period of years such 'nomadic' officials may occupy a great variety of posts. There was an editor of a district newspaper in the Ternopol Region who proved incompetent and had to be removed, so the regional party committee gave him a job as an instructor in its propaganda and agitation department. He was found unsuitable for this and sent as secretary of a district party committee. Next he was given work as inspector of crop estimates, but had to be removed for incompetence, and was appointed director of a distillery. He was dismissed from this for not providing the enterprise with proper leadership. Finally he was returned to his original post of editor of a district newspaper.[122]

Displaced nomenklatura officials are notoriously particular about accepting new appointments. In 1941 a Ukrainian paper carried an article entitled 'Unemployed Communists', which described how displaced officials used to hang about the cadres departments of city and ward committees on the look out for attractive 'leading' posts, sometimes refusing to accept alternative appointments for months on end.[123] At times such officials set certain conditions for making their services available, such as that a car be supplied for their personal use and there be a certain minimum office staff.[124]

When a protege has discredited himself too seriously to be given another immediate appointment, a common practice is to have him enrolled as a full-time student in a party school, in the hope that the passage of time and the enhancement of his political qualifications will make it possible to install him in another post upon his graduation.[125] It was claimed that when this occurred in the Khabarovsk Territory the fate of the entrant was determined not by the examination, but by a telephone call from the Khabarovsk Territorial Committee. The telephone conversation, it appears, was between the head of the sector for training party cadres of the territorial party committee and the director of the two-year territorial party school.[126] Nevertheless, it is not always possible to reinstate such people on their return. The year after Stalin's death Khrushchev inveighed against this practice at a plenary session of the Central Committee:

> Not infrequently an unsuitable official is transferred from one region to another, instead of being sent to more junior work. It also happens that, if an official who has failed cannot be transferred to another region, he is recommended for a yearly course, for the Higher Party School or the Academy of Social Sciences. And then, when this official completes the course or school and comes back to the party committee (which sent him), it is not known what to recommend him for, because the organization he has come from will not take him, and it is dangerous to send him to another post – he would not cope with it. This literally takes place at the expense of the party's interests and does harm to the cause. Such an approach to the training and selection of cadres may not be acknowledged as correct and it deserves to be condemned.[127]

What happens when the local patronage boss is himself transferred? Quite often, he seeks to have as many of his former subordinates as possible transferred to his new organization. Stalin gave some striking examples of this in 1937,[128] but the practice continued and cases were reported in the press from time to time.[129]

According to the Central Committee's organization journal, 'no "voice from below", complaining about faults in the work, is capable of penetrating such a coterie'.[130] It would seem, moreover, that even senior officials of an area may be unable to escape victimization if they do not accommodate themselves to the local ruling group. Thus we find the bureau of an important city committee deciding to get rid of the deputy chairman of the city executive committee, the chairman having asserted that he was doing too much criticizing. He was called before the bureau of the city committee, and 'without any particular discussion', removed from his post. The pretext for this was drunkenness, although this was later claimed to be baseless; nevertheless, in order to facilitate his transfer elsewhere, a glowing reference was sent to the republic capital. The ex-deputy chairman of the city executive committee was unable to secure work for a considerable period, and was eventually sent out to a rural district as local agent of the Ministry of Procurement.[131]

There is ample evidence of the difficulties which will face a junior official if he refuses to collaborate with the local bosses, and of the fact that even the intervention of the highest authorities may not be sufficient to secure him justice. To bring this out, it may be worthwhile recounting the history of one such case.

The director and chief engineer of an industrial plant in Belorussia made threats of reprisals to the secretary of the plant's party organization and the party group organizer of one of the workshops, by name Yaduta and Trubnichenko, if they would not refrain from making criticisms. Yaduta and Trubnichenko thereupon informed the city party committee, but the latter gave its support to the plant administration, and Yaduta was removed from his post. He complained to the regional party committee, which declined to take any action.

Meanwhile Trubnichenko wrote to *Pravda*, criticizing a secretary of the city committee, a secretary of the regional committee and a number of other leading officials. This caused the Belorussian Central Committee to take the matter up; it was discussed by its bureau, Trubnichenko's criticisms found to be correct, the director of the plant dismissed, its chief engineer and the secretary of the city committee reprimanded, and the decision to remove Yaduta from the post of secretary of the primary party organization of the plant revoked.

The city and regional committees then set about preparing to rid themselves of their critics. The head of the industry and transport department of the regional committee and the instructors of the department invited Trubnichenko up to the regional committee several times to offer him posts elsewhere. He refused, and was eventually relieved of his job on the pretext of a reduction in establishment. Less direct methods were at first tried with Yaduta.

One of his responsibilities was to supervise a subsidiary enterprise of the plant. A commission was set up to investigate alleged misdemeanors in his administration of this enterprise. Fabricated evidence was placed before the commission, which then handed over the case to the investigating organs of the state. The local public prosecutor, however, found on investigation that there was no case against Yaduta, and refused to prosecute him. So Yaduta was also removed on the grounds of alleged reduction of establishment.

Both he and Trubnichenko were refused work in any capacity whatsoever in the plant. For four months they were unable to obtain work, despite continual requests to the city committee. For appearance's sake, a number of posts were offered them, but when it came to the point, it transpired the vacancies did not exist. The director of the plant, who had been dismissed by order of the republic central committee, was meanwhile appointed to a leading post in an important trust.

While all this was happening, action was simultaneously being taken against Yaduta and Trubnichenko in respect of their party status. An old offence of Yaduta's, long ignored, was now dredged up, and liberally mixed with fiction to provide grounds for excluding him from the party. Trubnichenko was also gratuitously brought into it, and a 'severe reproof' was entered in his party card.

The two victims appealed to the Belorussian Central Committee which twice sent officials to investigate. Although a 'crying suppression of criticism' was established, the case was merely referred back to the authorities which had carried out the suppression. Eventually the bureau of the regional committee was obliged to open new investigations of Trubnichenko's case, but up to the time of reporting of this case (April 1952) Yaduta's penalty was still in force.[132]

In this case the intervention of *Pravda* probably meant that the All-Union Central Committee would see to it that the damage was undone. What is significant here, as in dozens of similar cases,[133] is that local patronage groupings and 'mutual insurance societies' are so blatant in their mishandling of 'voices from below'. This must mean that the chances are greatly in favour of their being able to suppress unwelcome critics without being taken to task by higher authorities. Indeed, it is difficult to see how such 'mutual insurance societies' could continue to abound if this was not so.

NOTES

1   'The cadres departments . . . are called upon to aid the Party committee correctly to select people for those posts which are subject to the approval of the committee.' N. Shatalin, 'On Work with Cadres', *Partiinoe Stroitel'stvo*, no. 20 (1943) p. 14.
2. *Partiinoe Stroitel'stvo*, no. 24 (1943) p. 29.
3. Calculated on the basis of the Kirgiz First Secretary's figures as reported in *Sovetskaya Kirgiziya*, 21 September 1952.
4. G. Alferov, Inspector of the Belorussia Central Committee, writing in *Sovetskaya Belorussiya*, 15 August 1952.
5. *Partiinaya Zhizn'*, no. 12 (1947) p. 17.
6. Shatalin, op. cit., p. 16.
7. *Zarya Vostoka*, 10 January 1949.
8. *Moskovskaya Pravda*, 31 March 1951.
9. *Sovetskaya Kirgiziya*, 21 September 1952.
10. *Zarya Vostoka*, 28 January 1949.
11. Shatalin, op. cit., pp. 16–17.
12. See *Partiinoe Stroitel'stvo*, no. 11 (1946) pp. 39–40.
13. See *Sovetskaya Belorussiya*, 1 December 1950.
14. *Pravda*, 6 March 1954.
15. *Pravda*, 27 August 1952.
16. See *Pravda Ukrainy*, 2 March 1948.
17. *Sovetskaya Belorussiya*, 15 August 1952.
18. See *Pravda Ukrainy*, 29 August 1946.
19. *Partiinaya Zhizn'*, no. 8 (1946) p. 34.
20. The party committees in the autonomous soviet socialist republics are referred to as regional committees and appear to be treated on exactly the same basis as the other regional committees.
21. At the time of writing, in Ukraine, Belorussia, Kazakhstan, Uzbekistan, Turkmenia, Georgia, Azerbaijan, Kirgizia and Tadjikistan. Those in Georgia and Azerbaijan are for subordinate ASSRs and autonomous regions only. In 1952 administrative regions were established also in these two republics, as well as in Latvia, Lithuania and Estonia, but these were abolished in 1953.
22. See *Pravda*, 15 August 1952; 21 September 1952; 26 September 1952; *Pravda Ukrainy*, 10 September 1952.
23. It is pointed out later that at one time even the junior secretaries of all district committees had to be put up for approval by the All-Union Central Committee.
24. *Pravda* , 2 June 1952.
25. *Partiinoe Stroitel'stvo*, nos 19–20 (1938) p. 78.
26. See *Partiinaya Zhizn'*, no. 3 (1947) p. 66; no. 3 (1948) p. 78; *Pravda*, 12 December 1952; 9 September 1952; 30 September 1952; 9 July 1952; 25 May 1952; 20 June 1952; 3 July 1952; 22 September 1952; 26 September 1952.
27. See for example, *Sovetskaya Moldaviya*, 20 September 1952; *Sovetskaya Estoniya*, 12 February 1954.

28. See *Pravda Ukrainy*, 11 September 1946; 29 December 1946; *Pravda*, 2 June 1952; 13 September 1952; 14 September 1952; *Sovetskaya Belorussiya*, 19 February 1953; *Pravda*, 15 August 1952; 16 September 1952.
29. See *Kommunist Tadjikistana*, 20 September 1952; *Pravda* 8 July 1953, 17 December 1953.
30. See *Pravda*, 12 August 1953.
31. See *Pravda*, 12 June 1953; *Sovetskaya Kirgiziya*, 12 February 1954.
32. See *Pravda*, 30 January 1950; 3 July 1952; *Pravda Ukrainy*, 14 September 1952.
33. See *Sovetskaya Kirgiziya*, 12 February 1952.
34. City executive committees may be subordinate either to the republic, regional or district authorities, according to their size and importance, at the discretion of the Republic Supreme Soviets. See *Administrativnoe – territorial'noe Delenie SSSR*, various editions, *passim*.
35. See *Pravda*, 16 August 1952; 10 September 1952.
36. See Partiinoe Stroitel'stro, no. II (1946) p.28; *Partiinaya Zhizn', no. 2 (1947) p. 53; no 5, (1947) p. 28; no. 4 (1948) p. 70; Pravda*, 18 June 1952; *Sovetskaya Belorussiya*, 15 August 1952.
37. See *Pravda*, 26 September 1952.
38. See *Pravda Ukrainy*, 25 August 1946; *Pravda*, 20 June 1952; 10 September 1952; 13 September 1952; 17 September 1952; *Partiinaya Zhizn'*, no. 8 (1947) p. 35; *Pravda*, 3 July 1952; 21 March 1954; *Pravda Ukrainy*, 24 August 1946.
39. See *Pravda*, 22 September 1952.
40. See *Pravda*, 26 September 1952.
41. See *Partiinaya Zhizn'*, no. 3 (1947) p. 66; no. 8 (1947) p. 34; no. 3 (1948) p. 78; no. 4 (1948) p. 71; *Pravda*, 13 May 1952; 20 June 1952; 15 August 1952; 22 September 1952; 12 December 1952; 14 September 1952; *Sovetskaya Belorussiya*, 19 February 1953.
42. See *Sovetskaya Kirgiziya*, 12 June 1953; 12 February 1954.
43. See *Sovetskaya Belorussiya*, 31 March 1948; *Pravda Ukrainy*, 6 April 1948.
44. *Zarya Vostoka*, 17 September 1952.
45. See *Pravda*, 30 September 1952.
46. See *Sovetskaya Belorussiya*, 21 April 1951; *Pravda*, 17 May 1952; 17 June 1952.
47. See *Zarya Vostoka*, 17 September 1952.
48. *Kommunist Tadjikistana*, 5 March 1953.
49. *Pravda*, 22 August 1952.
50. See *Zarya Vostoka*, 26 February 1953; *Pravda*, 24 September 1952; 15 September 1952; 12 June 1952; 17 September 1952; 10 September 1952.
51. See *Pravda*, 11 May 1952; *Pravda Ukrainy*, 3 September 1952.
52. See *Sovetskaya Belorussiya*, 15 August 1952; *Pravda*, 4 September 1952; 17 September 1952. Note that none of the enterprises involved came under All-Union (federal only) ministries.
53. See 'Carefully Train Collective Farm Chairman', *Pravda*, 6 June 1952; *Pravda*, 13 May 1952; 1 July 1952; 16 June 1952; 3 July 1952.
54. See *Pravda Ukrainy*, 16 August 1952.
55. *Pravda*, 17 May 1952.
56. See *Pravda*, 6 March 1954.
57. See *Partiinaya Zhizn'*, no. 22 (1947) p. 52; *Pravda Ukrainy*, 11 September 1946; *Zarya Vostoka*, 14 February 1950; *Pravda*, 13 August 1952.
58. See *Partiinaya Zhizn'*, no. 12 (1947) p. 63.

59. See *Pravda,* 16 August 1952; 2 February 1953.
60. See Merle Fainsod, *How Russia is Ruled,* rev. edn (Cambridge, Mass., 1964) ch 6.
61. See *VKP(b) V Rezolyutsiakh* (1941), vol. 1, pp. 398-9, 504; vol. 2, p. 374.
62. See L. M. Kaganovich, 'Report on Questions of Organization', *Pravda,* 12 February 1934. The seven departments then created were: Agriculture, Industry, Transport, Planning–Finance–Trade, Politico–Administrative, Culture and the Propagation of Leninism, and Leading Party Organs. Each of these was responsible for selecting cadres, training, checking fulfilment, industrial propaganda, etc., within its field, though the Department of Leading Party Organs was entrusted with a vaguely defined responsibility for supervising the work of all.
63. See *Partiinoe Stroitel'stvo,* no. 10 (1934) p. 2.
64. *The Land of Socialism Today and Tomorrow* (Moscow, 1939,) p. 206. Zhdanov said that the branch-department arrangements had given rise to constant squabbles over personnel, and had caused 'artificial pigeon-holing of the cadres under separate departments, whereas the proper selection of cadres demands skilful and flexible manoeuvring'.
65. See ibid., pp. 41, 453. The Cadres Departments came under the Cadres Administration of the All-Union Central Committee.
66. See, for example, *Partiinaya Zhizn',* no. 10, (1947) p. 32.
67. N. Shatalin, writing in *Partiinoe Stroitel'stvo,* no. 20 (1943) p. 14.
68. See article by N. Semin, Cadres Secretary of the Sverdlovsk Regional Committee, *Partiinoe Stroitel'stvo,* no. 24, (1943) p. 29.
69. For an example in the latter part of 1947, see *Partiinaya Zhizn',* no. 22 (1947) p. 61.
70. See Popov's report in *Moskovskii Bol'shevik,* 2 February 1949; Charkviani's report in *Zarya Vostoka,* 28 January 1949; Rumyantsev's report in *Moskovskaya Pravda,* 31 March 1951.
71. Fainsod, op. cit. pp. 198-9. See also Louis Nemzer, 'The Kremlin's Professional Staff: the Apparatus of the CC, CPSU', *American Political Science Review,* no. 1, March 1950.
72. Semin, op. cit., p. 31.
73. *Pravda,* 24 February 1952; 12 August 1952; 3 September 1952; 4 September 1952; 21 September 1952; *Pravda Ukrainy,* 1 February 1951; 25 March 1954; *Pravda Vostoka,* 18 February 1954.
74. See *Pravda Ukrainy,* 10 September 1952.
75. For listings of republic CC departments at the time of the 1952 and 1954 republic congresses, see (a) for 1952: *Pravda Ukrainy,* 27 September 1952; *Turkmenskaya Iskra,* 24 September 1952; *Kommunist Tadjikistana,* 24 September 1952; *Sovetskaya Estoniya,* 20 September 1952; *Leninskoe Znamya,* 26 September 1952; *Sovetskaya Latviya,* 24 September 1952; *Sovetskaya Kirgiziya,* 25 September 1952; *Kommunist* (Erevan), 24 September 1952; *Kazakhstanskaya Pravda,* 25 September 1952; *Sovetskaya Moldaviya,* 23 September 1952; *Pravda Vostoka,* 19 September 1952; *Bakinskii Rabochii,* 26 September 1952; *Sovetskaya Litva,* 27 September 1952; *Sovetskaya Belorussiya,* 25 September 1952; and (b) for 1954 (details were given for seven Republics only): *Pravda Vostoka,* 18 February 1954; *Sovetskaya Kirgiziya,* 14 February 1954; *Turkmenskaya Iskra,* 17 February 1954; *Sovetskaya Belorussiya,* 14 February 1954; *Leninskoe Znamya,* 19 February 1954; *Sovetskaya Litva,* 21 February 1954; *Sovetskaya Latviya,* 13 February 1954.

76. For example, see *Sovetskaya Belorussiya,* 6 February 1954.
77. There were two to four MTSs in most rural districts. In those with more, some MTS zones might embrace two MTSs.
78. See Resolution of the CC CPSU of 7 September 1953, *Pravda,* 13 September 1953, p. 4; N. S. Khrushchev, Report to the All-Union Central Committee of 3 September 1953, *Pravda,* 15 September 1953, p. 6; and *Pravda,* 21 March 1954.
79. See *Kommunist* (Erevan), 16 February 1954.
80. *Pravda,* 15 September 1953, p. 6.
81. See Shatalin, op. cit., p. 17; Semin, op. cit., p. 31.
82. See *Sovetskaya Kirgiziya,* 17 September 1949.
83. *Pravda,* 10 December 1952.
84. See *Lenin i Stalin: Sbornik proizvedenii k izucheniyu istorii VKP(b)* (Moscow, 1937) vol. III, p. 721.
85. See Shatalin, op. cit., pp. 17-18.
86. See *Pravda Ukrainy,* August 24, 1946; *Pravda Vostoka,* June 27, 1948; *Zarya Vostoka,* January 10, 1949.
87. For example, see *Pravda Vostoka,* March 24, 1953.
88. See T. H. Rigby, *The Selection of Leading Personnel in the Soviet State and Communist Party* (Ph.D. Thesis, London University, 1954) pp. 316-30.
89. See *Izvestiya,* 3 July 1952.
90. See *Pravda,* 13 August 1952.
91. *Pravda,* 16 August 1952.
92. See *Pravda,* 31 May 1952; 3 July 1952.
93. See *Bakinskii Rabochii,* 30 May 1950.
94. See *Partiinaya Zhizn',* no. 22 (1947) p. 52. In this case the person appointed turned out to be a crook, and the moral was drawn that the approving bodies should not have abdicated their role of 'controlling' appointments. For an identical case, see *Pravda,* 13 August 1952.
95. See *Pravda Ukrainy,* 26 August 1946.
96. Begma, First Secretary of the Kamenets-Podolsk Regional Committee, writing in *Pravda Ukrainy,* 8 September 1951.
97. Shatalin, op. cit., pp. 15-16.
98. Semin, op. cit., p. 29.
99. *Pravda Vostoka,* 18 February 1954.
100. See Bubnovsky's speech, reported in *Pravda Ukrainy,* 25 March 1954.
101. See *Pravda Ukrainy,* 3 September 1952; for other cases see *Pravda,* 3 September 1952; 21 September 1952.
102. See *Pravda,* 22 August 1952.
103. See *Kommunist Tadjikistana,* 5 March 1953.
104. *Pravda Ukrainy,* 1 February 1951. For similar cases see *Pravda Ukrainy,* 21 September 1946; 27 June 1952; 5 August 1952; 13 September 1952.
105. *Pravda Ukrainy,* 29 August 1946.
106. See *Sovetskaya Belorussiya,* 19 February 1953.
107. The case was reported in *Pravda,* 2 February 1950. The upshot of *Pravda*'s intervention is not known, but Markov, at least, does not seem to have been discredited as he remained first secretary of the regional committee at least up till 1952.
108. Malenkov, *Report to the Nineteenth Congress,* p. 124.
109. See *Bakinskii Rabochii,* 1 March, 1953.
110. See *Pravda,* 4 May 1952; 16 September 1952; *Sovetskaya Kirgiziya,* 15 May 1952.

111. Malenkov, op. cit., p. 124.
112. See *Lenin i Stalin: Sbornik proizvedenii k izucheniyu istorii VKP (b),* 1937, vol III, pp. 724–5.
113. *Partiinoe Stroitel' stvo,* no. 11 (1946) pp. 3–4.
114. *Pravda Ukrainy,* 15 September 1946; *Pravda,* 16 September 1952; 30 September 1952.
115. *Pravda,* 17 May 1952.
116. *Pravda Ukrainy,* 16 September 1952. See also *Pravda,* 19 September 1952.
117. *Pravda,* 16 December 1952.
118. *Pravda Ukrainy,* 7 September 1952.
119. Ibid.
120. *Pravda Ukrainy,* 4 March 1951.
121. See *Pravda Ukrainy,* 26 August 1946; 21 September 1946; 25 July 1951, 11 June 1952; 2 September 1952; *Izvestiya,* 27 June 1952; *Partiinaya Zhizn',* no. 3, (1948) p. 32; *Sovetskaya Belorussiya,* 19 February 1953; *Sovetskaya Kirgiziya,* 15 May 1952; *Pravda,* 6 May 1950; 12 August 1952; 15 September 1952; 16 September 1952; 17 September 1952; 24 September 1952; 30 September 1952; 10 December 1952; 8 July 1953; 4 August 1953.
122. See *Pravda Ukrainy,* 16 August 1952. For other cases see *Pravda,* 16 December 1952; 2 September 1953; *Pravda Ukrainy,* 11 September 1946; *Partiinaya Zhizn'* no. 12 (1947) p. 18; *Pravda,* 6 June 1952.
123. See *Sovetskaya Ukraina,* 5 March 1941.
124. See *Pravda,* 5 July 1951.
125. For example, see *Sovetskaya Belorussiya,* 10 September 1952.
126. *Pravda,* 25 August 1952.
127. Khrushchev, 'Report to the Central Committee of the CPSU', *Pravda,* 21 March 1954.
128. *Lenin i Stalin: Sbornik proizvedenii k izucheniyu istorii VKP (b),* vol. III, p. 725.
129. See, for example, *Pravda,* 4 September 1952.
130. *Partiinoe Stroitel'stvo,* no. 11 (1946) p. 4.
131. This case is reported in *Pravda Ukrainy,* 29 December 1946 and 18 March 1947.
132. A. Lukovets and A. Zin'kovsky, writing in *Pravda,* 17 April 1952.
133. Examples will be found in *Partiinaya Zhizn',* no. 23 (1947) p. 3; *Pravda Ukrainy,* 6 April 1948; 13 April 1948 and 30 April 1948; *Pravda,* 5 January 1950; 30 January 1950; 21 March 1950; 2 April 1950; 6 April 1950; 15 June 1952; 16 June 1952; 18 July 1952; 4 August 1952; 15 August 1952; 28 August 1952; 5 September 1952; 7 September 1952; 30 September 1952; 16 October 1953.

6.   Was Stalin a disloyal patron?*

The patron–client relationship has long been recognized as an important structuring element in Soviet political life, but only now is it beginning to be subjected to close analytical and comparative study, a reflection in part of the recently burgeoning interest among political sociologists and political anthropologists specializing mainly on various 'modernizing' societies.[1] In Chapter 3, the author examined the origins of political clientelism in the Soviet Union in the first years after the Revolution, and indicated how the prevalence of clientelist norms and practices among provincial party and government officialdom made it easier for Stalin to use the personnel-assignment powers of the Central Committee apparatus to build a nationwide 'machine' personally loyal to him.[2] The next phase, in which Stalin deployed this following to defeat successive groups of rival leaders and ultimately to make himself dictator, is one of the best-known, and best-attested, passages in Soviet political history. Nor would many doubt that Stalin remained to the last the unquestioned 'boss', his lieutenants entirely dependent on his personal favour, each of them striving meanwhile to build up his own network of followers, while Stalin in turn depended on them to administer the spheres entrusted to them in accordance with his wishes.

Such reciprocal dependence is the core of the patron–client relationship, however unequal their power resources may be, and its corollary is a high level of objective loyalty between the parties to it, whatever their secret feelings. The follower must never act against the boss's interests, and must be ever ready to put his hand in the fire for him, if required, while the boss must maintain and protect him, so long as he does so act. A power structure built on patron–client relations is viable only so long as

*Soviet Studies, vol. XXXVIII, no. 3 (July 1986) pp. 311–24.

each side's expectations of the other's loyal behaviour is generally confirmed by experience. There is abundant evidence that such mutual expectations are widely respected in the Soviet case. One thinks, for example, of all those 'Dnieper-Benders' whose attachment to Brezhnev over several decades took them eventually into his *Politbureau* and other leading positions in Moscow. One thinks of the endemic phenomenon of the *kadrovaya karusel'* where local party bosses whose loyal cadres have to be removed from one messed-up job after another are constantly found a new one. One thinks of the special sarcasm reserved for the *disloyal* Shepilov, the Khrushchev supporter who deserted to the ranks of the 'anti-party group' in 1957. And we might add, while perhaps differing over how much weight to give this one, the failure of Khrushchev's Central Committee to support him in 1964 as it had in 1957, following *his* blatant displays of disloyalty by engaging in frequent sackings and riding roughshod over their dearest interests.[3]

But what about Stalin? We know he could be cruel and treacherous to his rivals and those who did not bow to his authority. But was he a good 'boss' to his followers? Did he answer loyalty with loyalty? In this chapter I consider some evidence bearing on this question; evidence which, I believe, suggests conclusions considerably at variance with what I shall call the standard view.

This standard view might be epitomized by the reply that Charles de Gaulle is said to have given when asked what he would do about the right-wingers whose activities made possible his return to power in 1958: 'I shall astound them with my ingratitude!' Morbidly suspicious, fickle, disloyal and vengeful, Stalin was, so we are told, constantly astounding *his* supporters with his ingratitude, discarding and destroying successive cohorts of them once they had served their current purpose. The odd exception, like the egregious Vyacheslav Molotov, only served to emphasize the general pattern.

There are some impressive witnesses to the correctness of this conventional wisdom, beginning with Lenin who in his so-called 'Testament' dwelt specifically on Stalin's capriciousness and disloyalty. Khrushchev has left many bitter words in his secret report to the Twentieth Congress and in his memoirs about his old boss's arbitrary, suspicious and cruel treatment of his entourage. Over forty years ago Boris Souvarine in his still invaluable biography of Stalin summed it up as follows:

Stalin incites and provokes his auxiliaries, stirs up rival passions, exploits rancour and hatred to guarantee in his own way the continuance of his despotism and the unique position of the supreme arbiter. He cuts short differences, separates the protagonists, and profits from the situation to impose new men. Not knowing in whom to trust and seeing traitors on all sides, he keeps changing his favourites without changing his methods, and always with identical results.[4]

And more recently George F. Kennan, in the course of a brilliant characterization of Stalin in his book *Russia and the West under Lenin and Stalin*, has described Stalin as:

a man of incredible criminality . . . without pity or mercy; a man in whose entourage no one was ever safe; a man whose hand was set against all that could not be useful to him at the moment; a man who was most dangerous of all to those who were his closest collaborators in crime, because he liked to be the sole custodian of his own secrets, and disliked to share his memories or his responsibility with others who, being still alive, had tongues and consciences and might still be susceptible to the human weaknesses of remorse or indiscretion.[5]

Similar characterizations of Stalin's treatment of his supporters can be found in the pages of other leading students of Stalin and the Stalin era, and I should say right away that in my opinion this 'standard view', if it is fair to call it that, contains much that is true and important about Stalin. It *is* difficult on the evidence not to see him as devious, deceitful, secretive, suspicious, treacherous, vindictive, totally manipulative in his relations with others and never happy unless *he* had the whip hand. Nor is there any shortage of instances to show that these ugly traits could bring political and even physical death to his own supporters as well as to those who opposed him.[6] They *could*, but is this what *usually* happened to Stalin's supporters? The standard view asserts or implies that it is, and further asserts or implies three propositions about the rate of attrition in the Soviet political élite under Stalin; first, that it was exceptionally high, secondly, that it tended to be greater as you approached the innermost circle of his collaborators, and thirdly, that it fell most heavily on those who had been longest in his service.

I propose to test these propositions by analyzing the turnover in the Politburo and in the full and candidate membership of the Central Committee: the Politburo as embodying most (though not necessarily all) of the 'innermost circle', and the Central Committee as embodying the most important of those further levels within the political élite, membership of which could be expected to require Stalin's approval.

It is obvious that what happened during the 'Great Terror' and the decade-and-a-half of 'high Stalinism' which it ushered in will provide our most crucial evidence. Let us, however, begin a little earlier, with the Sixteenth Congress in 1930, which ushered in the first phase of Stalin's unchallenged dominance, before the killing began. By this time the so-called oppositionist leaders had been removed from the Politburo (Rykov remaining a lame-dog member for a few more months), their places taken by supporters of Stalin, and opposition supporters had been cleared out of nearly all second-level jobs carrying Central Committee status. In the course of the 1920s Stalin had progressively stacked the Central Committee with his adherents – that is to say with his direct clients or protégés or the clients of his clients – and when we come to the Central Committee elected in 1930 the process is virtually complete. Four years later he had the opportunity at the Seventeenth Congress for a final mop-up and for bringing in some younger blood to replace some of his older supporters.

It is when we compare the actual membership in 1930 and 1934 that we encounter the first bit of counter-evidence to the propositions under consideration. The Central Committee consisted of 71 full members in both years, and there were 67 candidate members in 1930 and one more in 1934. Now, according to our 'standard view' of Stalin as patron we should expect a higher turnover among the full members, who tended to be older, longer-term party members, more privy to what had been going on at high levels in the 1920s, than among the rising and ambitious but less tainted candidates. This is in fact not the case. Of the 71 full members in 1930, 50 were re-elected full members in 1934, six as candidate members, and only 15 disappeared into obscurity. Of the 67 candidate members, 29 remained candidates in 1934, seven were promoted to full membership, and fully 31 were removed from the Central Committee altogether: in other words the more junior candidates stood twice the chance of being discarded by Stalin as the more senior full members. What is more, when we look at the 28 candidates who made it to the Central Committee *for the first time* in 1930, and who must therefore be seen in terms of our propositions as enjoying especially high chances of political survival and advancement, we find that no less than 12 of them have already faded out by 1934, almost as high a casualty rate as among the old hands who were carry-overs from the 1920s – 43 per cent as against 46 per cent.

The Politburo as approved in July 1930 following the Sixteenth Congress comprised Stalin, Molotov, Kaganovich, Kalinin, Kirov, S. V. Kossior, Kuibyshev, Rudzutak, Voroshilov and Rykov as full members, and Mikoyan, Chubar', Petrovsky, Andreev and Syrtsov as candidates. Rykov, the one open opponent of Stalin retaining a place in the leadership following the Congress, lasted only till December, to be replaced by the Stalin supporter Ordzhonikidze. Andreev was temporarily dropped at the same time, being appointed Chairman of the Central Control Commission (CCC), and was restored in 1932, when Rudzutak took over as CCC Chairman and was in turn temporarily dropped from the Politburo. But this period did see the expulsion from the leadership of one of Stalin's long-term supporters, namely Syrtsov, who was removed from candidate membership of the Politburo and his job as Chairman of the Council of People's Commissars of the RSFSR in December 1930. This action was not entirely unprovoked. Syrtsov had criticized aspects of Stalin's industrialization and collectivization drive, and met with Lominadze, the Transcaucasian Stalinist who had made similar criticisms through formal party channels. The Politburo as approved in February 1934 following the Seventeenth Congress comprised Stalin, Molotov, Kaganovich, Kalinin, Kirov, Kossior, Kuibyshev, Voroshilov, Ordzhonikidze and Andreev as full members, and Mikoyan, Chubar', Petrovsky, Postyshev and Rudzutak as candidates. The changes since 1930 were thus relatively minor: apart from the removal of the 'oppositionist' Rykov they comprised the addition of one new member and one new candidate, one promotion from candidate to member and one demotion from member to candidate, and finally the expulsion of one – and one only – of Stalin's own men. Thus the attrition rate among Stalin's collaborators (not counting Rykov) in this four year period was 7 per cent at Politburo level, 20 per cent at the level of full CC membership, and 46 per cent at that of candidate CC membership, indicating a scale and pattern of élite turnover in striking contradiction to those implicit in the propositions under consideration. Not only was attrition relatively slow among the top six dozen or so of Stalin's subordinates (about 5 per cent per annum), it was slowest of all (the equivalent of less than 2 per cent per annum) among his fourteen immediate lieutenants.

Here it may be objected that the pattern during these years is of limited significance, since Stalin's power over his subordinates remained incomplete and it was soon to be changed radically in the course of the holocaust of 1937–8. I agree, and shall shortly consider the pattern of élite attrition during the holocaust and the fifteen years of Stalin's despotism that followed. But first we must note that the power relationship between Stalin and his followers was already different in the period we have just been considering from what it had been in the 1920s. Any personal political machine is vulnerable to severe internal tensions once it achieves full power and its rivals are politically destroyed. The common dangers and common ambitions which cemented the bond of leader and followers are now behind them, and it is the dangers and ambitions that *divide* them that suddenly loom. One is reminded of the reported remark of Al Capone when asked what he thought of Mussolini's prospects following the Fascist seizure of power. 'He'll be O.K.', he replied, 'so long as he can keep the boys in line.' Hitler faced this problem within months of taking power, and his response was the 'Night of the Long Knives', an action that promptly knocked *his* 'boys' back into line.

It is important to make some distinctions here. Stalin's defeat of the 'Right Opposition' did not put an end to political rivalry and conflict within the Soviet political élite, although it changed its character. Stalin was now seen internationally as a 'dictator' and the 'personality cult' was in full flood,[7] but then, as later, he devolved large areas of decision making to his subordinates, as any ruler must do, and they competed among themselves for his ear, for institutional territory, for resource allocations, for policy priorites, for advancement of their protégés. There, as in any political setting, the conflict of personal and group interest was inextricably mixed up with conflict over policy, and, as in any authoritarian bureaucratic system, the politics of policy implementation assumed at least equal importance with the politics of policy formation.[8] This blend of court politics and bureaucratic politics became a permanent feature of Stalin's rule, much as it was a feature of Hitler's rule[9] or, for that matter, of the rule of Alexander III.[10]

What I am discussing here, however, is something more specific, namely, the dynamics of power and dependency between the *khozyain* and his subordinates. For both of them, so long as there was some possibility that the Stalin machine could be defeated, the Opposition (*any* opposition) was the chief danger, and their chances of achieving their individual and collective ambitions depended on their hanging together. Once that machine was in full possession of the field, however, it was only from each other that a block to their ambitions or a threat to their personal and political security could come. The cost–benefit calculus of mutual loyalty was now drastically changed. For the followers, any misgivings they might have over Stalin's policies or methods, any doubts as to their prospects of surviving and flourishing under his command, were now no longer overshadowed by the greater danger of an Opposition victory. And as for Stalin, one can scarcely believe that he would have been content to rule at the pleasure of his Politburo colleagues and of a Central Committee with quasi-parliamentary powers, needing constantly to court support rather than simply compel it and facing the constant possibility that the doubts and misgivings among his supporters could blossom into a move to replace him.

In short, the scene was now set for that crisis in leader–follower relations to which, as suggested above, victorious personal political machines are vulnerable. Nor were signs lacking of an incipient crisis during the early 1930s. Indeed, one might interpolate here, the cost–benefit calculus of leader–follower loyalty within the Stalin machine had clearly been shifting for some time before the Sixteenth Congress, Uglanov's breaking of the ranks in 1928 being a significant case in point. But the Lominadze and Syrtsov cases were the first examples of officials who had stood with Stalin against *all* the oppositions and who now, precisely when the latter's defeat was complete, could be moved by their concern over Stalin's policies and methods to come out in criticism. If the 'boss' needed evidence that he must now find new ways to 'keep the boys in line', this was surely it. The 'personality cult' launched some months previously clearly had a part to play here. Its political function was to overawe not so much Stalin's opponents as his supporters, to emphasize the gulf between his authority and that of even the most senior of them, and to deter criticism by making it seem almost sacreligious in the eyes of the rank-and-file communists.

But Stalin was soon to conclude, if he had not done so from the
outset, that the 'cult' needed some teeth in it, something sharper,
moreover, than the dismissal and disgrace suffered by Syrtsov and
Lominadze. For disaffection began to manifest itself in potentially
more dangerous forms. On the one hand, there was the transition
to conspiratorial methods, notably in the group organized by M.
N. Ryutin, a Central Committee *apparatchik* become *raikom*
secretary, which brought together defecting Stalinists and former
oppositionists. On the other hand, at least by 1934, some senior
officials were beginning to think the unthinkable: the replacement
of Stalin as General Secretary. I do not intend here to enter
the controversy over the actual sequence of events linking these
developments with the *Ezhovshchina*, in particular over whether
Stalin tried and failed to get the Politburo to agree to the death
penalty for Ryutin, whether he inspired or authorized the murder
of Kirov, and intended the party-membership purges from 1933
on to help prepare the way for the replacement of most of the
party élite.[11] My argument is simply this: in the early 1930s Stalin
had reasonable grounds for doubt whether he was entirely proof
against the defection of his supporters, and the *Ezhovshchina*,
whatever else can be said about it, dealt with this problem by
demonstrating that the least indication of disloyalty could be fatal.
Given what we know about Stalin's character, I find it difficult to
believe that this consequence was not intended.

On the face of it, the holocaust of the party élite in 1937–8
offers incontrovertible confirmation that Stalin was an egregiously
'disloyal' patron. Surely we have only to compare the 1934 Central
Committee with that elected at the Eighteenth Congress in 1939.
Four-fifths of the 1934 members and candidates, practically all of
whom were Bolsheviks of pre-Revolutionary or Civil War vintage
who had boarded the General Secretary's bandwagon during the
1920s or been co-opted by him in the early 1930s, were now swept
away, most of them to a cruel and sordid death, to be replaced by
a second generation of Stalinists rapidly advanced from obscurity
and half of them not even party members when Lenin died 15 years
earlier.

But there *were* survivors, and if we take a careful look at
who these were we shall encounter further problems for the
propositions embodied in what I have called the standard view
of Stalin's way with his followers and subordinates (namely,

not only was there a high attrition rate, but this increased the longer you had been in his service and the closer you were to his immediate entourage). To start with, the generally younger, more junior candidates again had (as in 1930–4) a worse survival rate than the full members. Only 12 per cent of the 1934 candidates were re-elected candidates or members in 1939, compared with 22.5 per cent of the full members. And now let us look in particular at our cohorts of 1930 and 1934 – those co-opted to the Central Committee for the first time at the Sixteenth or Seventeenth Congresses – the rising stars of the first years of Stalin's dictatorship. According to the propositions we are considering, *they* should have had a distinctly better survival rate than the older, and generally more senior, Stalinists who had come to prominence in the 1920s. But they did not. In fact, those elected for the first time in 1930 and re-elected in 1934 were particularly badly mauled during the purges – only 8 per cent were still in the Central Committee by 1939. Those elected for the first time in 1934 did considerably better – 21 per cent of them were again chosen in 1939. So comparison just of the 1930 and 1934 cohorts offers some *prima facie* support for the proposition that longer service under Stalin made you more vulnerable. When, however, we combine the 1930 and 1934 cohorts, as might seem reasonable since they both entered the Central Committee in the same phase of the consolidation of Stalin's power, we find that their survival rate was slightly *worse* than that of those 1934 members and candidates who had been co-opted to the Central Committee back in the 1920s.

Another more striking characteristic of the 1934 to 1939 survivors will perhaps be apparent from a simple perusal of their names: A. A. Andreev, A. E. Badaev, L. P. Beria, K. E. Voroshilov, A.A. Zhdanov, L. M. Kaganovich, M. M. Kaganovich, M. I. Kalinin, M. M. Litvinov, D. Z. Manuilsky, A. I. Mikoyan, V. M. Molotov, K. I. Nikolaeva, N. S. Khrushchev, N. M. Shvernik, and of course Stalin himself. The six 1934 candidates who were made full members in 1939 were: M. D. Bagirov, S. M. Budenny, N. A. Bulganin, S. A. Lozovsky, L. Z. Mekhlis, and A. N. Poskrebyshev. Finally, there were just two of the 1934 candidates who remained candidates in 1939, namely I. G. Makarov and G. D. Veinberg. The majority of the Central Committee members who survived the holocaust politically and physically were men who had already been part of

Stalin's inner circle during the 1920s or in a couple of cases been added to it in the years preceding the purge.

There were exceptions. Klavdia Nikolaeva was an ex-Zinovievite who threw in her lot with Stalin and was rewarded with a series of party posts and made a trade union boss in 1936; while Stalin was a notorious sexist in his cadres policy, even he found it useful to retain a few token women in secondary posts. Maksim Litvinov 'ought' to have died along with most of the diplomatic corps, but Stalin evidently perceived the need to keep *someone* with international standing and experience for negotiating with the British and French. If Nikolaeva was kept on as a token woman, Badaev was probably retained as a token Old Bolshevik – he had been one of the Bolshevik members of the Duma and Stalin used him both for internal and foreign consumption as a symbol of respectability and continuity, making him Chairman of the Presidency of the Russian Republic. Solomon Lozovsky, till 1937 head of the Trade Union International (*Profintem*), also probably owed his survival to his usefulness internationally, but his wartime role in the Jewish Anti-Fascist Committee was to lead to his arrest in 1948 and execution in 1952. Mikhail Kaganovich enjoyed (although it ultimately failed him) the protection of his still very powerful brother Lazar. Bagirov was a leading protégé of Stalin's new police chief Beria. Veinberg like Lozovsky had been a leading trade-union official till 1937, when he was reduced to a minor administrative position in one of the commissariats, a post which by no stretch of the imagination justified keeping his candidate membership of the Central Committee. Perhaps he had some symbolic use, too, which further study may reveal. Or even, perhaps, Lazar Kaganovich protected him too, however out of character this may seem, for as young men the two had worked together in the Bolshevik underground in Kiev. I have no hypothesis to account for the survival of Makarov, who moved from a central government post to the Mogilev *obkom* during the Terror.

These were the exceptions. The rest were all big wheels in the Stalin machine. Molotov, Voroshilov, Andreev, Kaganovich and Kalinin were all full members of Stalin's Politburo by the early 1930s and Mikoyan was a candidate member – he became a full member in 1935. Khrushchev was Kaganovich's right-hand-man in the Moscow party organization in the early 1930s and became its First Secretary in 1935: in January 1938 he was made a candidate member of the Politburo and sent to take over the party organization in the Ukraine. Andrei Zhdanov had been for many years Stalin's man in Nizhny-Novgorod (renamed Gorky), which had the largest party organization in Russia proper, after Moscow and Leningrad, and on Kirov's assassination succeeded him as Secretary of the Central Committee and the Leningrad party organization, he too being made a candidate member of the Politburo in 1935. Nikolai Bulganin was another of Stalin's and Kaganovich's placemen in the Moscow organization – he ran the executive committee of the Moscow soviet from 1931 to 1937 and later became a deputy premier for several years. Nikolai Shvernik was Stalin's nominee to take over the leadership of the trade unions from the 'Rightist' Tomsky in 1930, a job he held till 1944, and at the same time he was made a member of the Orgburo. Lavrenti Beria was Stalin's party boss in Georgia from 1931 and early in 1938 was brought up to Moscow to take over the NKVD. Semen Budenny had long been Stalin's favourite Army commander, was Inspector of Cavalry from 1934, Commander of the Moscow military district from 1937 and Deputy Commissar for Defence from 1939. Dmitri Manuilsky took over control of the *Comintern* on Stalin's behalf in 1928 and ran it till its abolition in 1943. Lev Mekhlis worked in Stalin's personal secretariat during the 1920s, then took charge of the Central Committee press department and was Stalin's chief man on *Pravda*, and headed the political directorate of the armed forces from 1937 to 1940 when Stalin was busy purging and restaffing the High Command. Finally, there was the detested Aleksandr Poskrebyshev, a long-time official of Stalin's personal secretariat and in charge of it from about 1930 on.

These fifteen, then, who constituted just on three-quarters of all the 1934 Central Committee full and candidate members who retained their membership in 1939, were all men who had been prominent supporters of Stalin for many years preceding the *Ezhovshchina* and most of them had in fact been in constant, almost daily contact with him throughout the period under consideration. The implications of this for the standard view of Stalin's way with his henchmen and supporters is obvious. These implications become even clearer when we look specifically at the fate of Stalin's 1934 Politburo.

Several members of the innermost circle perished during these years. Of the full members of the 1934 Politburo, Kirov was assassinated in December 1934 and Stalin may have contrived it; Kuibyshev died of a heart attack in January 1935, and some scholars have speculated that Stalin had a hand in this too; Ordzhonikidze committed suicide in February 1937, under great pressure from Stalin which culminated in the arrest of his brother; and Kossior was arrested and shot in February 1939. Apart from Stalin, the five other full members (Molotov, Kaganovich, Voroshilov, Kalinin and Andreev) survived and were re-elected at the Eighteenth Congress. Of the five candidate members, Rudzutak, Postyshev and Chubar' were arrested and shot (the last-named after having been promoted and serving for three years as a full member); Petrovsky was sacked but never arrested (Stalin made him Director of the Museum of the Revolution); and Mikoyan was promoted to full membership in February 1935 and re-elected in 1939. Four additional candidates were added between 1935 and 1938: Ezhov and Eikhe, who were to be arrested and shot; and Zhdanov and Khrushchev, who were made full members in 1939. Thus, of the nineteen men who served on the Politburo during these years, six certainly died at the hands of Stalin and the true figure could be up to nine.[12]

So it was dangerous being in Stalin's innermost circle – but *not* as dangerous as being in the wider circles of the party élite. Of the 1934 Politbureau, 47 per cent (seven out of fifteen) were re-elected in 1939, compared with 22.5 per cent of all full members of the CC and 12 per cent of the candidates. Those re-elected to the *Politbureau*, moreover, comprised 60 per cent of its 1934 full members and 20 per cent of its candidate members. Contrary to widespread opinion, the old adage *bliz tsarya – bliz smerti* (close to the Tsar – close to death), which is valid enough under most tyrannies, did not apply under Stalin's.[13] For those in the political élite, at least during these terrible years, the closer you were to Stalin the better were your chances of surviving physically and continuing your political career.

Nevertheless, those closest to Stalin, along with lesser mortals, could now be in no doubt that the slightest suspicion, the slightest offence to the *khozyain*, could prove fatal.[14] Stalin now had the power to grant life, or to withhold it, from even the most powerful in the land, a power he did not have in 1934. The repressions culminating in the *Ezhovshchina* served Stalin as his Night of the Long Knives: it knocked 'the boys' back into line.

We now turn to the last fourteen years of Stalin's rule, when the limits on his despotic power were at their weakest. Up to this point, one might hypothesize, these limits had prevented him from giving free rein to his natural inclinations in the treatment of his henchmen and subordinates, and that is why the pattern of such treatment differs, as we have seen, from the standard picture of it. Even the relatively high survival rate of his closest lieutenants during the *Ezhovshchina* simply reflected, perhaps, his need for some continuity at the highest level while he cleaned out all the power structures and staffed them with a new generation of totally dependent, totally subservient young officials: the time for those lieutenants would come later. Perhaps it was only during these last 14 years that the standard picture could be expected to apply fully. So the question arises: did it? Was this a period of exceptionally high attrition in the Soviet political élite? Was attrition particularly marked in Stalin's innermost circle? Did it fall more heavily on those who had been longer in his service? Let us consider the evidence.

Of the 71 full members of the Central Committee elected at the Eighteenth Congress in March 1939, 34 were re-elected as full members at the Nineteenth Congress in October 1952, and a further six as candidate members. Thus 31 had fallen by the wayside in these 13 1/2 years, which represents an attrition rate averaging a little under 3 per cent per annum. Far fewer of the 68 1939 candidates were re-elected in 1952: seven as full members and ten as candidates, representing an average annual attrition rate of almost 6 per cent. These figures speak for themselves: Stalin at the height of his power effected changes in the ranks of his Central Committee level subordinates at a rather *slow* rate, and the rate was only half as high among the more senior, on the whole longer-serving, full members as it was among the more junior candidates.

The attrition rate was low not only by absolute standards, but also by comparison with other periods of Soviet history.[15] The 3 per cent average annual rate among full members compares with 5 per cent in 1930–4 and 8 per cent in 1953–6. In 1956–61 (between the Twentieth and Twenty-First Congresses), Khrushchev's vintage years, the annual attrition rate among full members of the Central

Committee rose to 12 per cent: four times the rate during the period of 'high Stalinism'. The Brezhnev period is generally and correctly regarded as one of unusually high stability of tenure in the upper ranks of the Soviet political élite. However, only 44 per cent of the full members of the Brezhnev's first Central Committee, elected at the Twenty-Third Congress in 1966, were still there in 1981, when his last Central Committee was elected at the Twenty-Sixth Congress. This represents an average annual attrition rate of 4 per cent, or about the same as in 1939–52 when one allows for deaths in office and retirements in old age. The Soviet political élite, at least at the level of full members of the Central Committee, have never had greater security of tenure than they had under Stalin at the height of his power.

Before considering this proposition more closely, we should note that the 1939 Central Committee was augmented at the Eighteenth Conference in February 1941 by six full members and 17 candidates. The comparisons that follow relate the membership formed at the Nineteenth Congress, on the eve of Stalin's death, to the membership as it stood after the Eighteenth Conference, just before the German invasion. What they show is that the relative security of tenure of the late Stalin era did not apply equally to all sections of the political élite. Higher-level officials had a much higher survival rate than those at lower levels, and central officials a much higher survival rate than provincial officials. Seven of the ten members of the Central Committee Secretariat elected in October 1952 had been full members of the Central Committee before the war. By contrast, only four of the 57 republican and regional level party officials among the full members of the Central Committee in 1952 had been full members in 1941, and four had been candidates. Of the 21 who were elected as candidates in 1952, only one had been a candidate before the war and none had been full members. Turning to the government élite, all 13 members of the Presidium of the Council of Ministers (the Chairman and Deputy Chairmen) had also been full Central Committee members in 1941. On the other hand, only seven of the 18 more junior members of the Council of Ministers who were full members of the Central Committee on the eve of Stalin's death had been full members before the war and one had been a candidate. Of the 22 central government officials who were candidate members in October 1952, only one had been a full member before the war and one a candidate. These figures show that we must be careful in the conclusions we draw from overall attrition rates. They also make nonsense, however, of the view that those who were closest to Stalin, hierarchially and physically, were particularly likely to be discarded by him.

This last observation acquires further force when we consider what happened at the Politburo level, where the stability of membership was again greater in the years of Stalin's fully-developed despotism than in any other period of comparable length in Soviet history. All but two of the 11 full and candidate members of the Politburo as constituted in 1939 outlived Stalin and retained their places on the Politburo up to its merging in the new Central Committee Presidium shortly before Stalin's death. The two exceptions were Kalinin (died 1946) and Zhdanov (died 1948, under circumstances suggesting the possibility of foul play). Again, comparison with what happened under Stalin's successors will help to bring out the significance of this. Of the 14 full and candidate members of the Central Committee Presidium immediately after Stalin's death in 1953 only three retained their membership in 1964. Seven of the 19 full and candidate members of the reconstituted Politburo of 1966 were no longer there in 1981, and only two of these cases were due to death. The durability of Stalin's inner clientèle was truly remarkable. The 11 full members of the Politiburo who were his 'closest comrades-in-arms' in the early 1950s included seven who had been major supporters or assistants for 25–30 years (Molotov, Voroshilov, Kaganovich, Andreev, Malenkov, Mikoyan and Shvernik), three more whom he first entrusted with major positions in the early 1930s (Beria, Khrushchev and Bulganin), and only one (Kosygin) whose first experience of working closely with Stalin came as late as the Second World War.[16] How many of the other great tyrants of history have left such a record of objective loyalty to their lieutenants?

It is time to draw out some conclusions, at the risk of labouring the now obvious. The standard view is dead wrong on all three of the major propositions it entails about Stalin's way with his personal supporters. Far from being even relatively high, attrition in the upper ranks of the Soviet political élite was *lower* when Stalin's power was at its zenith than in any other period before or since. Proximity to Stalin (physical, geographical or hierarchical) made one *less* likely to suffer repression, not more. And far from constantly changing his 'favourites' and his 'closest collaborators in crime', he surrounded himself with long-term favourites and collaborators to the end of his days.

These conclusions are not merely negative: they embody important information about how Stalin actually did behave towards his henchmen and supporters. As they stand, however, they offer only a partial picture of this behaviour. For, as suggested near the beginning of this chapter, the standard view of Stalin's treatment of those around him does embody important and, for us very relevant, aspects of his personality and methods, even if the behavourial expression of these was different from what is usually imagined. Whether or not the 'beloved father and teacher' was really concerned to be loved is a matter for conjecture; that he was concerned to be feared is beyond doubt. I have argued that the repressions of the 1930s, which destroyed the greater part of the Soviet political élite and even members of Stalin's immediate entourage, were intended to place his power and personal security beyond challenge, doubt and question by demonstrating that the slightest hint of suspicion or opposition could be fatal. They undoubtedly had that effect, and thenceforth the occasional arrest and shooting – notably those of the young Politburo member Voznesensky and the other victims of the 'Leningrad Affair' – sufficed to reinforce the lesson.

Stalin's subordinates undoubtedly feared him and felt themselves to be entirely in his hands. As Khrushchev recalled having confided to Bulganin, 'It has happened sometimes that a man goes to Stalin on his invitation as a friend. And when he sits with Stalin, he does not know where he will be sent next, home or to jail.'[17] The same acute apprehension and sense of their utter dependence is reflected in the accounts of other senior officials summoned by Stalin.[18] Apart from his demonstrated power to kill, Stalin also found subsidiary ways to reinforce in his henchmen and subordinates their feeling of helplessness before him. One was by exactng their acquiescence in the repression of close relatives: Kaganovich in the execution of his brother, Molotov in the imprisonment of his wife. Then there was his arbitrary inclusion or exclusion of them from the meetings of decision-making bodies of which they were members, and convening or non-convening of such bodies according to his whim.[19]

If Stalin displayed a high level of 'objective loyalty' towards his subordinates and 'closest comrades in arms', it was evidently, therefore, not out of tender feeling towards them. It was rather out of a form of rational political calculation far more common in human affairs than the liberal mind can easily contemplate: the rationality, if you like, of the Mafia boss. Stalin wanted to be obeyed, he wanted to be secure against conspiracy, and he believed that instilling fear was essential to winning and maintaining that obedience and security. Having achieved this by egregious display of his power to kill, he thenceforth avoided the obvious mistake of so abusing that power as to drive his entourage to collective desperation.[20] The prudent despot or gangster boss will seek to ensure that those around him, those on whom he depends for information and for executing his will, are men whose unqualified subservience and sensitivity to his needs has been tested over many years, and whose strengths and weaknesses he knows inside out. Such men, he would understand, will need reasonable expectations of his continued favour and protection, or they may decide that the dangers of betraying him are less than the dangers of continued loyal service. Perhaps it is in such terms that we should understand Stalin's relatively high level of objective loyalty towards those henchmen and subordinates who feared and obeyed him.

NOTES

1. See the symposium in *Studies in Comparative Communism*, vol XII, nos 2–3 (Summer/Autumn 1979) pp. 159–211, where references to the relevant literature may be found. See also T. H. Rigby and Bohdan Harasymiw (eds), *Leadership Selection and Patron-Client Relations in the USSR and Yugoslavia* (New York: Pergamon Press, 1983) and T. H. Rigby, 'Political Patronage in the USSR from Lenin to Brezhnev', *Politics*, vol 18, no. 1 (May 1983) pp. 84–9.

2. See T. H. Rigby, 'Early Provincial Cliques and the Rise of Stalin, *Soviet Studies,* vol XXXIII, no. 1, (January 1981) pp. 3–28 (this volume, chapter 3).

3. On Khrushchev in the roles of client and patron. See T. H. Rigby, 'Khrushchev and the Rules of the Game', in R. F. Miller and F. Feher (eds), *Khrushchev and the Communist World* (London and Sydney: Croom Helm, 1984) pp. 39–81.

4. Boris Souvarine, *Stalin: A Critical Survey of Bolshevism* (Sydney and London: Angus and Robertson, 1940) p. 580.

5. George F. Kennan, *Russia and the West under Lenin and Stalin* (London: Hutchinson, 1961) pp. 254–5.

6. The evidence for this is perhaps best assembled in Roy Medvedev, *Let*

History Judge, The Origins and Consequences of Stalinism (London: Macmillan, 1972).

7. See Graeme Gill, 'Political Myth and Stalin's Quest for Authority in the Party', in T. H. Rigby. Archie Brown and Peter Reddaway (eds), *Authority, Power and Policy in the USSR* (London: Macmillan. 1980) ch. 6.

8. For a revealing case study of Soviet élite politics in the early 1930s, see Sheila Fitzpatrick, 'Ordzhonikidze's Takeover of Vesenkha: a Case Study in Soviet Bureaucratic Politics', *Soviet Studies*, vol. XXXVII, no. 2 (April 1985) pp. 153–72.

9. See Karl Dietrich Bracher, *The German Dictatorship* (Harmondsworth: Penguin, 1973) pp. 429–30; Albert Speer, *Inside the Third Reich* (London: Weidenfeld & Nicolson, 1970) *passim*.

10. P. A. Zaionchkovsky, *Rossiiskoe samoderzhavie v kontse XIX stoletiya* (Moscow, 1970) offers profuse case material on the politics of the reign of Alexander III.

11. The best introduction to the issues of evidence and interpretation here is the discussion between J. Arch Getty, Robert C. Tucker and Niels Erik Rosenfeldt in *Slavic Review*, vol. 42, no. 1 (Spring 1983) pp. 60–96. See also J. Arch Getty, *Origins of the Great Purges. The Soviet Communist Party Reconsidered, 1933–1938* (Cambridge: Cambridge University Press, 1985) especially ch 7 and appendix. The validity of the view I am offering here of Stalin's motives and their relation to the holocaust does not depend on giving positive answers to these three questions. That view is certainly strengthened by the indications that, as Seventeenth Congress delegate L. Shaumyan put it, 'the idea was maturing that the time had come to transfer Stalin from the post of General Secretary to some other job' (*Pravda*, 7 February 1964), and that Kirov would have been the most favoured candidate to replace him. Even, however, if there were only a few puffs of smoke here with little or no flame behind them, Stalin would have had to be a very trusting and complacent leader to assume his position was beyond challenge at this period. Being anything but trusting and complacent, he perceived the possible dangers and took what, for a man of his character, were entirely appropriate countermeasures. Soviet political life, as I have indicated, had many dimensions and components in the 1930s as at other periods, and everything certainly cannot be reduced to Stalin's drive for despotic power. Perhaps all would agree, however, that the latter must be brought into centre stage in any account of this period and particularly of the fate of the political élite at this period, if we are not to present 'Hamlet' without the Prince. Granted, Stalin's lieutenants were undoubtedly playing their own power games too, and many individual fates must have been affected by the moves of Ezhov, Kaganovich, Malenkov and their like to settle old scores, foster their own clienteles, strengthen their organizational positions etc. These men acted, however, within ground rules which were surely marked out by Stalin, and which were intended to serve, first and foremost, *his* power interests.

12. I do not intend, nor is it necessary to my argument, to examine, in detail, the cases of those who perished, and express a view about Stalin's role in the doubtful ones. See Leonard Schapiro. *The Communist Party of the Soviet Union*, 2nd edn (London: Methuen, 1970) chs XXI–XXIII; Medvedev, op. cit., chs V–VI and Robert Conquest, *The Great Terror. Stalin's Purges of the Thirties* (London and Melbourne: Macmillan, 1968) especially ch. 2 and pp. 185–91, 414–15.

13. See T. H. Rigby 'Stalinism and the Mono-Organizational Society', in Robert C. Tucker (ed.), *Stalinism. Essays in Historical Interpretation* (Princeton: Princeton U.P., 1977) p. 64. On the power to take any life he chooses as an essential attribute of the tyrant's rule, see ibid., p. 62.

14. It has been pointed out that most of the *Politbureau* members who perished in these years were men who had shown some reluctance always to bend their wills to Stalin's. See Schapiro, op. cit., p. 397.

15. Comparison of the CC (Central Committee) membership over time is a weak tool for certain types of élite analysis, e.g., for identifying its changing occupational composition, because of its tendency to expand and therefore to embrace increasing numbers of more junior officials. It seems a valid method of measuring and comparing the rate of attrition, however, provided one asks what proportion of the *old* CC are also in the new one, rather than the other way round. Two factors would appear to reinforce the validity of the comparisons we make in this section, namely, that the rate of expansion of the CC in the Khrushchev and especially the Brezhnev periods was substantially greater than between 1939 and 1952, i.e., the statistical chances of a demoted official retaining CC membership were *improved* under Stalin's successors; and the great majority of the 1939 CC re-elected to the 1952 CC were concentrated in the highest ranks of the élite, i.e., few of them had been demoted and only remained in the CC by virtue of its expansion.

16. One might add here the names of two officials of lesser formal rank, but great behind-the-scenes power, namely, the Chairman of the Party Control Committee Shkiryatov and the head of Stalin's personal secretariat Poskrebyshev. It is doubtful if anyone was privy to more of Stalin's guilty secrets, going back to the 1920s, than these two men, yet he had kept both of them constantly beside him for more than three decades. Niels Erik Rosenfeldt describes Poskrebyshev as 'Stalin's closest personal secretary . . . from around 1930' (see his *Knowledge and Power. The Role of Stalin's Secret Chancellery in the Soviet System of Government* (Copenhagen: Rosenkilde and Bagger, 1978) pp. 129–30; see also p. 182. 'The ever-faithful Shkiryatov' was Stalin's principal man in the Control Commission apparatus from the 1920s, played a leading role in the purges of the 1930s, including the *Ezhovshchina* (ibid., pp. 138, 148, 178) and also in such postwar repressions as the 'Leningrad Affair' (see Medvedev, op. cit., p. 481). To have worked in Stalin's personal secretariat was, of course, no guarantee of exemption from repression. Apart from Ezhov, Rosenfeldt has identified 13 other former officials of Stalin's 'secret chancellery' who perished during the holocaust, most of them of sub-CC status.

17. N. S. Khrushchev, 'On the Cult of Personality and its Consequences', in *The Stalin Dictatorship,* ed. T. H. Rigby (Sydney: Sydney University Press, 1968) p. 80.

18. See especially N. S. Patolichev, *Ispytanie na zrelost'* (Moscow, 1977) pp. 280–4.

19. See Khrushchev, op. cit., pp. 80–81.

20. But perhaps Stalin's treatment of his entourage in the last days of his life indicated a lapse from rationality, if such developments as the reorganization of the party's leading organs and the 'doctors' plot' case were intended as preparations for a clean-out of his old henchmen on the Politburo, as Khruschev plausibly tells us (ibid., p. 82. See further Robert Conquest, *Power and Policy in the USSR* (London: Macmillan, 1961) chs 7 and 8). If he was up to something like this, it was not necessarily

wholly out of paranoia. He may have wished to perform a final service to the Revolution by installing a younger, more vigorous, better-trained leadership before he departed. Or he may have been motivated by the not-unreasonable belief that advancing age made him more vulnerable to a palace coup. The trouble was that even if his initial moves seemed directly threatening to only one or two senior leaders, the sense of relative security of all of them must have been badly shaken, thus raising the risk of the very outcome he wished to forestall. Beria, certainly, but others as well, had ample motivation to take countermeasures, and perhaps he, or they did, as Robert C. Tucker has suggested in his article 'Svetlana Alliluyeva as Witness of Stalin', *Slavic Review*, vol. XXVII, no. 2 (June 1968) pp. 309–12.

7. Khrushchev and the resuscitation of the Central Committee*

History is not lacking in cases of hoary and respected institutions apparently condemned forever to a secondary or purely formal role which acquire, with changed political circumstances, a vital and perhaps decisive influence over events. This might be said, for instance, of the English Parliament in the seventeenth century. The recent history of the Central Committee of the Soviet Communist Party provides a twentieth-century example, appropriately explosive in both the speed and evidently episodic character of its recrudescence.

Supreme authority in the party is formally vested in its Congresses, which used to be held annually in the early years of the regime and are now supposed to be convened every four years. The Central Committee, according to the Party Rules, is elected by the Congress and exists to carry out its decisions.[1]

There is, of course, nothing unusual in the relationship between a party's Congress and its executive bodies being very different in practice from what they are on paper. We do not really expect Congresses to work out policies; at the most they choose between rival groups of leaders and the policies which these have brought *to* the Congress. CPSU Congresses have never even performed this role. Although in the early years they sometimes provided the platform for criticism of the party leadership, and later for the condemnation of defeated groups of leaders, they have always been effectively controlled by the dominant group in the leadership, and the latter have never behaved as if the Congress placed the slightest restrictions upon their actions.

However, if Soviet Party Congresses do not in fact exercise the sovereign rights formally vested in them, it is not the Central

*_Australian Outlook_, vol. 13, no. 3 (September 1959) pp. 165–80.

Committee which has usurped these. Although the Central Committee was intended to be the party's supreme executive body (in mid-1917 it had nine voting members and four non-voting members), from the eve of the October Revolution onwards, decisions have usually been taken by various standing and *ad hoc* inner bodies. The importance of such inner groups was given formal recognition at the Eighth Party Congress in 1919, which approved the amendment of the Rules to provide for a Political Bureau, Organizational Bureau and Secretariat of the Central Committee.[2] However, the Rules have never attempted a frank and accurate description of the role of these bodies, their mutual relationships and relationships with the Central Committee as a whole, let alone the position of various semi-formal groups which from time to time have exercised authority in various fields (such as Stalin's 'fivesomes' and so on, the 'bureau of the Presidium', etc.)[3]

With the emergence of these inner groups, the Central Committee did not immediately acquire a new role. For a time after 1919 it provided an alternative forum to them within which current issues might be discussed and settled. Its gradual withdrawal from such current executive functions is reflected in the growing infrequency of its meetings. In the six months preceding the Tenth Congress in March 1921 the Central Committee, like the Politburo, met on the average once a week. In the following year it met only 15 times, while the Politburo met 109 times and the Orgburo 159 times.[4] Thenceforth its meetings became rarer with each succeeding year and by the late 1920s it was not unusual for several months to pass without the Central Committee being convened.

Displacement of the Central Committee from close day to day control over the execution of policies went hand in hand with a

Table 7.1   *Growth in size of the Central Committee, 1917–56*[5]

May	1917	9	voting and	4	non-voting members
	1919	19		8	
	1921	25		15	
	1923	40		17	
	1925	63		43	
	1927	71		50	
	1939	71		68	
	1952	125		111	
	1956	133		122	

rapid growth in size, which soon changed it from a compact committee to a large unwieldy body and ultimately to a small public meeting (see Table 7.1.).

For some time, however, no one seems to have questioned the assumption that the Politburo and other inner bodies were merely, as it were, sub-committees of the 'full' Central Committee, wholly answerable to it for all their activities, and throughout the 1920s matters under dispute in the Politburo continued to be referred to it for decision and it remained the principal platform from which major policy changes were launched. The process of its transformation into a kind of 'Soviet Parliament' was already well under way before the death of Lenin, and appears to have enjoyed his approval.

This new role of the Central Committee did not long outlive the political factors which gave rise to it. The most obvious of these factors was the disunity within the Politburo, disunity which was largely concealed during Lenin's lifetime, but which broke out into the open almost immediately after his death. This enhanced the importance of the Central Committee as the supreme court of appeal short of the Party Congress. But scarcely less important was the absence of close, organic links between the Politburo (the chief policy-making body in the party) and the party's administrative machinery (the 'apparatus'). The party apparatus, which almost atrophied during the first year of Bolshevik rule, was built up in 1919–21 to become the most powerful instrument of rule in the country, its officials at each level having authority over the activities of all governmental and extra-governmental bodies in their area. Appointment of these officials and direction of their work was the main responsibility not of the Politburo but of the other two bodies set up beside it, the Orgburo and the Secretariat. By the time of Lenin's death in January 1924, one member of the Politburo, Stalin, had secured, by energetic exploitation of his position as General Secretary of the party, close personal control over both these bodies, and through them over the party apparatus throughout the country.

The apparatus was converted into a highly centralized and strongly disciplined bureaucratic 'service', directed by Stalin. Stalin's control of the party apparatus enabled him to ensure that the selection of local delegates to Party Congresses provided a majority for elements sympathetic to him. More than this, as the development of the Central Committee into a 'Soviet Parliament' proceeded, and more and more representatives of local party organizations were brought into it, it was inevitable that these representatives should be men owing to Stalin the positions by virtue of which they were chosen for the Central Committee. When matters were referred from the Politburo to the Central Committee, how could the apparatus-men therein be expected to be impartial in arbitrating between their 'boss' and rival members of the Politburo?

This situation, and the tactics employed by Stalin to take maximum advantage of it, have often been described.[6] Here I wish merely to consider the relative roles of the various institutions involved. By the time of Lenin's death, the Politburo was firmly established as the most authoritative of the party's inner organs of rule, and the most senior party leaders were concentrated in it. However great Stalin's control over the party apparatus, he could not win supreme authority in the country until he could dominate the Politburo. Any attempt to use the party apparatus to seize full power against a majority in the Politburo would almost certainly have failed. His strategy, therefore, was to make alliances within the Politburo to isolate, in turn, his most serious rivals and avoid being isolated himself, while using control of the apparatus gradually to pack the 'full' Central Committee with loyal followers, and then to manipulate the Central Committee first to harass and ultimately to purge his opponents in the Politburo and replace them with his own men.

Once the Politburo had been converted into as pliant an instrument of Stalin's will as were the other inner party bodies, the need for a 'Soviet Parliament', as a court of appeal from the Politburo, lapsed. This role of the Central Committee virtually came to an end with its meeting of November 1929, which expelled Bukharin from the Politburo.[7] For several years thereafter, however, indeed right up to the Second World War, the Central Committee continued to be convened every few months to give its formal approval to major decisions. This reflected Stalin's concern to retain as many as possible of the trappings of 'inner party democracy' to help legitimize his power, and also helped highlight the importance of the matters concerned.

This pseudo-'parliamentary' phase of the Central Committee's existence did not survive the outbreak of war. In the last twelve years of Stalin's lifetime the Central Committee appears to have met only three times.[8] Its role as an honorific body, membership of which conferred special status but no special powers, a role which had assumed increasing importance throughout the 1930s, now appeared to be its sole reason for existence.

The membership of the Central Committee in the latter part of the Stalin era consisted of the occupants of the most senior posts in the various sections of the central and regional Party and Governmental machines, and in the other major hierarchies and fields of activity – the armed forces, political police, trade unions, etc. There was little change in the proportions in which these were represented as between the Eighteenth Congress in 1939 and the Nineteenth in 1952 (see Table 7.2).[9]

Table 7.2   *Posts held by Central Committee members, 1939 and 1952*

	Voting Members	Non-Voting	Total	Per cent	Voting Members	Non-Voting	Total	Per cent
			1939				1952	
Central party officials	7	–	7	5.1	13	4	17	7.2
Regional party secretaries	15	24	39	28.1	57	21	78	33.2
Central govt officials	29	11	40	28.8	26	36	62	26.2
Regional govt officials	3	5	8	5.8	11	11	22	9.2
Military	8	10	18	13.0	4	22	26	11.0
Police	1	6	7	5.1	2	6	8	3.4
Komsomol, TU, etc.	4	–	4	2.9	2	4	6	2.5
Industry	1	1	2	1.5	–	–	–	–
Ideology and 'Culture'	3	–	3	2.2	9	5	14	6.0
Unidentified	–	11	11	7.9	1	2	3	1.3
Total	71	68	139		125	111	236	

An essentially honorific body, consisting of those who had reached the top in the various sectors of the politico-administrative structure, and functionally moribund – such were the apparent features of the Central Committee inherited by Stalin's successors in 1953. Still, the Party Presidium, in which supreme power now resided, was, after all, the Presidium of the *Central Committee,* and it was inevitable that its members, in their concern for legitimation of their rule, should bring the Central Committee into play. It was a joint meeting of the Central Committee, the Council of Ministers and the Presidium of the Supreme Soviet which ratified the allocation of jobs effected by the Old Guard immediately after Stalin's death. It was the Central Committee, meeting alone, which approved Malenkov's resignation from the Party Secretariat a week later. After a further four months, the Central Committee was called together again, to express its approval for the arrest of one of the members of the Presidium, Beria, and his principal supporters.[10]

Thus, in the months immediately following the death of Stalin, the answerability of the Presidium to the full Central Committee, in matters affecting the composition of the party's inner bodies, was reaffirmed. This was the first phase in the resuscitation of the Central Committee.

The second phase began in September 1953, and was the direct reflection of the activities of the new First Secretary, Khrushchev.[11] In the general parcelling out of fields of responsibility among the inner leadership, Khrushchev appears to have been charged with overall guidance of agriculture. This was perhaps the least glamorous sector of the economy in a country dedicated to large-scale industrialization; nevertheless it was the sector where improvements were most obviously and most urgently needed. Khrushchev threw himself energetically into the task of securing these improvements by sponsoring a series of sensible, practical reforms and removing some of the more irrational features of the farm system. However, he was not content merely to have these measures implemented through the ordinary administrative channels. Instead, he launched them with considerable publicity at specially convened meetings of the Central Committee. Such meetings were held in September 1953, February–March 1954, June 1954 and January 1955.

Apart from an isolated instance in 1947, the Central Committee had not been given an opportunity of discussing economic affairs since before the war. At this series of meetings, moreover, Khrushchev set an example of frankness and plain speaking unknown since the 1920s, and took the greatest pains to explain the reasons for the measures he was proposing. There can be little doubt that many Central Committee members were deeply gratified and flattered by being thus taken into the First Secretary's confidence, and by his apparent awareness of a responsibility towards them for the work under his jurisdiction. For two years no other Presidium member followed suit, so Khrushchev went unrivalled as the protagonist of 'restoring Leninist norms in party life'.

At the same time, many lines of policy pursued by Khrushchev could not fail to win the support of large groups of Central Committee members. For the party *apparatchiki* who, after all, made up over half the Central Committee, the First Secretary stood for the restoration of the primacy of the party machine as against first the Police, and then the central government machine. Typical of the measures sponsored by Khrushchev to this end was the abolition in September 1953 of the local organs of the Ministry of Agriculture and the transfer of control over the *kolkhozes* to groups of officials of the district party committees stationed in the Machine and Tractor Stations.[12] This ensured that agricultural matters were referred up through Party rather than government channels. For local officials as a whole, including provincial and republic government officials, Khrushchev stood for the extension of their powers at the expense of the Central Ministries. It is worth noting at this point that Khrushchev's consistent advocacy of measures of administrative decentralization served his cause in two ways: not only did it foster good will among provincial officialdom, but it enhanced the powers of the central party apparatus by virtue of the supervisory responsibilities vested in the republic and provincial party bureaux.

During the first phase of the Central Committee's revival, in the months immediately following Stalin's death, it assumed again the 'pseudo-parliamentary' role which it had played during the 1930s. In the second phase, however, after September 1953, it began to behave like the Central Committee of the 1920s, that 'Soviet Parliament' which was constantly called upon to declare itself on questions under dispute in the Politburo, and which Stalin manipulated to such effect in his struggles with the various opposition groups.[13] Among those of his policies which Khrushchev referred to meetings of the Central Committee for ratification after his assumption of the First Secretaryship, some were known to be opposed by certain Presidium leaders – such as the virgin lands programme (February 1954 meeting) and the *rapprochement* with Yugoslavia (July 1955 meeting). Thus, it seemed that Khrushchev was seeking to establish the Central Committee's right to the last word in major issues on which differences existed within the Presidium.

While Khrushchev was working to enhance the Central Committee's role and to promote his credit among its members, he did not neglect those more direct measures available to the First Secretary to build up Central Committee support. A study of major appointments between 1953 and 1956 suggests that there may have been some sort of understanding about the allocation of patronage among Presidium members during this period as a result of which Khrushchev received a more or less free hand within the Party apparatus, the principal say over agricultural appointments and a major role in the purging and re-staffing of the police apparatus, but seems to have had little influence within the majority of departments of the central government. However, although the central ministries lying outside Khrushchev's jurisdiction contributed about a quarter of the Central Committee membership, and considerable authority over these appointments lay with the Premier (Malenkov till February 1955, then Bulganin), the latter had to share patronage opportunities in the government machine with the six other Presidium members holding positions in the Council of Ministers. Thus, while the patronage directly and almost exclusively disposed of by Khrushchev included about 35 per cent of the posts holding Central Committee status, no other member of the Presidium had in his gift more than a handful of such posts. There is ample evidence that Khrushchev made energetic use of these opportunities.

Starting with the closing months of 1953, there was a continuous stream of appointments to major party, agricultural and police posts of officials who had previously worked closely under Khrushchev when he was party boss in the Ukraine (1938–49) or the Moscow Region (1949–53). Stalwarts of the Ukrainian party organization now took over a number of major provincial committees in the RSFSR; for example A. P. Kirilenko became First Secretary at Sverdlovsk, A. I. Struev at Molotov (now Perm), M. M. Stakhursky at Khabarovsk, V. S. Markov at Orel, and so on. Former Ukrainian L. I. Brezhnev became party boss in the third largest republic, Kazakhstan. The Central Committee's Department of Party Organs for the RSFSR, which controls major appointments throughout the Russian Republic, was entrusted to V. A. Churaev, another old Ukrainian associate of Khrushchev. V. V. Matskevich and L. R. Korniets, both of whom held major administrative posts under Khrushchev in the Ukraine in the postwar period, became Ministers of Agriculture and of Agricultural Procurement respectively. I. A. Serov, Khrushchev's police chief in the Ukraine in 1939-41, became Chairman of the new Committee on State Security. His deputy (probably in charge of personnel) was K. F. Lunev, a local party official in Moscow when Khrushchev ran the provincial committee there. N. P. Dudorov, the new MVD Minister, another product of Khrushchev's local Moscow apparatus, later worked as one of Khrushchev's department chiefs in the Central Committee. These are some of the more conspicuous cases.

Apart from products of the Khrushchev machines in the Ukraine and Moscow, there was another group of officials who appear to have been particularly favoured by Khrushchev. These were men who had served in the Leningrad Party organization when it was under Zhdanov and who had somehow survived the massive purge of Zhdanovites conducted by Malenkov and Beria in 1949 (the 'Leningrad Case'). No doubt Khrushchev felt he could rely on the support of these men against his major rival, Malenkov. Old Leningraders now took over in Leningrad itself (F. R. Kozlov), in the Gorky and Maritime provincial committees (N. G. Ignatov and T. F. Shtykov respectively), and another (A. B. Aristov) became secretary of the Central Committee, apparently responsible for party cadres.

The various policies and programmes sponsored and directed by Khrushchev, such as his agricultural campaigns, administrative decentralization, and the restoration of party control in the state security organs, provided ample cover for his manipulation of 'cadres'. A few remarks made by Khrushchev at the February 1954 meeting of the Central Committee offer a glimpse of this cover at work.

In organizing the struggle to implement the decisions of the September plenary meeting, the Central Committee [apparatus] accords special importance to reinforcing republic, territorial, regional and district party committees . . .

Naturally the CC has paid the closest attention to the activity of the party bodies in republics, territories and regions where big defects have been tolerated in the development of agriculture. Since the September plenary meeting reports have been considered in the CC from the Central Committees of the Kazakh and Moldavian Communist Parties and the Bashkir, Tula, Kostroma, Molotov, Astrakhan, Voronezh, Novgorod, Velikie Luki, Kalinin, Bryansk, Smolensk, Crimean, Orel and Yaroslavl Regional Committees . . .

In considering the question together with the members of the Bureau [of the party committees concerned] we brought the defects to light and came to certain general conclusions, but did not adopt any [formal] decisions, agreeing instead to call a plenary meeting of the Party committee concerned, to discuss the matters which had arisen. A representative of the Central Committee [apparatus] attended this meeting, and pointed out the defects which had been revealed.[14]

In fact, not only did the representative of the central apparatus 'point out the defects', but in most cases he effected changes in local party bosses. Altogether some 45 of the 84 First Secretaries of republic and regional party committees coming directly under the Central Committee were changed in the two and a half years between Khrushchev's assumption of the First Secretaryship and the Twentieth Party Congress in February 1956. It seems safe to assume that by then there were few if any provincial party bosses left in office about whose support Khrushchev did not feel pretty confident in the event of a crisis (see Table 7.3). There is also little doubt that Khrushchev was behind many of the changes of republic premiers and provincial executive committee chairmen in this period.[15]

Table 7.3, based on an analysis of the Central Committee membership as it emerged from the Twentieth Party Congress, represents an attempt to draw up a balance sheet of Khrushchev's efforts to create Central Committee support since 1953. Group A comprises categories of officials who must be regarded as deeply committed to Khrushchev, and whose careers would be disastrously affected by the triumph of Khrushchev's rivals. Group B comprises provincial officials lacking any obvious personal commitment to Khrushchev, but who enjoyed his patronage at least negatively, in the sense of being retained in office through the various waves of changes effected by him.

Table 7.3   *Strength of Khrushchev's support among Central Committee members, 1956*[16]

| | Number of Members | | | |
	Voting	Non-voting	Total	Per cent of CC
GROUP A				
Ex-Khrushchev's Ukrainian party machine	23	20	43	17
Ex-Khrushchev's Moscow regional party machine	9	8	17	7
In CC apparatus under Khrushchev	5	3	8	3
Holding senior agricultural posts under Khrushchev	2	2	4	1.5
Leningraders	4	1	5	2
Favourably mentioned by Khrushchev – later promoted	3	1	4	1.5
Progressive total	46	35	81	32
GROUP B				
Other provincial party officials	34	27	61	24
Other provincial government officials	7	8	15	6
Total	87	70	157	62
Total CC membership	133	122	255	100

This table shows that by early 1956 about a third of the Central Committee membership were people closely committed to Khrushchev, while almost another third were more likely to support him than his rivals. The remaining 98 voting and non-voting members included some 54 central government officials and 11 Foreign Office officials. Many of these had close career links with other members of the Presidium, and this group as a whole must have felt their interests threatened by Khrushchev's measures of decentralization and asserting party control. The 19 service chiefs elected to the CC were an unknown factor.

The strong following which Khrushchev enjoyed in the full Central Committee by 1956 was not matched in the Presidium, whose voting membership included only one of his protégés (Kirichenko). And the Presidium was, after all, still the supreme policy-making body in the country. Although the responsibility of the Presidium to the full Central Committee had been reaffirmed, and the latter's authority had more than once been invoked against dissenters in the Presidium, there is no evidence that the Central Committee had ever been mobilized to overrule a *majority* in the Presidium. Any attempt by Khrushchev to do so would naturally have been regarded as a move to replace 'collective leadership' by one-man rule, and would undoubtedly have thrown most uncommitted CC members and perhaps some of his supporters into the rival camp. The supremacy of the Presidium extended to its own composition. Though Khrushchev's Presidium colleagues had to reconcile themselves to a large increase in his Central Committee following, they could, and did, prevent his building up a voting machine in the Presidium. And though five of Khrushchev's supporters were admitted to candidate (non-voting) status in the Presidium after the Twentieth Congress, there were no changes in its voting membership.

Khrushchev's position was now reminiscent of Stalin's in the mid-1920s. His main strength lay in the full Central Committee and the provincial bureaucracy. In the Presidium (Stalin's *Politburo*) he had to proceed by way of alliances, concession and compromise. It would be idle to speculate upon the reactions of the other members of the Presidium to Khrushchev's success in building up support at the intermediate and local levels. It cannot be assumed, however, that they necessarily saw much danger in this, so long as he was prevented from packing the Presidium. If any of them thought of the parallel with the situation in the mid-1920s and its aftermath, this may not have seemed very pertinent, at least so far as the role of the Central Committee was concerned. Such a view would have been understandable in the circumstances, though proved wrong by subsequent events.

There is no need to trace here in detail the developments leading up to the crisis of June 1957. It is worth recalling the salient background facts, however. The Soviet leadership appears to have been deeply divided on two major issues during 1956 – 'de-Stalinization' and economic planning and administration. Khrushchev was deeply committed to the 'de-Stalinization' programme ('liquidating the effects of the cult of personality'), which led to such embarrassing and dangerous consequences towards the end of the year. The Sixth Five-Year Plan, approved by the Twentieth Congress, ran into serious trouble within its first few months (it was later scrapped) and the whole mechanism of industrial planning and control came under discussion, a variety of more or less radical solutions evidently being espoused by different leaders. When the Central Committee was finally convened, after a ten months' break, in December 1956, the de-Stalinizers managed to avoid discussion of the effects of their policies, and the agenda was limited to the second issue.[17] It obviously suited Khrushchev to have attention concentrated upon difficulties for which he could not be held responsible and over which his opponents were divided. At this meeting, for the first time since 1953, he found it expedient to remain in the background and seems to have made only one rather demagogic intervention concerning housing.

The decision of this Central Committee meeting was vague and contradictory, but it was followed almost directly by a government reorganization which inflated the State Economic Commission[18] into a sort of economic inner cabinet, headed by Pervukhin, and with the vice-premiers responsible for the various groups of economic ministries (including agriculture) as his deputies.

At the beginning of 1957 Khrushchev's fortunes appeared to be at their lowest ebb since his assumption of the First Secretaryship in 1953. Embarrassed by the effects of de-Stalinization, he now seemed to have lost the initiative which had been his for over three years. Both his policies of enhancing party control and administrative devolution were threatened by the enormous strengthening of the co-ordinating machinery of the central government. A great access of power had accrued to the toughest of the younger members of the Presidium. Unless he could recover the initiative and demonstrate to uncommitted provincial officials his ability to maintain their interests, his support in the Central Committee was in danger of melting away to a hard core of old adherents. His survival in the First Secretaryship might then be very precarious.

Khrushchev then took a daring and dramatic step. Only six weeks after the December meeting of the Central Committee, he summoned it again to discuss the same subject of industrial administration and had it approve a decision diametrically opposed to the December reorganization. The new decision envisaged the virtual dismantling of the central government apparatus for administering industry, and the devolution of its functions upon local 'economic councils' which would be subordinate to the Republican governments and supervised by the provincial party bosses.[19]

It seems most unlikely that these proposals could have commanded a majority in the Presidium. Be this as it may, the other members of the Presidium (with the exception of Khrushchev's protégé Kirichenko), and together with them the industrial ministers themselves, maintained a collective silence on the proposals throughout the 'public discussion' and during the session of the Supreme Soviet in May which passed them into law.[20] Observers at the time took this to signify the opposition of the majority of the collective leadership to the measures. As if to confirm this, the proposals, although put forward in the name of 'the government and the Central Committee', were universally referred to as 'comrade Khrushchev's theses'. During the 'public discussion' the apparatus worked frantically to create the impression through the press and public meetings that the adoption of the proposals was a foregone conclusion and only an occasional hint came through of the deep misgivings felt by the industrial administrators.[21] In these circumstances, open dissension from the proposals on the part of government leaders would have appeared, in the light of the decision of the February CC meeting, nothing less than the dread crime of 'factionalism'. They had to let Khrushchev have his way, signifying their disapproval by silence and preparing to fight again.

For it was obvious that Khrushchev was now prepared to rule, if necessary, in spite of the Presidium, and his opponents would have to move quickly to prevent him from doing so. In fact, less than six weeks elapsed between the adoption of the law creating the Councils of National Economy and the attempt to unseat Khrushchev. Though many details of the June 1957 crisis remain to be explained, its main lines are known. The attack on Khrushchev began in the Presidium on 18 June and the Presidium was virtually in continuous session till 21 June. Three voting members were absent at first but took part in the later stages. The attack on Khrushchev centred largely on his economic reorganization, but ranged over a variety of other topics; for example, he was accused of a 'right deviation' for his programme of overtaking America in meat and dairy production before catching up in heavy industry. As the meeting proceeded it became clear that six out of the 11 voting members were opposed to Khrushchev, while others vacillated. Khrushchev's supporters among the non-voting members remained firm, with the exception of Shepilov. The opposition met in Bulganin's office to co-ordinate their attack and Malenkov made an unsuccessful approach to Marshal Zhukov to seek the support of the army. Meanwhile supporters of Khrushchev on the Central Committee began to appear on the scene demanding to know what was going on. Khrushchev insisted that any leadership changes proposed by the Presidium should be submitted to a meeting of the full Committee. The opposition, however, who could now evidently muster a majority for a reorganization of the leadership involving Khrushchev's relinquishment of the First Secretaryship, were determined that the changes should be announced by the press and radio before the Central Committee was convened. Meanwhile, CC members were now pouring into Moscow from the provinces. Here Zhukov gave vital help in providing military transport. According to one report, 107 arrived by plane on 21 June alone. Finally, the opposition had to accede to the demand for a meeting of the Central Committee.

It has been suggested that the outcome of this meeting was largely due to the way it was chaired by Party Secretary Suslov. However, there is surely nothing surprising in Khrushchev's victory. The methods used by Khrushchev to regain the initiative early in 1957 – his forcing through of the radical industrial reorganization – were certainly disposed to produce a hostile majority in the Presidium, but they were also ideally chosen to secure the support of those uncommitted provincial officials whose votes were essential to ensure him a majority in the Central Committee. But it was not only the decentralization measures whose fate was in the balance at the June meeting. Reluctant to face Khrushchev on this issue before the Central Committee, the opposition assumed a posture of impugning the Presidium's accountability to the Central Committee which had been so sedulously and effectively fostered by Khrushchev since 1953. A vote for the opposition therefore became a vote against their own collective rights and standing. As things turned out, Khrushchev's active support at the meeting appears to have come close to our estimate in Table 7.3. Of the 309 voting and non-voting members of the CC and Central Auditing Commission at the meeting, 215 put forward their names to speak against the opposition.[22]

Since June 1957, with the Presidium packed with Khrushchev supporters, the Central Committee has ceased to be an instrument of inner-party struggle. As in the 1930s, it has, nevertheless, continued to be called together at intervals, to act as a sounding chamber for a now essentially 'monolithic' leadership and, increasingly, for the greater glory of the First Secretary himself. The proceedings have again become predictable and formalized. This is reflected in the innovation of announcing meetings beforehand with agenda and names of *rapporteurs* and the subsequent publication of proceedings, which are increasingly coming to resemble those of the Supreme Soviet.[23]

Thus, after a brief revival as 'Soviet Parliament', the Central Committee has again slipped back to a pseudo-parliamentary role. Its vicissitudes since the death of Stalin have obviously been evoked by the politics of the succession struggle. Yet, the Central Committee itself came to play a decisive role at a crucial stage in this struggle. This would scarcely have been expected of the moribund Central Committee of 1952. Constitutional fictions should not be taken for facts, but they are capable of acquiring a reality of their own, especially if there is a recurrence of circumstances similar to those which gave rise to them.

NOTES

1. Rules of the CPSU, paras. 24, 25 and 28.
2. *KPSS v rezolyutsiyakh i resheniakh s'ezdov, konferentsii i plenumakh Ts K* 7th edn (Moscow, 1953) vol. I, pp. 442–3.
3. On the 'fivesomes' etc., see *The Dethronement of Stalin* (Khrushchev's 'secret speech') (*Manchester Guardian,* 1956) p. 31.
4. *Izvestia Ts K RKP (b),* no. 29, March 1921, and no. 40, March 1922. See further no. 5 (63) May 1924.
5. Based on the lists of CC members published after the Party Congresses held in these years.
6. See, e.g. I. Deutscher, *Stalin: A Political Biography* (London, 1949); M. Fainsod, *How Russia is Ruled* (Harvard, 1953) pp. 156–66; L. Trotsky, *Stalin* (London, 1947) chs XI and XII and Supplement II.
7. *KPSS v rezdyutsiyakh . . . ,* vol. 2, pp. 542–3.
8. In January 1944, to approve changes in the federal constitutional structure (*KPSS v rezolyutsiyakh . . . ,* vol. 2, p. 1018); February 1947, on agriculture (ibid., pp. 1045–93); and after the Nineteenth Congress in October 1952 to approve the reorganized inner bodies (*Pravda,* 17 October 1952).
9. The 1939 Central Committee is listed in *XVIII s''ezd VKP (b),* p. 688; the 1952 Central Committee in *Pravda,* 15 October 1952. The posts of members were identified from references in the Soviet press in the period of their election.
10. *Pravda,* 7 March 1953 and 10 July 1953; *KPSS v rezolyutsiyakh . . . ,* vol. II, p. 1151.
11. It is worth noting that Khrushchev's election as First Secretary in

September 1953 did not create, but merely acknowledged, the fact of his dominance of the Central Committee Secretariat. Since Malenkov's resignation from the Secretariat in March he had been the only Central Committee Secretary with a seat on the Presidium and was therefore answerable there for the work of the whole party apparatus.

12. *Pravda,* 13 September 1953.

13. It is not impossible that the March meeting, at which Malenkov resigned from the Secretariat, was already the scene of differences between the leaders. In the absence of any evidence on this, however, it is more likely that the issue was fully settled in the Presidium, and the CC was merely asked for its formal approval.

14. N. S. Khrushchev, *O dal'neishem uvelichenii proizvodstva zerna v strane i ob osvoenii tselinnykh i zalezhnykh zemel'* (Moscow, 1954) p. 50.

15. There is ample evidence that selection of Chairmen of executive committees of Soviets is the responsibility of the *party*, and not the government apparatus, at the next higher level. See, e.g. *Partiinaia zhizn',* no. 8 (1946) p. 34.

16. CC listed in *XX s''ezd KPSS. Stenograficheskii otchet* (Moscow, 1956) vol. II, pp. 500–3; posts and careers identified from official Soviet sources.

17. See *Pravda,* 25 December 1956.

18. Ibid, 26 December 1956. The State Economic Commission had heretofore been a purely planning body, set up in May 1955 to take over short-term planning (up to one year) from the State Planning Commission. Another body which appears to have played a major role in co-ordinating economic administration in 1955 and 1956 was the Current Affairs Commission of the Presidium of the Council of Ministers. (See Yu. M. Kozlov, *Kollegial'nost' i edinonachalie v sovetskom gosudarstvennom upravlenii* (Moscow, 1956.) The reorganized State Economic Commission seems very likely to have absorbed this body, as there are no subsequent references to it.

19. See *Pravda,* 16 February 1957.

20. The vast majority of the 32 speakers in the Supreme Soviet debate were republic and provincial bosses. None of the heavy industry ministers and 'overlords' whose interests were most involved and who were best qualified to speak to the question took part. The two members of the Council of Ministers who spoke (both in favour) were B. P. Beshchev, whose Railways Ministry was to be left intact, and V. P. Zotov, Foodstuffs Minister, whose career suggests close links with Mikoyan, and who was rewarded by appointment as Deputy Chairman of *Gosplan*. One speaker alone, Academician Bardin, the country's most distinguished metallurgist, was courageous enough to express plain reservations about the scheme, and to press for the preservation of the metallurgical ministries. See *Zasedania verkhovnogo soveta chetvertogo sozyva (sed'maia sessia)* (Moscow, 1957).

21. An example of the methods used was the publication of an article by N. G. Ignatov, a protégé of Khrushchev and party boss at Gorky, on the eve of the Supreme Soviet session, and while the 'public discussion' on the desirability of the proposals was still going on, which revealed that his committee had already begun implementing the proposals as soon as 'comrade Khrushchev's theses' were published. See *Pravda,* 6 May 1957.

22. This account of the June crisis is based on an analysis of a multitude of contemporary and subsequent reports in the Soviet press, and the contemporary reportage in non-Soviet communist newspapers, especially *Unità* (Rome) and *Tribuna Ludu* (Warsaw).

23.   The first CC meeting to be reported extensively in the press was that in November 1958, and a subsequent verbatim report was published in book form. *Pravda* announced on 10 May 1959 the agenda for a CC meeting to begin on 24 June. This meeting was also reported in detail, and on 14 July 1959 the agenda of the next CC meeting, to be held in November or December, was announced. Prior to this no fore-mention of forthcoming CC meetings was ever made, and at most the main 'report' and formal decisions of the meeting were published.

8. The Soviet Politburo: a comparative profile, 1951–71*

It is now (December 1971) two decades since the last full year of Stalin's Politburo, and perhaps time for comparisons.

The role and significance of the Politburo in the Soviet political system are well enough known, and need not detain us long. The subordination of the government executive to the party executive was acknowledged from the inception of the Soviet regime, but for various reasons this relationship was weakly institutionalized and even at times inoperative prior to the establishment of the Political Bureau (along with the Organizational Bureau) of the Central Committee in March 1919.[1] Thereafter, matters of major importance continued for a time to be referred to the full Central Committee, especially when the Politburo was sharply divided about them, but the latter had established itself by the early 1920s as the supreme policy-making and executive body in the country: and this it has remained.

All too little is known about the question of this as of other Soviet decision-making bodies, but over its history it has undoubtedly functioned in profoundly different ways in keeping with the changing relationships of power among its members and in the political system at large. Something vaguely like a British cabinet under Lenin, it became the supreme battleground (and supreme prize) of contending oligarchs in the mid-1920s, a sort of cabinet again – but now more like the US President's cabinet – in the 1930s, and finally, with the entrenchment of Stalin's dictatorship, the ruler's *camarilla*. Since it is of the essence of dictatorship that formal structures are dissolved in a kaleidoscope of personal dependence, we should scarcely be surprised by Khrushchev's allegation in his 1956 'secret'

Soviet Studies, vol. XXIV, no. 1 (July 1972) pp. 3–23.

speech that the Politburo did not meet regularly in Stalin's last years, that it functioned largely through changing and presumably overlapping sub-committees, and that members who had incurred the dictator's displeasure were excluded for longer or shorter periods from its deliberations.[2] Yet it remained, however feebly institutionalized, the embodiment of the Soviet supreme leadership, and this requires no better illustration than Stalin's decision to replace it by a more diffuse body, as a cover for effecting radical changes in the leadership.

Not that the abolition of the Politburo at the Nineteenth CPSU Congress in October 1952 initiated a prolonged break in its continuity – if indeed there was a clean break at all. Certainly, the Politburo of 11 members and one candidate (non-voting member) was replaced by a Presidium of the Central Committee with 25 members and 11 candidates.[3] However, in the course of the reorganization that ensued on Stalin's death five months later, it was revealed that a 'Bureau' had existed within the Presidium, and it is possible – though we do not know – that this was similar in membership to the old Politburo. In any case, the reconstituted Presidium of March 1953, with 10 members and four candidates, restored the Politburo in all but name,[4] and the name was eventually to follow at the Twenty-Third Congress in 1966.[5]

In its operation the post-Stalin Presidium–Politburo seems to have recapitulated, albeit in a substantially changed setting, several of the phases of the 1920s and 1930s. At the same time, however, one can identify an overall trend away from the arbitrary, structurally indeterminate pattern of decision-making characteristic of Stalin's system of personal rule. The oligarchic configuration of power, which has now prevailed – despite partial reversal during Khrushchev's ascendancy – for nearly 20 years, has placed a premium on formal structures and regular procedures, thus promoting a reinstitutionalization of the supreme executive bodies of party and state, in particular the Politburo.[6]

This chapter is concerned with the composition of the Politburo, the characteristics of its members. Our information on this topic is notoriously defective. We know a good deal, but not necessarily what it would be most useful to know. We have only the haziest notions about the characters and personalities of Politburo members, can only guess at their convictions, prejudices, interests and values, must make do with gossipy tit-bits about their personal and family lives, and know precious little about their links and relationships with each other, with subordinate officials, with formal groups and organizations and with informal cliques and coteries. Such matters are of great interest for understanding the nature and development of any executive body, and what can be discovered or guessed about them deserves the attention of scholars. Here, however, I propose to limit discussion to those 'hard' facts on which information is complete enough to permit of systematic analysis and comparison of the Politburo today with the Politburo shortly before Stalin's death: facts about the origin and background of members, their work experience, formal education and politico-administrative careers. The intention is to try and identify some significant continuities and discontinuities in the make-up of the Soviet political executive over the past two decades.

In recent years the Soviet 'political élite' has attracted a good deal of scholarly attention,[7] often on a quite high level of methodological and mathematical sophistication – a quality to which the present chapter cannot lay claim. It is noteworthy, however, that most of this work has focused on the second echelon of power, that of the Central Committee member or *obkom* First Secretary. The 'élite of the élite', the Politburo–Presidium, has received comparatively little systematic study. There is interesting information scattered through several accounts of 'Kremlin' politics,[8] there are a few political biographies (mainly of Khrushchev),[9] and useful sections in some of the general textbooks on Soviet government.[10] But there has been no general systematic analysis of biographical data since Schueller's pioneering monograph in 1951.[11] This article is intended to reduce this gap, but will not fully bridge it, since it focuses on the Politburo's profile at two points of time and does not directly discuss intermediate phases.

DRAMATIS PERSONAE

The members of the Politburo at the end of 1951 and 1971 respectively are listed below, with posts then held.[12]

Politburo Members, 31 December 1951

I. V. Stalin	General Secretary of the CPSU Central Committee
	Chairman of the Council of Ministers
V. M. Molotov	Deputy Chairman of the Council of Ministers
G. M. Malenkov	Secretary of the CPSU Central Committee
	Deputy Chairman of the Council of Ministers
L. P. Beria	Deputy Chairman of the Council of Ministers
K. E. Voroshilov	Deputy Chairman of the Council of Ministers
N. A. Bulganin	Deputy Chairman of the Council of Ministers
L. M. Kaganovich	Deputy Chairman of the Council of Ministers
A. A. Andreev	Chairman of the Party Control Commission
	Deputy Chairman of the Council of Ministers
	Chairman of the Committee on Collective Farm Affairs
A. I. Mikoyan	Deputy Chairman of the Council of Ministers
A. N. Kosygin	Deputy Chairman of the Council of Ministers
N. S. Khrushchev	Secretary of the CPSU Central Committee
	First Secretary of the Moscow Regional Committee (*obkom*) of the CPSU

Politburo Members, 31 December 1971

L. I. Brezhnev	General Secretary of the CPSU Central Committee
N. V. Podgorny	Chairman of the Presidium of the Supreme Soviet
A. N. Kosygin	Chairman of the Council of Ministers
M. A. Suslov	Secretary of the CPSU Central Committee
A. P. Kirilenko	Secretary of the CPSU Central Committee

A. Ya. Pel'she	Chairman of the Party Control Committee
K. T. Mazurov	First Deputy Chairman of the Council of Ministers
D. S. Polyansky	First Deputy Chairman of the Council of Ministers
P. E. Shelest	First Secretary of the Central Committee of the Communist Party of the Ukraine
G. I. Voronov	Chairman of the Committee for People's Control
A. N. Shelepin	Chairman of the Central Committee of the Federal Trade Union Council
V. V. Grishin	First Secretary of the Moscow City Committee (*gorkom*) of the CPSU
D. A. Kunaev	First Secretary of the Central Committee of the Communist Party of Kazakhstan
V. V. Shcherbitsky	Chairman of the Council of Ministers of the Ukraine
F. D. Kulakov	Secretary of the CPSU Central Committee

As these lists remind us, Politburo membership does not in itself constitute an office, and members have always held one or more posts in major executive bodies. Nor has the configuration of offices represented in the Politburo remained constant for long; indeed, considerable differences are apparent as between 1951 and 1971. In the former year four of the 11 members held central party posts and 10 held central government posts; in the latter year five of the 15 held central party posts and four held central government posts. In 1951 three members (Stalin, Malenkov and Andreev) occupied both party and government posts, whereas in 1971 all members occupied one position only. While the posts held in 1951 were confined to the central organs of the party and government (except for Khrushchev's occupancy of the Moscow *obkom* secretaryship in addition to the CC secretaryship), there were six members of the 1971 Politburo holding office in other central or regional bodies. These differences are of great relevance to the operation of the Politburo as a decision-making body (which is not our topic), but also carry implications for the mix of experience brought to its deliberations (which is) – a point we shall return to later. It is also noteworthy that Kosygin is the only 1951 member who was still in the Politburo in 1971.[13] This almost complete turnover, taken in conjunction with the changes in the range of offices held, gives added force to the question of the degree of continuity in the *characteristics* of the membership.

ORIGINS AND EDUCATION

Information about the early background of Soviet officials is generally sparse. Official biographies[14] give date of birth and nationality, as well as the social class, and in some cases the actual occupation, of the official's father. In view of the political advantages of lower-class, and particularly proletarian origins, official classifications need to be approached with caution and, where sources conflict or appear evasive, appropriate deductions drawn.[15]

The question of age and generational differences will be discussed more fully later. At this point we may note that, whereas most of the Politburo in 1951 were men who had grown up entirely in the old pre–Revolutionary society, the majority in 1971 were still children at the time of the Revolution and several have spent their whole conscious lives under Soviet rule. Both Khrushchev and Kulakov grew up in villages in the Kursk region, but Khrushchev's village was dominated by landlords and Kulakov's by Soviet officials.

Although the Politburo became slightly more urban in background between 1951 and 1971, it remained overwhelmingly provincial or rural. Apart from Kosygin, the one member common to both groups, who was born in the then capital St Petersburg, four members in 1951 came from provincial towns and six from villages, compared with seven and seven respectively in 1971. At the same time the proportion born in Russia proper went down from just over a half to just under a half, and there was a marked change in the non-Russian areas represented: in 1951 there were two from the Ukraine and three from the Caucasus, whereas in 1971 there were five from the Ukraine and one each from Belorussia, Latvia and Kazakhstan.

Ethnically, the most striking change was the influx of Ukrainians – from none in 1951 to four in 1971. This was of course

Table 8.1 *Origins*

	Year of birth	Place of Birth	Nationality	Class/occupation of Father
1951 Politburo				
Stalin	1879	Gori, Georgia	Georgian	peasant/artisan/worker
Molotov	1890	township, Kirov region	Russian	salesman
Malenkov	1902	Orenburg	Russian	white-collar worker
Beria	1899	village, Georgia	Georgian	poor peasant
Voroshilov	1881	village, Ukraine	Russian	railway watchman
Bulganin	1895	Nizhni-Novgorod	Russian	white-collar worker
Kaganovich	1893	village, Ukraine	Jewish	'poor'
Andreev	1895	village, Smolensk region	Russian	peasant
Mikoyan	1895	village, Armenia	Armenian	carpenter
Kosygin	1904	St Petersburg	Russian	worker
Khrushchev	1894	village, Kursk region	Russian	peasant/miner
1971 Politburo				
Brezhnev	1906	Dneprodzerzhinsk, Ukraine	Russian	iron and steel worker
Podgorny	1903	small town, Ukraine	Ukrainian	worker
Kosygin	1904	St Petersburg	Russian	worker
Suslov	1902	village, Ulyanovsk region	Russian	poor peasant
Kirilenko	1906	small town, Voronezh region	Russian	artisan
Pel'she	1899	village (?), Latvia	Latvian	peasant
Mazurov	1914	village, Belorussia	Belorussian	peasant
Polyansky	1917	village, Ukraine	Ukrainian	poor peasant
Shelest	1908	village, Ukraine	Ukrainian	poor peasant
Voronov	1910	village, Kalinin region	Russian	village teacher
Shelepin	1918	Voronezh	Russian	railway official
Grishin	1914	Serpukhov, Moscow region	Russian	railway worker
Kunaev	1912	Alma-Ata, Kazakhstan	Kazakh	white-collar worker
Shcherbitsky	1918	town, Ukraine	Ukrainian	worker
Kulakov	1918	village, Kursk region	Russian	poor peasant

*Unless otherwise stipulated, the towns and regions listed lie in Russia proper.

a direct result of the patronage earlier exercised by Khrushchev, who had been party boss in the Ukraine for so many years. The non-Russians in the 1951 Politburo were all drawn from nationalities which had been prominent in the early Bolshevik movement, a feature which applied to only one – Pel'she – of the 1971 Politburo. Whereas the proportion of Russians among Politburo members has gone down (from 64 per cent to 53 per cent) the proportion of *Slavs* (Russians, Ukrainians, Belorussians) has risen (from 64 per cent to 86 per cent). Kunaev, the one Asian so far to achieve membership of the Politburo, may owe his position largely to Brezhnev's patronage (but see below on his other qualifications).

Although the early Bolshevik leadership was composed predominantly of revolutionaries of middle-class background, the men Stalin later gathered around him came mostly from worker or peasant families, and this was reflected in the social composition of his Politburo in 1951. To judge from official biographical data, this strongly lower-class complexion remained no less marked in 1971. If the Soviet Union is run by a 'new class' – and this remains a dubious concept – one must conclude that the men at the top are still first-generation new class; in any case, it would seem highly unlikely on the evidence that they have been helped to gain their present eminence by their family connections, whatever contribution connections of other kinds may have made to their careers. Looking more closely, one notes the big increase in leaders of peasant origin – from two to six – despite the reduced rural representation noted above.[16] Although the proportion of members of 'worker' origin has gone down, the term usually implied more of an urban, industrial background in 1971 than it did in 1951. It is worth adding that the three most powerful members of the Politburo in 1971 are all of unequivocal working-class background, a state of affairs that never applied under Stalin or before. It seems worth speculating whether this fact may bear some relation to the re-emphasis of the 'leading role' of the working class in the post-Khrushchev era.

The educational profile of the Politburo has been entirely transformed in the last two decades (see Table 8.2). Only three members of the 1951 Politburo had received advanced training under the Soviet regime, compared with every member of the 1971 Politburo. There was also a sharp contrast in the type of education received.

Table 8.2   *Education of Politburo members*

Highest level achieved	1951	1971
Complete higher technical	2*	10
Incomplete higher technical	2	
Secondary technical	1	2
Higher social sciences or humanities		3
Theological seminary or academy	2	
Real (modern secondary) school	1	
Elementary	3	
Also graduated Higher Party School		3

*Including Malenkov, who possibly did not graduate.

Thus, 45 per cent of the Politburo in 1951 had some measure of technical training, compared with 80 per cent in 1971. Educationally, the Politburo in the late Stalin period presented a very heterogeneous picture. It included Voroshilov, whose whole formal education had consisted of two winters in a *zemstvo* school, Stalin and Mikoyan with their seminary education in the Caucasus, Malenkov, who graduated from Orenburg *gimnazium* and later attended Moscow Technical College in the 1920s, and Khrushchev, the worker-*apparatchik* who was put through a *rabfak* and then did a year or so in the Industrial Academy during the First Five-Year Plan. By comparison with this, the educational homogeneity of the 1971 Politburo is most striking. The great majority received a secondary schooling (some of them part-time) during the 1920s and went on to a higher educational institution during the 1930s. Fully two-thirds of them possess diplomas in various specialized technical fields: two in agriculture, one each in the textile and food industries, and no less than six (40 per cent) in various branches of heavy or transport engineering. The odd men out are Suslov, a graduate of the Plekhanov Economics Institute, who then studied part-time at the Institute of Red Professors, Pel'she, a graduate of the latter institute , and Shelepin, who attended the Moscow Institute of History, Philosophy and Literature: a fact of some political interest, since differences of intellectual formation might well influence the stand taken by Politburo members on certain issues (indeed, there are reports suggesting that these three may have taken distinctive positions on questions related to the handling of Czechoslovakia in 1968–9). The most highly educated member of the 1971 Politburo is Kunaev, who graduated from the Moscow Institute of Non-Ferrous Metallurgy, and was later awarded the higher degree of Candidate of Technological Sciences, serving for some time as President of the Kazakh Academy of Sciences.

POLITICAL GENERATIONS

Table 8.3 sets out the main landmarks in the political careers of Politburo members, indicating in what year they joined the Communist Party, when they were admitted as candidate members, then full members of the Central Committee, and when they became candidates, then members of the Politburo (of course it is possible to proceed to full membership of the CC or the Politburo without prior candidate membership). One thing stands out immediately: in 1951 the Politburo was made up of men who joined the party when it was illegal or during the desperate years of revolution and civil war; 20 years later it was made up almost entirely of men who had become communists only well after the party had consolidated its power.

Stalin, Molotov, Voroshilov, Kaganovich and Andreev all spent many years as professional revolutionaries, and Mikoyan was also entering the same path on the eve of the revolution. In the case of the other five members of the 1951 Politburo, the balance between revolutionary and opportunist motives for their joining the party is more obscure. Bulganin, whose biographers are curiously reticent about his pre-Revolutionary career, joined the Bolsheviks some time after the downfall of the imperial regime, and worked in the Cheka virtually from its inception. Beria joined in March 1917, and (like Mikoyan) was engaged in clandestine political activity in the Caucasus, prior to the extension of Soviet authority to the area. Malenkov, a middle-class youth just out of *gimnazium,* entered the party while serving in the Red Army, and worked as a political commissar. Khrushchev, eight years older, and grown to maturity amongst the Donbas workers without political involvement, hastened to his home village on the collapse of the monarchy, taking an active part in redistributing *pomeshchik*

Table 8.3   Landmarks in Political Careers

	Joined CPSU	Age at joining*	Central Committee		Politburo	
			Cand.	Mem.	Cand.	Mem.
1951 Politburo						
Stalin	1898	18		1912		1919
Molotov	1906	15–16	1920	1921	1921	1926
Malenkov	1920	18		1939	1941	1946
Beria	1917	18		1934	1939	1946
Voroshilov	1903	22		1921		1926
Bulganin	1917	21–22		1934	1946	1948
Kaganovich	1911	17–18	1923	1924	1926	1930
Andreev	1914	18–19		1921–22, 1923–	1925	1932
Mikoyan	1915	20	1922	1923	1926	1935
Kosygin	1927	22–23		1939	1946	1948**
Khrushchev	1918	24		1934	1938	1939
1971 Politburo						
Brezhnev	1931	24–25		1952	1956	1957
Podgorny	1930	26–27		1956	1958	1960
Kosygin	1927	22–23		1939	1957**	1960
Suslov	1921	18–19		1941		1955
Kirilenko	1931	24–25		1956	1957–61	1962
Pel'she	1915	15–16		1961		1966
Mazurov	1940	25–26		1956	1957	1965
Polyansky	1939	21–22		1956	1958	1960
Shelest	1928	19–20		1961	1963	1964
Voronov	1931	20–21		1952	(Jan.) 1961	(Oct.) 1961
Shelepin	1940	21–22		1952		1964
Grishin	1939	24–25		1952	1961	1971
Kunaev	1939	26–27		1956	1966	1971
Shcherbitsky	1941	22–23		1961	1961–63, 1965–	1971
Kulakov	1940	21–22		1961		1971

*In most cases day and month of joining are unknown. **Not re-elected 1952–7.

land to poor peasant families (like his own), and joined the party either there, or shortly afterwards while serving in the Red Army. Kosygin, the one 1951 member to enter the CPSU after the Civil War, nevertheless joined the Red Army at the age of 15 and served in it for nearly two years.

Apart from Kosygin, Pel'she and perhaps Suslov were the only members of the 1971 Politburo to identify themselves with the Bolsheviks while it was still dangerous to do so. Indeed, the great majority joined the party after the consolidation of Stalin's power, especially during the mass recruitment drives of the First Five-Year Plan/collectivization period (Podgorny, Brezhnev, Kirilenko, Voronov) and of the post-Purge era (Polyansky, Grishin, Mazurov, Shelepin, Kunaev, Kulakov, Shcherbitsky). Though most of them were of worker or peasant origin, all but two (Pel'she and Voronov) had already taken their first modest steps in various spheres of authority when they entered the CPSU, and four of them were at the time full-time students.

Broadly speaking, the Politburo of 1951 consisted of protégés of Stalin or men who had thrown in their lot with him when he was struggling for power against rival leaders, while the Politburo of 1971 consisted of men who bore similar relationships to Khrushchev: with the qualification that the latter group had already had time to unseat their patron. In both cases a distinction can be drawn between 'joiners' and 'creatures'. Molotov, Voroshilov, Kaganovich, Andreev and Mikoyan all achieved some distinction in the party under Lenin, subsequently linked their careers to Stalin, and then, after the consolidation of his power, survived the purges, while other faithful old Stalinists like Ordzhonikidze, Kossior and Chubar' perished. Similarly, Suslov, Kosygin and Brezhnev, who were already forces in the land before Stalin died, allied themselves with Khrushchev during his struggles with his rivals, and kept afloat after the consolidation of his power, while others with a similar record, like Aristov and Ignatov, were suffering drastic demotion. On the other hand, we have the Stalinists like Malenkov, Beria, Bulganin, Kosygin and Khrushchev, and the Khrushchevites like Podgorny, Kirilenko, Mazurov, Polyansky and Shelest, who would probably have remained comparative non-entities had it not been for the good offices of their respective patrons. The comparison is somewhat blurred by the fact that several of the 1971 Politburo, though they rose to comparatively senior positions under Stalin, had already been beneficiaries of patronage exercised by Khrushchev when he was party boss in the Ukraine (1938–49) or Moscow (1949–53); this applied to Brezhnev, Podgorny, Kirilenko, Polyansky, Shelest, Shcherbitsky and Grishin. The eight members co-opted to the Politburo after the fall of Khrushchev, although all identifiable in various degrees as Khrushchev protégés, were at the same time indebted to the post-Khrushchev leadership for their elevation, and probably in some cases to Brezhnev in particular.

On average, Politburo members in 1971 were three years older than 1951 members when they joined the party (22–23 as against 19–20) and their subsequent political advancement was far slower. It took 1951 Politburo members an average of 14 years after joining the party before they became members of the Central Committee, and 1971 members 22 years. By this point their mean average age was 33–34 and 44–45 respectively. By contrast, the time-lag between entering the Central Committee and becoming Politburo members was much the same for both groups, their age thus averaging 42–43 and 52–53 respectively.[17] In other words, the members of the 1971 Politburo had had far more time to accumulate professional qualifications and administrative and policy-making experience before they entered the top decision-making body.

On the eve of his death, Stalin had evidently decided that several, at least, of his entourage had outlived their usefulness, and was resolved on bringing in younger blood. In this connection it is noteworthy that the average age of Politburo members was five years higher in 1971 than in 1951 – 61 as against 56. Furthermore, the six most senior members of the 1971 Politburo were aged over 65, compared with only two (Stalin and Voroshilov) in 1951. Table 8.4 further amplifies the contrast. By the standards of modern political executives elsewhere the Soviet Politburo in 1951 was scarcely a gerontocracy. By 1971 it was bidding fair to become one.

Table 8.4　*Age of Politburo members*

	1951	1971
Under 50	2	–
50–59	6	7
60–69	1	7
70 and over	2	1

Table 8.5   Main Components of Work Experience

		Party posts			Government posts							
	Total	Reg. 1st Sec.	CC App.	CC Sec.	Total	Council of Mins.	Trade union posts	Komsomol posts	Army posts	Police posts	Management	Manual work
1951 Politburo												
Stalin	29	1−		29	16	16			8			
Molotov	11			9	23	21			2			
Malenkov	26		10	12	5	5						
Beria	7	7			10	10				17		
Voroshilov					11	11			32	1−		15
Bulganin				12	14	13			8	4	8	
Kaganovich	19	9		18	16	16			2			5
Andreev	25	3			13	13	9					6
Mikoyan	6	3			25	25			1		9	
Kosygin	1−				13	12			2		9	?
Krushchev	24	17		2	3				5			11
1971 Politburo												
Brezhnev	24	8	1	12	5				5		3	6
Podgorny	10	9		2	14	1		2			8	4
Kosygin	1−				33	32			2		9	?
Suslov	40	5	3	24	(6)−			2	4			?
Kirilenko	30	15		9	1−			1	1−		4	4
Pel'she	36	7		5					10	?		5
Mazurov	16	12			12	6		7	4			3
Polyansky	16	5	4		13	9		1	1−			5
Shelest	25	13			11	2		5	?		12	2
Voronov	24	9		2	3	3			1−		1	
Shelepin	7		1−	6			11	19	2	3		
Grishin	19	4									4	
Kunaev	9	9			17				4		5	
Shcherbitsky	17	4			8			1			1	1−
Kulakov	14	4	1	6	15	4		1			3	

NOTES

1. Reg(-ional) 1st Sec: First Secretary of *obkom, kraikom* or republic CC.
2. CC App(-aratus): Posts in apparatus of CC CPSU other than secretary.
3. CC Sec(-retary): including Chairman Central Control Commission and Deputy Chairman of CC Bureau for RSFSR.
4. Council of Mins (Ministers): All posts from Deputy Minister up in the USSR Government, exclusive of police (MVD, KGB, etc.) and army (Ministry of Defence, etc.) posts.
5. The cipher 1- indicates a period considerably short of a full year.
6. Kosygin was presumably already in manual employment before joining the Red Army at the age of 15. Similarly, Suslov, a 16-year-old peasant lad in 1918 when reported organizing a Poor Peasants' Committee in his district, presumably had substantial experience of farm work behind him by this time.
7. Suslov – Government posts – Total (6): This represents a period working in the party's Central Control Commission and the People's Commissariat of Worker-Peasant Inspection, at that time linked in a single structure. It seems likely, however, that Suslov was concerned wholly or mainly with control work in party bodies.
8. Pel'she – Police posts?: Emigré sources claim that Pel'she worked for the political police in the 1920s and 1930s, whereas his official biographies list political posts in the armed forces and agricultural bodies. While Soviet biographical sources do not usually conceal tenure of police posts, there are reasons for doubt in this case, and a period of police work may have been involved.
9. Shelest – Army posts?: Some sources indicate that Shelest had a very brief period of conscript service during the 1930s.
10. In the few cases where party and government posts were held concurrently the figures given include the full period of tenure of each.
11. Table does not include posts held (in practice party posts) prior to the Revolution.

CAREERS AND EXPERIENCE

By what paths do men approach the threshold of the Politburo and what bodies of experience do they bring to its counsels? Some facts relevant to this question have already been considered: facts about revolutionary and civil-war service, about formal education, and about length of service to the party before gaining admission to the Politburo. What interests us here is the fields of activity and organizational milieus in which they have gained their administrative experience and the main kinds of posts they have held.

Tables 8.5 and 8.6 aim at bringing together the salient data on this question. Their biggest shortcoming is that they do not indicate the chronological order of work in different fields. Another is that they fail to distinguish between service before and after entry

Table 8.6   *Amount and Spread of Experience in Main Work Spheres*

| | No. and percentage of Politburo members with Relevant Experience | | | | Mean average experience of all Politburo members in years | |
| | No. | | Percentage | | | |
	1951	1971	1951	1971	1951	1971
Party posts	9	15	82	100	13.3	19.5
incl. Reg. 1st Sec	6	13	55	87	3.5	6.9
CC App	1	5	9	33	0.9	0.7
CC Sec.	6	8	55	53	7.4	4.4
Government posts	11	11[a]	100	73[a]	13.6	8.7
incl. Council of Mins.	10	7	91	47	12.9	3.8
Trade union posts	1	1	9	7	0.8	0.7
Komsomol posts	0	9	0	60	0.0	2.6
Army posts	8	11	73	73	5.4	2.2
Police posts	3	1[b]	27	7[b]	2.0	0.2
Management	2	10	18	67	1.5	3.3
Manual work[c]	5	10	45	66	3.4	2.0

[a] Government posts: 12 (80%) if Suslov included (see note 7 to Table 8.5).

[b] Police posts: 2 (13%) if Pel'she included (see note 8 to Table 8.5). This doubtful case, and that of Suslov, are not included in the calculation of mean average experience.

[c] Averages here are based on totals exclusive of manual work experience by Kosygin and Suslov.

into the Politburo. Some information on both these aspects will be introduced in the discussion that follows.

It will be realized that Table 8.5 is intended to summarize a great variety of facts about the careers of Politburo members, while Table 8.6 is based on a summary of Table 8.5. The categories used naturally reflect judgements about what are the most significant distinctions to make, but of course many other distinctions are possible, for example, between 'generalist; and 'specialist' posts (or 'staff' and 'line'), between all central and all regional posts, between posts located in the RSFSR and posts in the non-Russian republics, and so on. These tables, therefore, are far from exhausting all that is worth knowing about the careers of Politburo members, and other scholars might well wish to emphasize other variables.

The most striking change revealed here is that the Politburo today contains a far greater pool of experience in party jobs relative to government jobs than it did 20 years ago. It is remarkable that, although Politburo members in 1971 averaged five years older than those in 1951, they had worked on average five years *less* in government bodies. The contrast is even greater if one concentrates on posts in the central government (Council of Ministers). Nearly all the government experience accumulated by 1951 members was located in central bodies, whereas more than half the government experience accumulated by 1971 members was located in local, regional or republic bodies. A further, and related, difference is that most of the 1951 members, unlike those in 1971, had acquired the bulk of their government experience *after* entering the Politburo. This reflects the increased relative importance of the central government machine in the late Stalin era and the revived importance of the party machine under Khrushchev and Brezhnev, in addition to the differences already noted in relative length of the careers of 1951 and 1971 members before reaching the Politburo.

There is a similar contrast between central and non-central experience in party jobs. Politburo members in 1951 had acquired well over half their experience in party work while employed in the central party machine, compared with only a quarter in the case of 1971 members. Again, the 1971 members got a far higher proportion of their party experience *before* entering the Politburo, and this relates to a most important difference between the Politburo today and that of 20 years ago: experience as regional party bosses. The *Politburo* in 1971 had spent on average seven years of their lives working as the First Secretaries of *obkoms, kraikoms*, or republic central committees: twice the time spent by 1951 members. Two-thirds of them held such jobs for five years or more, compared with only three of the 1951 members. It will be apparent from the tables that service in the Central Committee apparatus has not been a common avenue to top political office either under Stalin or since. Malenkov was the only 1951 member to have held sub-secretary level apparatus jobs and, although such experience was more widespread among 1971 members, it was on average relatively brief and came at a point when they were already well advanced in their careers.

Both in 1951 and 1971 the Politburo included only one man who had worked (in both cases for prolonged periods) in trade union organizations. There is, however, an important difference between the trade union phase of Andreev's and Grishin's careers.

The former's original involvement in workers' organizations, in wartime Petrograd, antedated his joining the party, and after the revolution he first rose to party prominence through his work in 'bolshevizing' the Metal-Workers' Union. Grishin, by contrast, had no trade union experience before his appointment as Chairman of the Central Committee of the Trade Union Council, by which time he had been a member of the Party Central Committee for some years.

Age factors alone are sufficient to account for the fact that no member of the Politburo in 1951 had ever worked as a Komsomol official. Almost two-thirds of their successors 20 years later had served at least a brief stint in the youth organization, and for two of them, Mazurov and Shelepin, the Komsomol was their original channel to high office. (Shelest, in his five years of Komsomol work, finished up a *raikom* secretary, but his chief avenue to advancement was his subsequent service in factory management.)

Beria is the sole member of the Politburo throughout its existence who made his career predominantly in the political police. It was only after achieving high office in the NKVD that he received his first party appointments, and, at the other end of his career, when he became a Deputy Premier (classified in the tables under 'government posts') his primary concern continued to be security. One other member of the 1951 Politburo, Bulganin, took the first steps in his political career as a young *chekist*, but made his name primarily as an industrial executive. Shelepin, the one member of the Politburo in 1971 to have worked in the police (with the possible partial exception of Pel'she – see note 8 to Table 8.5) was appointed straight to the top KGB office on the basis of the political standing he achieved through his long service in the Komsomol.

The figures shown in the tables under 'army posts' require some explanation, since this term comprises several very different kinds of activity. To start with, six members of the 1951 Politburo and two of the 1971 Politburo saw action during the Civil War. None of the 1951 group, but fully one-third of the 1971 group, served as young peacetime conscripts, and in addition Pel'she did a long period as a political officer during the 1920s. Shelepin's military experience was limited to a brief spell as a political officer during the Soviet–Finnish war.

At the time of the second World War all members of the

1951 Politburo were already in top political posts, and it is not surprising that few of them served with the armed forces in the field. Voroshilov had a brief period as a front-line commander and subsequently was sent as State Defence Committee 'plenipotentiary' to various fronts. Khrushchev served for much of the war as Member of the Military Council of various fronts (essentially a political job), as did Kaganovich and Bulganin for brief periods. Stalin of course was Commander-in-Chief and People's Commissar for Defence, and Bulganin became Deputy People's Commissar towards the end of the war. All the 1951 Politburo except Khrushchev, Kosygin and Andreev served on the State Defence Committee during the war.

The fact that few members of the 1971 Politburo saw active service during the Second World War is rather more remarkable, since most of them were men of military age occupying relatively junior administrative posts, that is obvious 'officer material' (political or otherwise). There were three *frontoviki*. Shcherbitsky spent the war years in the army, but details of his service are unavailable. Mazurov was wounded during the early stages of the war, and played a major role organizing the partisan movement and underground Komsomol in Belorussia, part of the time behind the German lines. Brezhnev served from 1941 to 1946 as a senior political officer in the Soviet Army. Two other members, Suslov and, very briefly, Kirilenko, worked as members of Front Military Councils, and Suslov was also responsible for the partisan detachments in the North Caucasus for a time. The other 10 members of the 1971 Politburo spent the war years in civilian jobs.

There were three members of the *Politburo* in 1951 who had served as People's Commissar or Minister of Defence: Voroshilov before the war, Stalin during and Bulganin after the war. (This service is classified under 'army posts' in the tables.) But Voroshilov was the only one whose political rise was a function of his military role. A worker-revolutionary without prior military experience, Voroshilov distinguished himself as a Civil War commander, and subsequently advanced to become People's Commissar of Defence as the fortunes of his patron Stalin prevailed over those of Trotsky. No member of the Politburo in 1971 has served as Defence Minister, nor did the achievement of senior military rank play a major role in the political careers of any of them. Brezhnev has the most significant military connections, the consequence not only of his war service but also of his year spent as Deputy Head of the Political Directorate of the Armed Forces just after Stalin's death. However, Brezhnev's career as a party official was already well advanced in 1941, and in 1946 he resumed it where he had left off. The political significance of his military experience consists not in its contribution to his rise to Politburo status, but in the use he has subsequently made of it to cultivate support among the military and ex-servicemen.

Finally, what changes have occurred in the production experience that Politburo members have behind them? The proportion who have worked for wages with their hands has increased – from under one-half to two-thirds – although there is no one in the Politburo today with the extensive proletarian experience of a Voroshilov or a Khrushchev. Moreover, unlike their predecessors in 1951, the ex-workers in the 1971 Politburo gained their experience mostly under *Soviet* conditions, for the greater part in industrial undertakings, though Polyansky spent three years as a *sovkhoz* worker, and Shelest also worked in a *sovkhoz* before taking a job on the railways.

The great increase in the proportion of members with experience in industrial management (at enterprise, trust or directorate level) is one of the most important changes in the Politburo over the past 20 years. In 1951 only two members possessed such experience, though in both cases it was quite extensive. In 1971 there were three Politburo members with 8–12 years of managerial experience, five members with 3–5 years, and two others who had served in junior managerial positions for a year or so. It would be rash to assume from this that the Politburo has necessarily become more responsive to the interests and attitudes of industrial managers as a 'group', since one might equally suppose that their own experience had left them better equipped to control and out-argue the latter. Certainly, this striking extension of managerial experience should make for more sophisticated perceptions of problems of administering the economy, and more realistic decision-making in this area. However, this development probably acquires its greatest significance as part of a more general trend in career-making patterns, which will now be considered.

SUMMARY AND CONCLUSIONS

The Soviet political executive today is in many important respects a very different body of men from what it was 20 years ago. There are significant continuities. They are still all communists of long standing, most of them are of humble origin, there are no women among them, and they are once more an ageing group – even more so now than then. But there the likenesses end.

The Politburo in 1951 consisted mostly of men formed under the old regime, party members of pre-Revolutionary or civil war standing, lacking advanced formal education, who had made their mark politically by the 1920s or early 1930s, and were promoted by Stalin to the Politburo, either in the wake of his rise to power or of the Purges and Second World War. With two or three exceptions, they were men whose careers prior to joining the Politburo were devoted to tasks related to the overthrowing of the old order and the establishment of the political and economic structures of the new society.

The men who make up the Politburo in 1971 came to maturity in the years between the Revolution and the Second World War, mostly joined the party when Stalin was already in power, obtained tertiary education in the 1930s, and entered the Politburo either on Khrushchev's coat-tails or in the reshuffles and expansion since his removal. With only minor qualifications, they are men whose careers prior to entering the Politburo were devoted to *operating* the established political and economic structures of Soviet society.

The Politburo today is far more homogeneous than it was in the late Stalin era. We have noted the striking standardization in the formal education of Politburo members. They are also significantly less disparate in age. Most important of all, they differ far less among themselves in their career experience.

The men around Stalin in 1951 rose to prominence by a number of distinct paths: Stalin and Molotov in the revolutionary underground, Malenkov in the Central Committee apparatus, Beria in the police, Voroshilov in the Red Army, Kaganovich, Khrushchev and (with qualifications) Mikoyan in the regional party machine, Bulganin and Kosygin in the economic administration, and Andreev in the trade unions. By contrast, the paths to high office pursued by the majority of Politburo members in 1971 followed a fairly standard pattern: a youthful period as a manual worker and/or

Komsomol official, sometimes a spell working for the local soviet or party committee, then a diploma course in a technical institute, followed by managerial jobs in industry, then into the party machine, with several years as a regional party secretary. Where careers departed from this pattern, they usually included several of its ingredients in roughly the order given. Only Kosygin, with his almost 'straight' career in economic administration, the 'Old Bolshevik' Pel'she, Suslov, with his extensive service in the central party machine, and Shelepin, who worked his way up the Komsomol hierarchy, departed more fundamentally from the usual pattern, the last three also having the 'wrong' education.

In a sense, then, Stalin's Politburo was composed predominantly of specialists in various fields of politico-administrative activity, while Brezhnev's is composed predominantly of generalists, each with organizational experience in a number of different settings. This picture needs to be qualified to take account of experience acquired after entering the Politburo, when Stalin's lieutenants tended to diversify their policy involvement and at the same time standardize their organizational role (as deputy premiers), whereas in recent years there has been a marked diversification of organizational roles performed by Politburo members.

In another sense, the careers of most current Politburo members have been highly specialized in a particular direction, namely, organizational activity aimed at maximizing economic production, which has been their primary concern whether working as plant manager, *obkom* secretary, republic premier or all-Union minister.

Those who now sit on the Politburo have more in common with large sections of the society in which they live than did the men in Stalin's entourage 20 years ago. Most of them are Slavs, reared in villages or provincial towns in European Russia or the Ukraine, whose earlier training and experience resembled those of millions of Soviet *sluzhashchie*. They are neither revolutionaries nor commissars, but second-generation organization men, like those who staff factories, farms and offices up and down the country. Yet in one respect they, too, may be out of tune with their time. Schooled in the simple formulas of Stalinist orthodoxy and tempered in the month-in-month-out struggle to fulfil tasks assigned from above and to secure fulfilment by those below, they have entered a period of rapid technological and intellectual change which calls for qualities sharply at variance with the conformism and authoritarianism they have perhaps learned to regard as 'normal'. Russia's 'second industrial revolution' is presided over by men who may have 'overlearned' the tasks of implementing the first.

NOTES

1.   See Leonard Schapiro, *The Communist Party of the Soviet Union* (New York, 1959) ch. 13.
2.   See *The Dethronement of Stalin* (Khrushchev's 'Secret Speech') (*Manchester Guardian,* 1956) pp. 31–2.
3.   *Pravda,* 17 October 1952.
4.   Ibid., 7 March 1953. Eight of the 10 Presidium members had been *Politburo* members before the Nineteenth Congress. Apart from Stalin, the only old *Politburo* members left out of the 1953 Presidium were Andreev and Kosygin.
5.   *XXII s''ezd Kommunisticheskoi Partii Sovetskogo Soyuza: stenograficheskii otchet* (M., 1966), vol. II, p. 318.
6.   There is a discussion of this in my article, 'The Soviet Leadership: Towards a Self-Stabilizing Oligarchy?', *Soviet Studies,* vol. XXII, no. 2 (October 1970) pp. 167–91 (this volume, chapter 9).
7.   See especially John A. Armstrong, *The Soviet Bureaucratic Elite: A Case Study of the Ukrainian Apparatus* (New York, 1959), George Fischer, *The Soviet System and Modern Society* (New York, 1968), R. Barry Farrell (ed.), *Political Leadership in Eastern Europe and the Soviet Union* (Chicago, 1970), Grey Hodnett, 'The Obkom First Secretaries', *Slavic Review,* vol. XXIV (December 1965) pp. 636–52, Peter Frank, 'The CPSU Obkom First Secretary: A Profile', *British Journal of Political Science,* vol. 1, no. 2 (April 1971) pp. 174–90, Michael P. Gehlen and Michael McBride, 'The Soviet Central Committee: an Elite Analysis', *American Political Science Review,* vol. LXII, no. 4 (December 1968) pp. 1232–41, Jerry Hough, 'The Soviet Elite', Part I, 'Groups and Individuals', *Problems of Communisim,* vol. XVI, no. 1 (Jan.–Feb. 1967) pp. 28–35, and Part II, 'In Whose Hands the Future?', ibid., vol. XIII, no. 5 (Sept.–Oct. 1964) pp. 45–52, Borys Lewytzskyi, 'Generations in Conflict', ibid., vol. XVI, no. 1 (Jan.–Feb. 1967) pp. 36–40, Frederic J. Fleron, Jr, 'Toward a Reconceptualization of Political Change in the Soviet Union: The Political Leadership System', *Comparative Politics,* vol. I, no. 2 (Jan. 1969) and idem. 'Co-optation as a Mechanism of Social Change', *Polity,* vol. II, no. 2 (Winter 1969) pp. 176–201. (Much important recent work on the Soviet 'political élite' was incomplete or as yet unpublished at the time this chapter was written.)
8.   See Robert Conquest, *Power and Policy in the USSR* (London, 1961), Wolfgang Leonhard, *The Kremlin Since Stalin* (London, 1962), Roger Pethybridge, *A Key to Soviet Politics: The Basis of the Anti-Party Group* (London, 1962), Boris I. Nicolaevsky, *Power and the Soviet Elite,* ed. Janet D. Zagoria (New York, 1965), Carl A. Linden, *Khrushchev and the Soviet Leadership* (Baltimore, 1966) and Michael Tatu, *Power in the Kremlin: From Khrushchev's Decline to Collective Leadership* (London, 1969).

9. See I. Deutscher, *Stalin: A Political Biography* (London, 1949), Mark Frankland, *Khrushchev* (London, 1966), Edward Crankshaw, *Khrushchev: A Career* (New York, 1966), Lazar Pistrak, *The Grand Tactician: Khrushchev's Rise to Power* (London, 1961), George Paloczi-Horvath, *Khrushchev: The Road to Power* (London, 1960), Martin Ebon, *Malenkov: A Biographical Study of Stalin's Successor* (London, 1953). For a very useful collection of brief biographies, including eight *Politburo*-Presidium members, see George W. Simmonds (ed.), *Soviet Leaders* (New York, 1967).

10. See especially Merle Fainsod, *How Russia is Ruled,* rev. edn (Cambridge, Mass., 1963) ch. 10. See also Frederick C. Barghoorn, 'Trends in Top Political Leadership in the USSR', in R. Barry Farrell (ed.), *Political Leadership in Eastern Europe and the Soviet Union.* Another paper in the same volume, R. Barry Farrell, 'Top Political Leadership in Eastern Europe', contains an interesting comparison of educational characteristics of Soviet and other East European *Politburo* members.

11. George K. Schueller, *The Politburo* (Stanford, 1951). Since Schueller's study terminates in 1951, the base year for the present article, readers will find comparison useful. Schueller analyses data on all 27 persons who served on the Politburo between 1919 and 1951, tabulating and discussing various characteristics of the whole group, and on some aspects commenting on trends. Some additional information on the men studied has come to hand since Schueller wrote. Many of the questions he addresses to his data are also posed in the present article, though some differences in the angle of enquiry and comment will be apparent; in the one case the Politburo is approached more as a 'revolutionary élite', in the other more as the executive of an ongoing political system.

12. Candidate members are not included, for the following reasons:
    a)   their status and policy-making role have at all stages been clearly inferior to those of full members;
    b)   on the other hand, their status and policy-making role have not always been clearly superior to those of certain non-members, namely, certain Central Committee secretaries and deputy premiers;
    c)   as there was only one candidate in 1951 as against seven in 1971, inclusion would reduce comparability not only in simple numerical terms but in terms of the relative representation of more senior and more junior leaders.

13. 'Again' would be more accurate than 'still': Kosygin was not elected to the Presidium when it replaced the Politburo in 1952; he became a candidate in 1957 and a full member again in 1960.

14. The principal sources for the data employed in this article are the first and second editions of the *Bol'shaya Sovetskaya Entsiklopediya,* the yearbooks (*Ezhegodniki*) of the second edition (1957–), the third edition of the *Malaya Sovetskaya Entsiklopediya* (Moscow, 1958–61), *Kratkaya Sovetskaya Entsiklopediya* (Moscow, 1943), *Entsiklopedicheskii slovar'* (Moscow, 1953–5), *Deyateli Soyuza Sovetskikh Sotsialisticheskikh Respublik i Oktyabr'skoi Revolyutsii* (reprint, Ann Arbor, 1970), *Sovetskaya istoricheskaya entsiklopediya* (incomplete, Moscow, 1961–), and the various editions of *Deputaty Verkhovnogo Soveta* (Moscow, 1958, 1962, 1966, 1970). Biographical sketches and other references appearing in central and republic newspapers have also been used, as well, in the few cases where they exist, as biographies and autobiographies, viz., *Iosif Vissarionovich Stalin: Kratkaya Biografiya,* 2nd edn. (Moscow, 1950),

A. I. Mikoyan, *Dorogoi bor'by: kniga pervaya* (Moscow, 1971), K. G. Voroshilov, *Rasskazy o zhizni (Vospominaniya), kniga pervaya* (Moscow, 1968). Secondary sources, especially those referred to in notes 9, 10, 11, have also been checked. Detailed footnoting of the data reported in the article would obviously be impracticable.

15. Thus, for example, if several sources list Bulganin's father as a 'worker' while others state a 'white-collar worker' (*sluzhashchii*), it is a reasonable assumption that the latter is more accurate. Or, again, most sources describe Shelepin's father as a 'railwayman' (*zheleznodorozhnik*), but none as a railway *worker*, while one refers to him as a 'railway official' (*zheleznodorozhnii sluzhashchii*), which is presumably accurate. Kaganovich's biographies are unanimous that he was born into 'a poor Jewish family' – and in avoiding more precise descriptions. If his father had been a factory worker they would certainly have said so, and it is probable that he was an artisan or small shopkeeper. Some inconsistencies may also be due to fathers changing their jobs, as we know Stalin's and Khrushchev's did. In Mikoyan's case, his carpenter father was evidently employed for wages for some period, but there are indications that he may also for a time have been in business on his own account; there may be other such cases, and in particular the fathers of some of the 1971 Politburo members may subsequently have been promoted above their original 'peasant' or 'worker' status. Nor can we exclude the possibility of complete falsification in certain instances. The data on nationality also present difficulties. In particular, different degrees of russification and widespread intermarriage mean that 'Belorussian' and 'Ukrainian' can be rather relative concepts as applied to particular individuals. Information about mixed parentage or descent is generally lacking – Malenkov, for instance, is said to be partly Bashkir or Tatar in origin, but there is no official confirmation of this – although, in so far as ethnic background may be thought to influence attitudes, it is obviously of potential relevance. Localism or tribalism is another pertinent factor which is difficult to isolate or evaluate. A clear example is Beria, usually classified as a Georgian, but more precisely a Mingrelian; there is a traditional enmity between the Mingrelians and the Georgians proper, and the fabrication of an alleged 'Mingrelian nationalist plot' in Georgia shortly before Stalin's death was a move evidently aimed ultimately against Beria (see Conquest, op. cit., ch. 7).

16. This may be seen as a carry-through of the influx of *apparatchiki* of peasant background into the provincial party leadership a few years earlier; see Hodnett, op. cit., p. 643.

17. These differences are explicable, in part, in terms of the relationship of Politburo members' careers to various phases of relative stability and rapid turnover in Soviet officialdom. See T. H. Rigby, 'The CPSU Elite: Turnover and Rejuvenation from Lenin to Khrushchev', *Australian Journal of Politics and History*, vol. XVI, no. 1 (April 1970) pp. 11–23.

9. Towards a self-stabilizing oligarchy?*

In any political system there is constant interaction between the structure of leadership, the distribution of power and influence, the character of political and governmental processes, and substantive policies. This interaction is abundantly evident in the evolution of the Stalinist system in the USSR and the course of its modification since 1953. Accordingly, in introducing this chapter on recent developments in the structure of the Soviet political leadership, it is fitting to begin with a caveat. By isolating this aspect of the system for separate study, we do not mean to imply that these other aspects are unimportant, uninteresting or merely epiphenomenal to the leadership structure, or that Soviet politics can be adequately described or accounted for solely in terms of 'power struggle' within the leadership.

Any attempt at a full account of developments within the Soviet leadership would need to explore in some detail how these have interacted with changing patterns of power and influence as between different segments of the polity, with modifications in the processes of rule and of political action, and with shifts in major policy orientations. For our present limited purposes these interactions may largely remain in the background, and we must content ourselves with a few hints as to their operation. There are certain assumptions here, however, that should be made explicit: that the structure of leadership is also not uninteresting or unimportant in itself, that changes in leadership structure are not merely epiphenomenal to developments in other aspects of the political system, that the leadership constitutes in fact a *semi*-autonomous subsystem within the political system as a

*'The Soviet Leadership: Towards a Self-stabilizing Oligarchy?', *Soviet Studies*, vol. XXII, no. 2 (October 1970) pp. 167-91.

whole, possessing a dynamic of its own, influenced by other sub systems but also exerting a profound influence upon them.

This chapter is concerned with the efforts since 1964 to maintain and strengthen *kollektivnost' rukovodstva* in the USSR by building stabilizing factors into the oligarchical structure of leadership. The inherent instability of oligarchical rule, its tendency to dissolve into a pattern either of individual dominance or of a far more diffuse distribution of power, has been remarked by students of politics from Aristotle on. While many political systems provide instances of *'interregna'*, when two or more leaders temporarily share supreme power, stable ongoing systems lacking an office which institutionalizes a dominant-leader role within the executive are rare indeed. The Swiss executive may constitute a contemporary example, and other instances may be found in the ancient world, notably republican Rome. History shows that it is not beyond the wit of man to devise and operate stable oligarchical systems, at least under certain conditions, but that the cards are stacked very heavily against it.

The strong tendency towards a dominant-leader pattern in human decision-making bodies appears general and is not peculiar to political executives. Work on the social psychology of small decision-making groups has thrown some light on why this should be so. This work shows that the pressure to arrive at group decisions in a collection of individuals starting off on an equal basis engenders a rapid process of role differentiation, and that this normally produces leaders who more or less dominate and orchestrate the decision-making process. Until a stable pattern of leadership emerges, decision-making tends to be slow and ineffective, and much time and energy is wasted on smoothing personal relations, avoiding destructive conflict, and resolving procedural confusion.[1]

Despite its doctrinal commitment to 'collective leadership', the Soviet political executive has been subject to single-leader dominance (varying in style and degree) for about three-quarters of its history. Scholars differ as to how basic this tendency is to the Soviet political system, and how likely it is to persist. There still appears to be a fairly widespread, if usually unexamined, assumption that what Henry Roberts has labelled 'the dictator–succession–crisis–dictator sequence' will continue.[2] Myron Rush, who recently pointed out that he has been wrongly regarded as accepting the inexorability of this sequence, envisages the possibility of prolonged oligarchical rule, but considers that this 'would change the character of the Soviet regime'.[3] Thus, he evidently accepts the point made above that developments within the structure of leadership are capable of exerting a profound influence on the polity as a whole, but goes further in implying that the polity as at present constituted is inconsistent with the perpetuation of oligarchy at the top. Other writers again have reversed the emphasis in suggesting that broader, more long-term developments in the Soviet social and political system now militate against the recurrence of personal dominance patterns, at least in their more extreme forms.[4] Discussions of this issue have so far given relatively little attention to the internal structural aspects of the leadership, and it is these that the present article seeks in some measure to illuminate.

There are two crucial positions most apt for institutionalizing a dominant-leader role within the Soviet political executive, namely, the First (or General) Secretaryship of the Party Central Committee, and the Chairmanship of the Council of Ministers (People's Commissars until 1946), and, indeed the three dominant leaders to date always occupied one or other of these positions, or both. However, the dominant-leader role has not yet become firmly identified with one of these positions rather than the other. While the succession of Stalin to Lenin appeared to signify a shift in the focus of leadership from the government to the party post, the emphasis drifted back to the former in Stalin's final years, and Malenkov in 1953–4 asserted a precarious primacy within the leadership in his capacity as 'Head of the Soviet Government' (*Glava sovetskogo pravitel'stva*). Though Khrushchev asserted *his* dominance from the vantage-point of the party Secretaryship, he was quick to assume the government leadership as well, and the ambiguity remained unresolved. Nor do these two positions exhaust the possibilities for institutionalization of the dominant-leader role. The Chairmanship of the Presidium of the Supreme Soviet (Chairmanship of the Central Executive Committee of the Congress of Soviets until 1936) has some potentialities in this regard (see below), not to mention the possible crystallization of existing key leadership functions, such as the chairmanship of the Central Committee or of the Politburo, as formal positions.

Nor do the structural uncertainties of the Soviet leadership end there. The powers, internal structure and processes and inter-relationships of the three bodies in which the collective aspects of

Soviet leadership are focused – the Politburo, Central Committee Secretariat and Presidium of the Council of Ministers – remain vague and shifting. Changes in the structure, membership and functioning of these bodies will obviously interact in the closest way with changes in the powers attaching to the key leadership positions.

The extreme scope, scale and centralization of power in the Soviet polity, especially power over communications, the repressive machinery and job assignments, exacerbates the tension between the oligarchic and dominant-leader tendencies in the leadership. It sharpens certain dilemmas with which any group of oligarchs is faced: how do you achieve expeditious decision-making and consistent, coherent policies without a *primus inter pares* who orchestrates, guides and adjudicates; yet, if you allow such a *primus* to emerge, how do you stop him accumulating autocratic powers? If to concede some of the leadership's powers to wider elements in the polity, including perhaps some controlling assembly, might provide one avenue for countering the drift to autocracy, how do you prevent this dispersal of power from getting out of hand and threatening the security of the oligarchs individually and as a whole, and disrupting national unity?

The history of the Soviet and other communist regimes gives some measure of these potential threats to the oligarchy from 'above', and from 'below' – they have at times involved life itself. It also shows how the extreme concentration of power at the centre permits a leader aspiring to personal dominance to deploy pressures from both 'above', and from 'below' to subvert the oligarchy. As political differences within the oligarchy seep out into wider circles, certain oligarchs are in a stronger position than others to manipulate communications, personnel appointments and repression so as to build up support for themselves at the secondary power level, and ultimately to employ this to coerce their fellow oligarchs. This factor was of crucial importance to both Stalin and Khrushchev in defeating their rivals within the oligarchy and establishing their dominance. The critical point in Khrushchev's elevation was the June 1957 Plenum of the Central Committee, which signified his ability to marshal sufficient support at the secondary level to defeat, and then purge, an oligarch majority resolved to remove him.

The political struggles of 1957–64 have received close analysis elsewhere,[5] and there is no need for us to outline them here. However, certain structural aspects should be noted. The defeat of the 'anti-party group' did not definitively settle the leadership question: an uneasy and shifting balance emerged between residual oligarchical elements and Khrushchev's personal dominance. The threats to the oligarchy from above and below were both exacerbated by this relationship. Moreover, once the role of 'leader' or 'boss' is successfully asserted within an oligarchy the issue of succession to this role immediately arises. How can the oligarchs install a new leader when the existing one loses their confidence? How can the incumbent protect himself against replacement? How can he groom a successor without risking 'premature' succession? The tensions likely to be generated between the leader and the lesser oligarchs are obvious, as are the temptations for him to take the bit between his teeth and for them to forestall this by attempting to depose him.

During this period the danger from below also took on a new edge. If Khrushchev could use the Central Committee plenum once to overrule and purge a hostile majority in the Presidium oligarchy, perhaps he could do it again. Inevitably, therefore, the tension between the leader and the lesser oligarchs overflowed into the second level of power. The dilemma for the oligarchs here was that further development of the Central Committee as a party 'parliament' offered a structural device for constraining the drift to dictatorship and institutionalizing the succession, but only at the cost of sanctioning factional politics at this secondary power level. Given the reduction of terroristic and ideological pressures, there was a danger that such public factional politics might unleash social forces which could ultimately engulf the whole bureaucratic structure of power and decision-making. A crucial element here was communications control. Even the minor degree to which politics had already overflowed from the corridors of power into the market-place had produced many object-lessons in the contradiction between the democratic myths and bureaucratic realities of the system. More open factional politics would place impossible strains on centralized communications control, thus threatening to dissolve the whole synthetic ideological uniformity of Soviet society – as had happened earlier in Hungary and was destined to happen again in Czechoslovakia. Such a prospect must have been seen by many leaders and ordinary communists as a serious potential danger to public order and national integrity. There are signs indeed that Khrushchev himself was aware of some dangers in these developments but thought he could contain them, and at the same time exploited them to strengthen his own position.

That the oligarchy was able to survive in a limited way for seven years after Khrushchev's victory over the 'anti-party group', and ultimately to reassert itself, was in large part due to a number of contingent circumstances. Whether at any stage Khrushchev aspired to dictatorial powers will perhaps never be determined, but the foregoing analysis suggests that there were pressures that could have pushed him in that direction. Offsetting these pressures, however, was the de-Stalinizing posture that greatly aided his rise to predominance but in which he then found himself frozen. Khrushchev could then move from predominance to dictatorship only, as it were, walking backwards, pretending he was going the other way – which was, indeed, what he was later implicitly accused of trying to do.

If the danger from above was moderated by certain incidental inhibitions, so too was the danger from below. The paralysis of initiative which Stalinist repression had imparted both to various élite groups and the general population did not suddenly disappear with the moderation of repression after 1953, but only gradually dissipated over a period of years. Most of the older generation had overlearnt the lesson of watching for their cue, and it was only in the early 1960's that the first post-Stalin generation became a significant element in the adult world (at this stage the natural alliance between the grandfathers and the grandsons against the Stalinoid fathers who dominated national life was a recurrent theme in Soviet literature). A second inhibiting factor was that improvements in most areas of grievance in the early post-Stalin years encouraged optimism about the future provided no one 'rocked the boat'. Khrushchev skilfully exploited these factors, tapping popular and élite grievances and aspirations to exert pressure on his fellow-oligarchs, but containing these grievances and aspirations by constant hints of a Stalinist reaction. In some fields he seems actually to have played off 'liberal' and 'conservative' groups against each other, thus enhancing his adjudicating role (this is best documented for the field of the arts but to some extent at least the same thing was going on in ethnic and economic policy).

While there were thus factors which tended to moderate the threat to the residual influence of Khrushchev's fellow–oligarchs, their position was scarcely a happy one. If Khrushchev was less than a dictator, the structure of the executive and of the polity as a whole presented no reliable obstacles to a possible assertion of dictatorial powers – indeed quite the reverse. His occupancy of the key positions in all major party and government executive bodies ruled out the possibility of using countervailing structures to shore up the oligarchy. Mention has already been made of the problem of the succession and the tensions it gave rise to. Other tensions were generated by the lack of established open – rather than conspiratorial – procedures for replacing the dominant leader. The availability of such procedures provides the only sanction to ensure that a dominant leader will pay regular attention to the views of his colleagues and not take the bit between his teeth on policy questions. Short of radical moves to institutionalize the Central Committee as a forum for discussing disputed policy issues, and tolerating factional politics within it, no means were available to Khrushchev's colleagues to ensure a hearing for policy solutions alternative to those he espoused. In these circumstances Khrushchev, for his part, could scarcely exercise his essential leadership function of imposing a strong and clear policy line without appearing to act dictatorially, while the moves of the lesser leaders to assert some controlling influence were bound to appear obstructionist, if not to betoken a wish to unseat him.

While the overthrow of Khrushchev took place against a background of sharp policy disputes over the period since 1960, and some observers have descried a dichotomization of the oligarchy into a pro-Khrushchev 'liberal' wing and an anti-Khrushchev or stop-Khrushchev 'conservative' wing, there is little evidence that specific policy issues precipitated the coup or that it involved a confrontation between 'liberals' and 'conservatives' with victory going to the latter.

If Khrushchev had been defended by a faction in the leadership, one would hardly expect the officials concerned to have long retained their positions after his removal. At the secondary leadership level a number of officials with a reputation for being closely dependent on Khrushchev did in fact lose their posts: Central Committee Secretaries Il'ichev and Polyakov, *Izvestiya* editor Adzhubei (Khrushchev's son-in-law), and a handful of other propaganda and mass media executives. The modesty of the changes in the Presidium itself, however, are hardly consistent with the hypothesis that Khrushchev retained the support of a significant faction up to the time of his removal. F. R. Kozlov was relieved of Presidium membership in November 1964, but he had been inactive since a major heart attack eighteen months earlier. Before that he had evidently contended with Brezhnev for the position of Khrushchev's right-hand man and *dauphin*, and Brezhnev was presumably glad to see him out; there is no reason, however, to doubt the health motive given at the time, as he died two months later. Two further Presidium members, Shvernik and Mikoyan, failed to be re-elected following the Twenty-Third Congress in April 1966. There seems little mystery about Shvernik: he was now aged 76 and it is unclear what contribution he had been making to the leadership for some years. Mikoyan's case is more equivocal: at 69 he seems to have been still capable of playing an active role. Perhaps this one leader was now paying the price for his earlier closeness to Khrushchev and to possible efforts on his behalf in October 1964.

If the removal of Khrushchev was not occasioned by policy issues or a factional struggle, why, then, did he go? Because the strains between the lesser oligarchs and the predominant leader had finally become intolerable. The coup was designed to restore rule by 'pure' oligarchy.

This interpretation is consistent with the terms in which the oligarchy justified their coup. This justification was contained in a number of editorial articles published in Central Committee organs in the weeks following the October plenum, of which the most systematic and authoritative appeared in the fortnightly journal *Partiinaya zhizn'*.[6] Though no attack was made on Khrushchev by name, and the form of retirement on age and health grounds was adopted, formulas were indeed used that would be understood by the politically literate as direct criticisms of Khrushchev. However, these were not linked with any particular policy issues, but focused instead on Khrushchev's 'leadership style', on his penchant for 'big talk and bragging, premature conclusions and wild schemes out of touch with reality (*pustozvonstvo i khvastovstvo, skoropospelye vyvody i otorvannoe ot real'noi deistvitel'nosti prozhekterstvo*)'. What is more important, it was made clear that the main issue was his attempt to place himself above the 'collective leadership'. It was necessary 'to control and, where necessary, to correct leaders, whether it be an enterprise director, a primary party organization secretary or a government or party figure of the highest rank'. Further, the need to curb such leaders and to safeguard 'collective leadership' was explicitly linked with the danger of a resurgence of dictatorship:

> Experienced, influential leaders who know their job enjoy among us well-earned authority. One listens willingly to their voice and takes account of their opinion, and this is an important condition of discipline, of business-like procedure, and of success in carrying out the party's directives. But legitimate respect has nothing in common with excessive praise and glorification of a leader, such that any word of the person standing 'at the summit' (*na vyshke*) is given out as a revelation, and his steps and actions are treated as infallible. Such an approach leads to no good, it can only revive the ways of the personality cult period, and the party is irreconcilably opposed to this.
> . .
> . . . But life shows that not all comrades have fully overcome the modes, forms and methods of work which established themselves in the period of the cult, and which life has rejected. It is precisely for this reason that the party is so insistent on questions of observation of the principle of collective leadership and of the Leninist norms of party life at all echelons of the party and state apparatus. Not a single communist, not a single party collectivity has the right to overlook cases where someone gets puffed up and stops taking account of the opinion of his comrades, failing to foster the development of criticism and of creative discussion, not just formal discussion, at plenums, meetings and decision-making sessions (*plenumy, sobraniya i zasedaniya*). It cannot be permitted even the most authoritative person to escape the control of his leading collectivity or party organization, to get the idea that he knows and can do everything, that he has no need for the knowledge and experience of his comrades.

Along with this diagnosis of the leadership problem, the oligarchy simultaneously offered their key to its solution – 'mutual control':

> Candid criticism and self-criticism, mutual control – this is one of the norms of intra-party life. All party organizations are obliged to observe and develop it by the CPSU Rules, and challenged to do so by the example of the Leninist CC of our party and its Presidium.

And it was clearly spelt out that 'mutual control' was far more than a safeguard against the inefficient or unsuccessful leader, it must be exerted even against the best of them, if the collective principle was to be maintained.

> One should also bear in mind that genuine insistence on high standards (*trebovatel'nost'*) does not tolerate concessions for rank or services. It is not a cudgel with which to belabour the negligent (*neradivykh*). Insistence (*spros*) and control should extend to the leading officials as well, since they too are not ensured against errors and shortcomings. Failing this any person is capable of taking it into his head that he is irreplaceable and infallible.

This, then, amounted to a veritable charter of oligarchy, legitimating the removal of Khrushchev as a violator of the oligarchical principle and an incipient dictator, and declaring that the Presidium members would henceforth take steps to ensure that there would be no more Khrushchevs, by elevating 'mutual control' to one of the 'norms of intra-party life', by persistent mutual checking of each other's power. The view of the evolution of the leadership problem implied here was clearly that the post-Stalin oligarchy had never been given a proper chance to work, that things had started to go wrong as soon as Khrushchev was allowed to get away with his first 'hare-brained schemes' and to 'emerge from the control of the collective'. The implied slogan was 'back to 1954'. For 10 years the post-Stalin leadership had been drifting on a false and dangerous course. It was time to return to first base, to make a new attempt at operating a collective leadership, but this time armed with a firm and frank compact to exercise 'mutual control'.

Whatever private reservations individual leaders may have entertained, it seems likely that, at the least, an implicit compact of this kind was the basis of the agreement and conspiracy to remove Khrushchev, and that this compact probably envisaged the following practical devices to this end:

1. Keeping the two top posts in different hands;
2. Reducing opportunities for patronage;
3. Distributing among leaders seats in the Party Presidium (Politburo from April 1966), Presidium of the Council of Ministers and Central Committee Secretariat in such a way as to avoid dangerous patterns of overlap;
4. Maintaining countervailing power between topmost leaders.

The application of each of these devices deserves to be considered in a little detail. First, then, the splitting of the top posts. The Central Committee plenum at which Khrushchev was forced to resign also adopted a resolution to the effect that it was considered inexpedient that the posts of First Secretary of the Central Committee and Chairman of the Council of Ministers should be held again by a single person.[7] This measure taken on its own would scarcely constitute an infallible safeguard against the emergence of a new boss. The personal dominance that Lenin, Stalin and Khrushchev enjoyed in the leadership did not depend on their first taking hold of these two posts. Lenin never combined them, Stalin ruled for 10 years before adding the premiership to the party secretaryship, and Khrushchev was entrenched for nine months before *he* assumed the premiership. Nevertheless, there is possibly something to be learned from this time-sequence. The growing complexity of government may well have made it progressively more difficult to stay on top without personally standing at the controls of both machines. Furthermore, Khrushchev would scarcely have managed to get on top without first capturing the premiership had he not contrived in the meantime to weaken drastically the central government – and this operation would not be too easy to repeat. So this resolution of the October 1964 plenum probably constitutes a genuine obstacle to the emergence of a new boss. In any case, it is a very potent *symbolic* obstacle, since it amounts to a compact, binding on the Central Committee, to prevent anyone achieving the degree of dominance that Khrushchev enjoyed – let alone Stalin – this being the one item in whatever understanding existed among the oligarchs which has been proclaimed publicly and solemnly by the party 'parliament', thereby making it virtually impossible to violate without a great deal of difficult manoeuvring.

None of the principal leaders has yet built up any considerable network of patronage or advantageous organizational position based on the pattern of overlapping membership in the key organs of power. These key bodies are, of course, the Presidium of the Central Committee, which resumed its old name of Political Bureau after the Twenty-Third Congress, the Secretariat of the Central Committee, and the Presidium of the Council of Ministers. The Politburo is in form a party body, which has reality to the extent – dubious and hard to measure – that it is effectively answerable to and capable of being overruled by the full Central Committee. But its membership has never been confined to party officials, and the actual posts held by its members constitute one of the most important variables reflecting and in turn affecting the distribution of power within and between the other central bodies and the various hierarchies they direct. The Politburo is the functional equivalent to Cabinet in the British system. Extending this analogy, we can think of the government Presidium and the party Secretariat as something like standing committees of Cabinet, composed partly of cabinet and partly of non-cabinet ministers. These bodies are supposed to deal with more routine matters coming up for decision within the government and party machines respectively, but at the same time they act as the main communication channels – or, if you like, communication sieves – between these machines and the top decision-makers.

Given this set-up it is obvious that the arithmetic of the leadership is going to be vitally important. In the first place it goes without saying that the more influential leaders will want to get as many of their own friends as they can into these bodies. What may not be quite so obvious is the power implications of the overlap between these bodies – *which* of the 'cabinet' ministers are in the 'standing committees' and *how many* of them are in them.

Let us take the question of patronage first. Even the best-run bureaucracy is not entirely free of patronage, and there are certain basic features of the Soviet system (lack of alternative paths to political power other than up one of the bureaucratic hierarchies, promotion by performance as assessed by superiors rather than by abstract rules, pressures arising from rivalries at the top, the frequent need to collude in using doubtful methods to achieve results) which have made the bureaucratic patron–client relationship one of the crucial factors in the political system. This relationship may or may not involve an affective personal bond; its essential basis is mutual aid. The patron offers protection and preferment, while the client's part is to throw all his energies into achieving his patron's programmes, if necessary starving, discrediting or sabotaging those of his rivals; both 'cover up' for each other. The difficulty of switching patrons in such a system will readily be seen. When the system is operating under an oligarchical structure of power at the top, the political role of patronage acquires a second level apart from that of day-to-day administration: the level of voting.

This is principally significant in the three inner bodies of party and state, but voting support at the next level down, that of the Central Committee plenum, is also a factor the oligarchs need to keep in mind, as Khrushchev showed in 1957.[8]

From what we know of past career connections and alignments, it is very difficult to discern in the current leadership any substantial groups of cronies. If we look at the next level down we do indeed find evidence of patronage. Men whose earlier careers had brought them in touch with Brezhnev, especially during his Zaporozh'e and Dnepropetrovsk periods, now occupy a number of important posts in the Central Committee apparatus and the government. In the early post-Khrushchev period another substantial group consisted of old Komsomol associates of Alexander Shelepin, but these have subsequently declined in influence. The Moscow party organization, originally one of Khrushchev's main sources of protégés, suffered something of an eclipse towards the end of the Khrushchev period. More recently the Muscovites seem to have been coming up again and a number of them now hold important jobs in the Central Committee apparatus and in the governments of the USSR and the RSFSR. Another regional group whose identity is somewhat more speculative consists of men who formerly worked in Khar'kov. If the individuals concerned do constitute such a group the question arises whether they should be linked with Podgorny, who was First Secretary of the Khar'kov *obkom* from 1950 to 1953. A number of former Khar'kovites were removed from sensitive positions at the centre in the months preceding the Twenty-Third Congress. On the other hand, graduates of the Belorussian party organization have become more numerous in senior jobs at the centre.

When we move from the second level of leadership to the inner circles it is hard to detect significant groupings. Brezhnev appears to have one protégé among the full members of the Politburo – Kirilenko – and possibly one candidate member in the person of Shcherbitsky. In the Secretariat Kirilenko seems to be the only member with early career associations with Brezhnev, but the latest addition, Katushev, probably owes his position to Brezhnev's patronage. In the government Presidium, two of the nine deputy premiers, namely Dymshits and I. T. Novikov, also had old links with Brezhnev. None of the other top leaders seems to be able to match this. Maybe the career of CC Secretary Ustinov, who is responsible for the defence industries, owes something to Kosygin. If so, he may be intended in part to balance Dymshits and Novikov in the Government. Polyansky, like Podgorny, has served in Khar'kov, but they were not there simultaneously, and it seems dubious whether they have derived from this any politically relevant measure of solidarity. We will have something to say later about Suslov and his possible clientèle in the leadership.

The point to be stressed here is that none of the leaders, not even Brezhnev, who has more cronies in senior positions than anyone else, has anything approaching a numerical majority of hangers-on in any of these bodies. Of course, securing a majority in the Politburo itself is something that happens only at the point of establishing your personal dominance – Stalin in the late 1920's, Khrushchev in 1957 – but this evidently has to be preceded by a stage when your supporters predominate in either the government Presidium or the party Secretariat – in both historical cases it has been the Secretariat. And no one has come close to achieving this preliminary stage as yet.

One possible criticism of this analysis relates to the 'Ukrainians'. Men who made their early careers in the Ukrainian party organiza-tion formed the largest of the three main groups that Khrushchev based himself on in his drive for power, and they have continued to be numerous in the post-Khrushchev regime. They currently comprise five out of the eleven members of the Politburo – as against the two or three one would expect if they were represented in proportion to population. If these five acted with any degree of solidarity they would certainly be close to dominating the leadership, and Brezhnev as their most senior member would be in a very strong position indeed. It is probably unrealistic to think of the men from the Ukraine – the reference is not of course to ethnic Ukrainians as such – as now acting as a solidary group. Their very numbers have probably encouraged centrifugal tendencies among them, and within the Politburo itself Brezhnev and Podgorny figure as separate centres of attraction. Yet in the face of certain kinds of threat they could still cohere and act as a powerful caucus.

Apart from Brezhnev, then, none of the oligarchy has managed to install a significant personal following in the highest executive bodies or at the level of the Central Committee plenum, and even Brezhnev's following, five years after achieving the top party post,

Political élites in the USSR

is not comparable with that achieved by Khrushchev within three or four years of becoming First Secretary. How do we account for this state of affairs? After all, under Soviet conditions, it must be extremely difficult to find candidates for major appointments who have not already acquired links with one or other of the oligarchs. A 'normal' Soviet rate of turnover in senior posts would therefore place extreme strains on an oligarchy concerned to ensure that such appointments do not allow one of their number to acquire too much patronage strength. The solution adopted by the oligarchy has been to cut back turnover well below the 'normal' Soviet level, indeed to a level that appears exceptionally modest by any standards. The official title given to this policy is 'stability of cadres', and much has been made of it as one of the improvements effected in the regime's leadership style after 1964. Again, a fairly explicit understanding both within the oligarchy and between the oligarchy and the secondary leadership level seems to be involved, whereby the latter are asked to curb any ambitions they might have for rapid advancement into the oligarchy in exchange for reasonable security of tenure and protection against encroachments from subordinate echelons.

Turning to the question of membership overlap between the top executive bodies, we may begin by noting two possible patterns of overlap which are potentially destructive to an oligarchical structure of power. First, if you can be the *sole* member of the Politburo in the government Presidium or the party Secretariat, you enjoy a tremendous advantage in the network of communication and executive responsibility, and this can be used not only to build up your predominance in the body concerned – through control of its personnel and its business – but to acquire a disproportionate influence over the business of the Politburo itself (what matters come up to the Politburo and in what form they come up) which at a certain point can amount to a power of veto.

Lenin enjoyed something like this position with respect to the Council of People's Commissars,[9] a factor which has perhaps been underestimated in discussions of how he managed usually to get his own way within the leadership. The same position was held with respect to the party Secretariat by Stalin in the mid-1920's and by Khrushchev between 1953 and 1955, and this was of vital importance to them in their drive for power.

The second situation is where you get a *majority* of the Politburo serving at the same time as members of either the government Presidium or the Secretariat. This means that anyone who has succeeded in securing a dominant position in the subordinate body concerned is thereby in a position to dominate the Politburo. This is the position Khrushchev achieved in 1957. Having largely managed to stack the Secretariat with his own supporters, he proceeded, following the defeat of the 'anti-party group', to promote a number of Secretariat members to the CC Presidium so that the two bodies then overlapped to the extent of about two-thirds. This meant that Secretariat decisions were virtually guaranteed a majority in the Presidium, and there is reason for suspecting that the Secretariat may have substantially supplanted the Presidium as the key organ of rule for a short time. This was very useful to Khrushchev during the period when he was consolidating his new position of dominance, but soon after he took over the Chairmanship of the Council of Ministers he replaced this arrangement by one in which the Presidium members were spread in threes and fours between the Secretariat, the government Presidium and also the Bureau for the RSFSR, with himself chairing all four bodies.[10] The 1957–9 period is the only time that the Politburo or Presidium has been closely identified in membership with the Secretariat, but in the late Stalin period it was even more closely identified with the government Presidium, and it is interesting that this was the period when, according to Khrushchev's 'secret speech', the Politburo ceased to function as a regular decision-making body.

We see, then, that there are two patterns of distribution of the leadership among these supreme executive bodies which present serious dangers for the maintenance of the oligarchy, namely: (1) where one of the subordinate bodies is represented by only one member in the Politburo, and (2) where its members constitute a majority in the Politburo. The situation most supportive of the oligarchical principle, given a Politburo of 10–12 voting members, is where three to four of them serve on the Secretariat and the same number on the government Presidium. Now this ideal level of overlap has in fact been approximated throughout the post-Khrushchev period, and such changes as have occurred have brought it closer to the ideal. In December 1964 two voting members of the party Presidium were in the Government and four in the party Secretariat. Since the Twenty-Third Congress in 1966 the numbers have been three and three.

The existing pattern of overlap between the three top bodies is undoubtedly an important device for preventing any undue concentration of personal power. One obvious condition of its operating in this way, however, is that decisions should in fact be taken within these bodies rather than through informal procedures which by-pass them. The political history of the Soviet regime shows that both the government Presidium and the Secretariat are vulnerable to being by-passed in this way, and each of them seems to have had periods when it did not regularly operate as a collective decision-making body at all. One of the interesting things about recent Soviet discussions of collective leadership at the top is the stress they place on the regular formal functioning of all these bodies, and it is clear that any deviation from this would be immediately recognized as a danger-signal for collective leadership. There is a definite trend for both the Secretariat and the government Presidium to be more formalized and institutionalized. One reflection of this is the suggestion that certain constitutional lawyers have been making, that the constitution should be amended to include a passage defining the composition and powers of the Presidium of the Council of Ministers.[11]

The fourth and final device for safeguarding the oligarchy is the maintenance of countervailing power between its leading members. It is difficult to establish this point without presenting a good deal of 'Kremlinological' documentation, but for reasons of length we must confine ourselves to sketching in a few salient aspects. At the time of Khrushchev's removal and the simultaneous declaration that the posts of First Secretary and Premier were henceforth to be kept in separate hands, many observers thought that Khrushchev's semi-demi-dictatorship had given way to a duumvirate or latter-day Roman consulate, in which the mutual checking of Brezhnev and Kosygin would be relied on to hinder the recurrence of one-man rule. As we have seen, what in fact emerged was a considerably more dispersed pattern of power, an oligarchy whose core comprised the 11 voting members of the Politburo, but which embraced all told over 30 officials. The two top men were therefore subject not only to mutual checks but also to checks exerted by this wider group of other

Table 9.1 *The Soviet leadership, 1970*

Presidium of Council of Ministers	Politburo	Party Secretariat
	Full Members	
	Brezhnev	Brezhnev
	Voronov	
	Kirilenko	Kirilenko
Kosygin	Kosygin	
Mazurov	Mazurov	
	Pel'she	
	Podgorny	
Polyansky	Polyansky	
	Suslov	Suslov
	Shelepin	
	Shelest	
	Candidates (non-voting members)	
	Grishin	
	Demichev	Demichev
	Kunaev	
	Masherov	
	Mzhavanadze	
	Rashidov	
	Ustinov	Ustinov
	Shcherbitsky	
	Andropov	
Dymshits		Kapitonov
Novikov, I. T.		Kulakov
Novikov, V. N.		Ponomarev
Lesechko		Solomentsev
Smirnov		Katushev
Kirillin		
Baibakov		
Tikhonov		
Efremov		

oligarchs. At the same time, however, one could discern a third, intermediate, level of checks and balances, based on the partly formal, partly informal relationships between an inner group of leaders. After some flux in 1965, there emerged in 1966 an informal quadrumvirate of Brezhnev, Kosygin, Podgorny and Suslov (the standard protocol indices dictate the order of listing, although some ambiguity attaches to Kosygin's precedence over Podgorny). We shall attempt to illustrate the phenomenon of countervailing power, looking briefly at the position of each of these leaders.

First, as to Brezhnev and Kosygin, the pre-eminence ensured by whose institutional roles scarcely needs explication. Brezhnev was made First Secretary of the Central Committee at the time of Khrushchev's removal, and General Secretary in April 1966, after the Twenty-Third Congress revived this post (it had lapsed even before Stalin's death). Though some observers saw this change as a sign of resurgent Stalinism, the title has stronger associations with the late Lenin period than with the period of developed Stalinism. This said, the revival of the title in Brezhnev's favour *did* appear to increase his standing within the leadership. In the circumstances it was a step towards institutionalizing the primacy within the country's top policy-making body. However, this institutionalization is far from complete, and the General Secretary's standing in the Politburo is not yet comparable with that of the Prime Minister in a parliamentary-cabinet system of government. One of the delegates to the Twenty-Third Congress, a *raikom* secretary, used the formula 'the Politburo headed by a General Secretary',[12] but Brezhnev's colleagues are apparently not prepared to concede him that much, because the formula does not appear to have been used since. The simultaneous renaming of the Party Presidium as the Political Bureau also raised the status of this body; it emphasized its role as the country's supreme policy-making body and tended to underline the subordination both of the government Presidium and the Secretariat.

At a time when the regime is stressing more than ever the continued relevance and validity of the patterns of rule current under Lenin, it is Kosygin who occupies the one formal executive post held by the founder of the Soviet state. There is no doubt, moreover, who was held to be Number One when Lenin was Chairman of the Council of People's Commissars and Stalin was General Secretary. Although Kosygin has never shown any indication of attempting to challenge Brezhnev for primacy within the leadership, it is also clear that he has had no intention of playing the Bulganin to Brezhnev's Khrushchev. The importance of the Council of Ministers as an institution, and *a fortiori* of its Chairman, were substantially enhanced in 1965 with the restoration of the central industrial administration to the pre-Khrushchev pattern. However, it seems likely that military and security policy remain the more or less exclusive responsibility of the *Politburo*, with the Defence Minister, KGB Chairman and MVD Minister reporting direct to that body.

Podgorny emerged as one of the leading members of the oligarchy right from the beginning. For the first year or so his importance seemed to rest on his role of chief counterweight to Brezhnev in the Secretariat, where he was evidently responsible for running the party machine. His transfer in December 1965 to the post of Chairman of the Presidium of the Supreme Soviet was seen by many at the time as a demotion, as a move away from the crucial levers of power, especially coming as it did at a time when a number of other former Khar'kovites were being transferred to more junior or less sensitive posts. However, the post of Presidium Chairman can be made to yield many power advantages, and Podgorny seems to have made able use of these to keep himself in the inner group.

So long as the posts of Premier and General Secretary are kept in separate hands and their incumbents have not built up undue informal power, the prestige and public prominence attaching to the formal role of the Presidium Chairman is inevitably an important political factor in itself. The relatively light administrative duties involved can perhaps enable the incumbent to devote more attention to major policy issues – to become something approaching a senior minister without portfolio. Nor should we forget that the job has its own bureaucratic power base – the hierarchy of soviets from the Supreme Soviets of the republics down. The job of supervising and directing the soviets and their executive committees is shared between the party apparatus and officials of the Supreme Soviet Presidium, and this makes the Presidium one of the more significant channels through which Moscow controls the periphery.

It is worth recalling that, in the first 17 months of the Soviet regime, when Sverdlov held the two jobs of Central Committee Secretary and Chairman of the Central Executive Committee of the Congress of Soviets, it was primarily through the soviet rather than the party apparatus that he ran the country outside the capital on behalf of the regime. After he died, the balance shifted sharply in favour of the party apparatus, but in a period like the present, when the role of the party and its relationships with the government administration are again subject to question, the balance could possibly be made to shift a bit the other way. Even without such a shift, however, the Supreme Soviet Presidium is already, as was suggested, a significant organizational base. The Presidium's constitutional position not only makes it a factor alongside the government and the party machine in supervising the soviets but also, and potentially more crucially, involves important powers *vis-à-vis* the central government and its ministries. Although its constitutional powers of legislation and of supervising the Council of Ministers have been little more than an empty formality since the 1930s, one of the most important political developments in recent years has been a cautious, modest, but persistent revival of this aspect of the Presidium's role, centred mainly on the expanded activities of the Standing Commissions of the Supreme Soviet, which are directed by the Presidium and its officials. Visiting Moscow in October 1967, when the Supreme Soviet adopted its new Statute on the Standing Commissions, the author was left in little doubt that what was involved here was not just refurbishing the democratic façade; it also raised most sensitive political issues. Here again one needs to recall the political relationships operating in the earliest phase of the regime. In 1918 Sverdlov's Presidium vied with Lenin's Council of People's Commissars for effective primacy amongst the organs of the State, and there was often friction between the two bodies.[13] Even a small reassertion by the Supreme Soviet Presidium of its powers *vis-à-vis* the government would obviously involve big shifts in the balance of power within the leadership.

Finally, Suslov, the leader whose standing increased most after the initial period of the post-Khrushchev regime. There appear to be two main reasons for this. The first relates to the 'arithmetic' of the leadership. As first Podgorny and then Shelepin left the Secretariat, while the other Central Committee Secretary with a vote in the Politburo, namely Kirilenko, was evidently a protégé of Brezhnev, this left Suslov as the only Politburo member capable of providing a counterweight to Brezhnev in the Secretariat, and the main factor the rest of the leadership had to rely on to prevent Brezhnev turning the Secretariat into a personal instrument of

power as Khrushchev had done in the middle 1950s. But supporting Suslov may also have resulted in more stress being placed on
those areas of activity for which Suslov was primarily responsible
at Politburo level, namely, dealings with the international communist movement and party training and indoctrination inside the
country itself. Meanwhile, however, things were happening which,
independently of personal power considerations, were tending to
up-grade the importance of Suslov's sphere of responsibility.
The continuing political and ideological diversification among
communist parties both in and out of power made dealings
with these parties an ever more complex and delicate problem
for the Soviet regime. The logic of the 1965 economic reform
was for the party apparatus to disengage from close day-to-day
administrative involvement with the economy, which had been
the largest of all its concerns since the 1930s. This made for
a shift in the relative weight within the apparatus as between
its ideological and economic departments, and at the same time
encouraged the party to rely more on ideology as the justification
for its position within the state and indeed for its *raison d'être*.
At the same time, the gradual secularization or de-ideologizing
of Soviet society has made countermeasures more and more
urgent if the party and the regime are not to allow the basis
of their legitimacy to evaporate. Indoctrination within the party
has been greatly intensified. Ideological considerations have played
an increased role in party membership policies, contributing to a
halving of the recruitment rate and a doubling of the expulsion rate
since Khrushchev went.[14] Perhaps most important of all, doctrinal
literacy and orthodoxy have been given far greater weight both in
job appointments and in the control and disciplining of officials,
not only party officials but also officials of the central ministries
and economic administration.[15]

One consequence of these developments is a convergence of
the ideological, party discipline and security concerns of the
regime. It is in this context that the appointment of Pel'she
and Andropov arouse particular interest. It is unprecedented,
at least since the 1930's, for a Chairman of the Party Control
Commission, concerned *solely* with internal party discipline, to
be made a full voting member of the Politburo. This indicates
the current importance the leadership attaches to this problem.
It is hard to be confident about career links in the case of

Pel'she, but it may be pertinent that he and Suslov worked together in the Baltic states at the end of the war, Suslov in Lithuania and Pel'she in Latvia, when Soviet rule was being reimposed there. Andropov's links with Suslov are, of course, very obvious. For many years prior to his appointment as KGB chairman Andropov was responsible for party-level contacts with other communist countries, and answerable at Politburo level to Suslov. While the implications of such prior associations may be ambiguous, one might speculate that the overlapping current concerns of these three leaders would tend to throw them into alliance within the oligarchy; if this were so, Suslov would begin to look like a very powerful member of the leadership indeed. Nor should we overlook the influence accruing from his standing as the oligarchy's only credible theoretician and from his reputation as a leader of principle who has played a major role in more than one crisis without grasping for personal power.

One may conclude, then, that Khrushchev's successors have evidently given much thought to the problem of leadership, and taken a number of sensible practical measures to moderate the problem. They have acquiesced in the emergence of a 'pecking order' in the oligarchy, with Brezhnev as No. 1, and this, one might expect,has made it easier to achieve coherence and expedition in current policy-making and administration. At the same time, however, and this is the most salient characteristic of their style of government, they have hedged around the power and authority of individual leaders with a number of quite formidable controls, with the object of preventing history from again repeating itself, of obstructing a new drift to one-man rule.

There is no space here to discuss the relationship between these developments in the structure of the leadership and the evolution of Soviet political processes generally since 1964, but certain aspects may be briefly noted. The Khrushchev era had seen a partial overflow of Soviet bureaucratic crypto-politics into the communications media and certain of the formal representative institutions. The post-Khrushchev oligarchy, as might be expected in view of its general style and approach, has sought once more to remove all indications of policy disagreement from public view. It is doubtful, however, whether one should conclude from this that Soviet politics have been completely re-bureaucratized. The stenographic report of the March 1965 Central Committee plenum contains many indications of significantly different viewpoints on a number of issues. The fact that verbatim reports of subsequent plenums were not published does not necessarily mean that they were the scene of open conflict, but certainly suggests that they manifested insufficient unanimity to satisfy the oligarchy's more exacting standards of the decencies of washing dirty linen in public.[16] Indeed, however concerned the oligarchy might be to keep policy discussion and criticism 'in the family', it would seem almost inevitable that there would be some overflow from the inner executive bodies into the forum of the Central committee, especially in view of the oligarchy's insistence, at the time of Khrushchev's removal, on the need 'to foster the development of criticism and creative discussion, not just formal discussion, at plenums', etc. There can be little doubt that an undertaking on the part of the oligarchy to take Central Committee meetings seriously formed part of the understandings on which the October 1964 settlement was based. Nor is this the only institution which shows some signs of having been politicized in the post-Khrushchev period. The increased activity of the Supreme Soviet Presidium and the bodies under its supervision, particularly the Standing Commissions of the Supreme Soviet, probably reflects, at least in part, the heightened role of these institutions in the representation and reconciliation of different interests and viewpoints. One might therefore conclude that, despite partially successful efforts to push back under the surface the visible tip of the iceberg of Soviet politics, there is also a modest trend, still behind the scenes, to institutionalize a non-bureaucratic level of politics.

If this chapter is correct in arguing that the Soviet leadership has been deliberately employing a battery of internal checks and balances in order to stabilize and perpetuate the oligarchy, then the record to date certainly suggests that they have enjoyed a considerable measure of success. Not a single change occurred in the core leadership group of 11 voting members of the Politburo in the four years following the Twenty-Third Congress. In the wider circle embracing those holding places on the Politburo, the party Secretariat and the government Presidium, now totalling 34 in all, there have been one death, two additions and no dismissals in the same period.[17] This stability is all the more impressive when one considers that the oligarchy has had to face a major, potentially disruptive, policy crisis during these years. Yet the Czechoslovak crisis did evidently generate strains within the Soviet leadership, and it may be instructive to consider these briefly before essaying a general estimate of the attempt to operate a 'self-stabilizing oligarchy' in the USSR.[18]

The Soviet leadership had begun by late 1967 to manifest serious concern over the trend of events in Czechoslovakia, against a background of ominously mounting problems in Eastern Europe as a whole and in the international communist movement. It was in April 1968 that the first major decisions were taken and launched at a plenum of the Central Committee. The campaign of internal vigilance and discipline was sharply intensified. At the same time a campaign of pressure on the Dubček regime was launched.

At this point, Suslov, who had held the satellite party brief in the Politburo for many years, ceased to be included in meetings with satellite representatives, and the brief was evidently taken over by Brezhnev himself, assisted by Konstantin Katushev, a new Central Committee Secretary, who had no previous experience of such matters but who had been appointed to a major provincial post in December 1965 under Brezhnev. It seems likely that in the Politburo, and possibly in the Central Committee at its April 1968 plenum, things were said that called in question Suslov's performance in this area. Brezhnev must bear the major responsibility for the policies which led up to the invasion. Suslov, of course, was present at Cierna along with most of the Politburo, where he is said by Czech and Western communists to have played a moderate role, and he is believed by these sources to have been at best lukewarm about the invasion. In view of Suslov's functions, this whole issue is of crucial importance to his standing in the leadership, and it would have been surprising if the initially ambiguous results of Brezhnev's Czechoslovak policies had not led to sharp recriminations.

Signs of strain in the leadership increased in late 1968. The party press printed some remarkably sharp homilies, albeit in the usual esoteric language, about 'the authority of the leader' and 'collectivity of leadership', the most plausible exegesis of which is that they constituted attacks on Brezhnev for attempting to subvert the collective and run things through his cronies. The same period produced signs of strain between the KGB and the MVD on the one hand, and the KGB and the army on the other. Attacks on government officials and industry for letting down agriculture were also prominent, and there was a curious phase early in 1969 when Kosygin was absent from view for several weeks and Polyansky, the First Deputy Premier responsible for agriculture, received some remarkable publicity - which ceased on Kosygin's return to public activity. There were signs that proposals may have been made for a major transfer of economic administrative functions to the republics which aroused intense resistance. It is possible also that there were serious differences in the oligarchy over policy towards China and West Germany. Meanwhile, the military seems to have been seeking to exert a greater role in policy-making, and in this context some observers drew attention to the personal connections between Brezhnev and Defence Minister Grechko. Furthermore, there were some hints of discontent in the bureaucracy at the obstacles to promotion arising from the policy of 'stability of cadres', and there may also have been divided councils at the top on this particularly sensitive issue.

It is difficult to evaluate these signs and portents. Our own view, for what it is worth, is that relations within the Soviet leadership were very strained by early 1969, threatening a polarization into 'Brezhnev' and 'Suslov' factions. Many observers would disagree with this interpretation, but few would maintain that there was little 'fire' behind all this smoke.

In the spring of 1969, as Soviet pressure began to achieve decisive results in 'normalizing' the situation in Czechoslovakia, the signs of divided counsels at home grew fewer, and it became clear that the post-Khrushchev oligarchy had survived its first severe test. This in itself was quite a considerable achievement. Nevertheless,the lesson of these events was that a major policy issue evidently did have the capacity to activate and compound latent cleavages within the regime to an extent that seriously threatened the existing pattern of leadership.

This lesson needs to be borne in mind in speculating about the future. At the same time, the possible impact of such 'external' factors should be evaluated in the light of pressures that seem likely to be generated by the internal dynamics of the oligarchy itself. For the attempt to stabilize the oligarchy by a system of 'mutual control', and certain of the particular devices employed to this end, produce – perhaps inevitably – some serious side-effects, which of their nature seem bound to become more acute as time goes on. Three of these should be particularly noted:

First, '*immobilism*'. When relations within an executive body are delicately balanced, concern to avoid 'rocking the boat' can lead to the virtual avoidance of action altogether. One of the findings of the small group research referred to earlier is that groups lacking a strong leadership pattern tend to be relatively slow and ineffective in settling the problems put up to them. Opinions differ as to how seriously the divided leadership pattern has impaired the coherence, expeditiousness and rationality of Soviet rule, but there is evidence of hesitant and contradictory decision-making and simple avoidance of decision in several major policy-areas.[19] Some problems do, indeed, go away if left, but others, such as those connected with economic planning and administration, are more basic or pervasive, and the ill-effects of irresolute decision-making are cumulative, so that the acuteness and potential divisiveness of these problems tend to grow with time.

Secondly, *the inevitability of core changes*. As the leadership ages, the likelihood of death or incapacity afflicting one or other of the core group of voting Politburo members increases. This would disrupt the existing pattern of balances, necessitating substantial and sensitive readjustments, and presenting a variety of threats and opportunities to the surviving oligarchs. The destabilizing effect of the loss of one of the inner quadrumvirate would be particularly marked. A sequence of losses among lesser members of the three top executive bodies could also, however, prove quite disruptive. Furthermore, even without the occurrence of deaths or incapacitating illnesses, advancing age is likely to impair the will or ability of some of the leaders to 'control' their more vigorous colleagues effectively, presenting opportunities for one or some combination of the latter to corner the substance of power, operating through informal channels which by-pass the gerontocracy still ensconced in the official executive bodies.

Thirdly, *the generational problem*. One aspect of this has just been noted, but there are also more widespread tensions arising from the policy of 'stability of cadres': the frustration of officials at the *obkom* secretary – Central Committee member level denied entry into the ruling oligarchy, and of officials at the *raikom* secretary–congress delegate level who see little early prospect of promotion to posts of Central Committee status. These growing frustrations offer potential support for a leader or group aiming to subvert the oligarchy and shake things up.

It would be rash to assume that the leadership will prove incapable of devising measures to moderate at least some of these problems. However, given that they are of their nature cumulative and in some degree mutually aggravating, the difficulties of operating the 'self-stabilizing oligarchy' seem bound to grow, and with them the likelihood of a 'front-runner' making a bid for personal dominance, or of a factional move to pre-empt such a bid. In the short run, the prospects for continuance of the stable oligarchical pattern of the last few years are therefore modest. Taking a broader view, however, the developments outlined in this paper may turn out to be of great long-term importance for the Soviet polity. If institutions can 'learn', so too can whole political systems. A new leadership emerging from any impending shake-up is likely to make use of and build on the experience acquired since 1964 in structuring stablizing factors into the oligarchy, just as the present leadership has used and built on the experience of the Khrushchev era. The Soviet polity may, indeed, have entered a phase of 'degeneration'. It is just possible, however, that it is experiencing a period of institutional creativity, as did the British polity under the first two Georges, when a stable system of oligarchical rule was evolved which proved to be very persistent and successful.

NOTES

1. See Sydney Verba, *Small Groups and Political Behavior : A Study of Leadership* (Princeton, N. J. 1961) especially pp. 124–9. It remains unclear how far findings based on the study of artificial experimental groups can be used to interpret and predict the behaviour of real-life executive bodies, and Verba shows himself fully aware of this. There is an excellent discussion of the relevant differences between experimental and real-life groups in James D. Barber, *Power in Committees: An Experiment in the Government Process* (Chicago, 1966) pp. 8–13. Though suggestive for our present purposes, the small-group evidence does not permit of any firm conclusions.
2. Henry Roberts, 'Succession to Khrushchev in Perspective', *Proceedings of the Academy of Political Science*, vol. *XXVIII*, no. 1. (April 1965) p. 11.
3. Myron Rush, *Political Succession in the USSR*, 2nd edn (New York, 1968) pp. 270–1.
4. See Roberts, loc. cit., Gerome M. Gilison, 'New Factors of Stability in Soviet Collective Leadership', *World Politics*, vol. 19, no. 4 (1967) p. 563–81, and Alfred G. Meyer's chapter in Lewis J. Edinger (ed.), *Political Leadership in Industrialized Societies: Studies in Comparative*

Analysis (New York, 1967). The case for the durability of present political arrangements is strongly argued by Tibor Szamuely in his contribution to the discussion 'The USSR Since Khrushchev', *Survey*, no. 72 (Summer 1969) pp. 51–69.

5.   See especially Michel Tatu, *Power in the Kremlin* (London, 1969), and Carl A. Linden, *Khrushchev and the Soviet Leadership, 1957–1964* (Baltimore 1966).

6.   *Partiinaya zhizn'*, no. 20 (1964); the citations that follow are taken from pp. 6–7.

7.   See P. A. Rodionov, *Kollektivnost'-vysshii printsip partiinogo rukovodstva* (Moscow, 1967) p. 219.

8.   See T. H. Rigby, 'Khrushchev and the Resuscitation of the Central Committee', *Australian Outlook*, vol. 13. no. 3 (September 1959) pp. 165–80 (this volume, chapter 6).

9.   By virtue of his power personally to approve or veto decisions of the *Malyi Sovnarkom.*

10.   See T. H. Rigby, 'How Strong is the Leader?', *Problems of Communism*, vol. *XI* , no. 5 (Sept.–Oct 1962) pp. 1–8.

11.   For example, see V. I. Popova, 'Printsipy deyatel'nosti Soveta Ministrov RSFSR', *Uchenye zapiski Vsesoyuznogo nauchno-issledovatel'skogo instituta sovetskogo zakonodatel'stva*, vyp. 4 (Moscow, 1965) p. 33. On the Secretariat, see Rodionov, op. cit., p. 231, and Tatu, op. cit., p. 518.

12.   See *XXIII s''ezd Kommunisticheskoi Partii Sovetskogo Soyuza 29 marta–8 aprelya 1966 goda: Stenograficheskii otchet* (Moscow, 1966) vol. 1, p. 462.

13.   See E. H. Carr, *The Bolshevik Revolution, 1917–1923 (London, 1950) vol. 1, p. 147.*

14.   See T. H. Rigby, *Communist Party Membership in the USSR, 1917–1967* (Princeton, N. J., 1968) pp. 316–22.

15.   For examples of evidence on this point, see 'Partiinye organizatsii ministerstv v novykh usloviyakh', *Partiinaya zhizn'*, no. 24 (1966), V. S. Tolstikov's article in *Pravda*, 29 March 1967, and the *Pravda* leading articles for 30 December 1966 and 23 January 1967. A Central Committee decision issued in 1967 strongly criticized personnel work in central ministries for giving insufficient attention to officials' communist *ideinost'* and their strict observance of state and *party* discipline (*Pravda*, 16 June 1967). For a valuable discussion of trends in the political role of ideology, see Alfred G. Meyer, 'The Functions of Ideology in the Soviet Political System', *Soviet Studies*, vol. *XVII*, no. 3 (January 1966), and comments by other authors in subsequent issues of this journal.

16.   The practice of publishing stenographic records of Central Committee plenums dated back to 1958, after the removal of the 'anti-party group' had drastically reduced the intensity of leadership conflict exposed at the plenums. At the same time, by making their procedure public, Khrushchev was able to employ the plenums as a device for hedging around the lesser oligarchs with a kind of imposed consensus. Publication of his innumerable speeches to various groups performed a similar function.

17.   Central Committee Secretary A. P. Rudakov died in July 1966, and was replaced by M. S. Solomentsev five months later. The other addition was K. F. Katushev, who joined the Secretariat in April 1968. There have been only two major changes of position *within* the oligarchy in the same period. In June 1967 Yu. V. Andropov left the Secretariat to become

KGB Chairman, and was elected candidate member of the Politburo, and in September 1967 A. N. Shelepin also left the Secretariat, becoming Chairman of the Trade Union Council, but remained a full member of the Politburo.

18.   It would be supererogatory to fortify the very sketchy account that follows with detailed 'Kremlinological' quotation and exegesis. Most or all of the aspects mentioned have been noted by other scholars and discussed by such observers as Victor Zorza, Edward Crankshaw and Anatole Shub. I wish merely to mention one article which helped more than anything else to order my own thinking about these developments, namely, V. Zasorin, 'Kollektivnost' v rabote – vazhneishaya cherta leninskogo stilya', *Partiinaya zhizn*', no. 3 (1969).

19.   For different views on this issue see Zbigniew Brzezinski, 'The Soviet Political System: Transformation or Degeneration?', *Problems of Communism*, vol XV, no. 1 (Jan.–Feb. 1966) and discussions in subsequent issues of *Problems of Communism*.

10. The Soviet regional leadership: the Brezhnev generation*

The secretaries of republic and regional party committees are the most important category of officials in the USSR after the supreme leadership. They formed 36 per cent of the full members of the Central Committee chosen in 1976, while the next largest group, comprising members of the Council of Ministers, made up 24 per cent. They are also the most important reserve from which members of the supreme leadership are co-opted. A study of the careers of Politburo members in 1971 showed that two-thirds of them had spent at least five years as regional or republic party first secretaries before being promoted to senior jobs at the centre.[1] The same applies to nine of the twelve present members of the Central Committee Secretariat.[2]

This chapter focuses on the first secretaries of regional (*oblast*) and territorial (*krai*) party committees – the *obkom* and *kraikom* secretaries – of the Russian Republic (RSFSR).[3] They make up almost two-thirds of all republic and regional party officials elected as full members of the present Central Committee, but their importance lies not only in their numerical weight within the political élite. An RSFSR *obkom* first secretaryship is the most crucial career position for promotion to top jobs at the centre, as several examples will show.

The antecedents of the *obkom* secretary go back to the *voevody* of seventeenth-century Muscovy, who were the plenipotentiaries of the tsars in provincial centres which for the most part had been capitals of independent principalities in former times. In the eighteenth century the *voevoda* gave way to the provincial governor (*gubernator*) and the role became increasingly bureaucratized, without, however, declining in power. The governors were

Slavic Review, vol. 37, no. 1 (March 1978), pp. 1–24.

the key body of tsarist officials right up to 1917, and the post was a common stepping-stone to high office in St Petersburg.[4] They were local embodiments of the sovereign's prerogative (the tsar, as 'autocrat', being theoretically invested with unlimited power) so that within their provinces they were comparable in authority and status to the European governors of overseas colonial territories, a fact that was not lost on some contemporary Western observers.[5]

The post of provincial governor was abolished by the provisional government in 1917, but the requirements of administrative co-ordination soon caused the Bolsheviks to create a functional equivalent in the form of the provincial party secretary. The reforms of the 1860s, reinforced by those following the 1905 revolution, had introduced elements of the Rechtsstaat and of local self-government into Russia, and after 1917 the soviets and their executive machinery to some extent perpetuated these elements. On the other hand, the party apparatus now came to embody the prerogative aspect of government (exercising the 'dictatorship of the proletariat' – defined as 'power unlimited by any laws'), with the regional party secretaries wielding the prerogative power in their regions on behalf of the supreme leadership, as the *gubernatory* had done before them. The speedy re-emergence of this role must thus be seen as a decisive setback to the struggle against arbitrary government in Russia – and one from which it has not yet recovered.

Jerry Hough has aptly termed the *obkom* first secretaries the 'Soviet prefects', suggesting a role as local agents of the central authorities comparable with that of the French departmental prefect.[6] In a sense the role is both less and more than this: less, because the existence of the *obkom* secretariat and bureau dilutes to some extent the powers of the first secretary as a 'line administrator'; and more, because of the global responsibilities of the party apparatus in Soviet society, such that there is scarcely an area of organized activity in his region on which the *obkom* secretary may not be called upon to make a decision, or a social institution or organization for whose performance he cannot be called to account.

The *obkom* secretaryship, of course, is in form an elective post, and this was not always a mere fiction. Officials sent out by the Central Committee as first secretary would sometimes encounter difficulty in gaining acceptance by the local organization, as Mikoyan discovered as late as 1920.[7] These vestiges of democracy, however, did not survive the consolidation of the party apparatus in the early 1920s, when General Secretary Stalin turned the provincial party officialdom into a major basis of support in his struggle for power. Molotov, Kaganovich and Mikoyan were among the many Stalinist stalwarts who served as provincial secretaries in this period, and they were followed by such future leaders as Kirov, Zhdanov and Khrushchev. The way in which *obkom* secretaries were made and unmade under Stalin may be illustrated by A. I. Shakhurin's (perhaps somewhat embellished) account of how, when serving as first secretary of the Gorki *obkom* in 1940, Stalin summoned him to Moscow to tell him he was to be people's commissar for the aircraft industry. When Shakhurin asked if he could return to Gorki to wind up his work there, Stalin replied: 'No, we will send a representative of the Central Committee there, who will inform the *obkom* of the decision we have taken.' He then asked Shakhurin whom he would recommend as his successor. Shakhurin recommended M. I. Rodionov,[8] then serving as chairman of the executive committee of the *oblast* soviet, and Rodionov was duly made first secretary. This case illustrates both the personal authority Stalin exercised over such appointments and their incumbents, and his willingness by this time to delegate responsibility to make nominations.[9] Career evidence suggests that certain of his lieutenants, such as Zhdanov, Malenkov and Khrushchev, were able to exploit their influence over nominations in order to build up personal followings among the *obkom* secretaries.

On his election as first secretary of the Central Committee in September 1953 Khrushchev acquired vast powers of patronage, and the *obkom* secretaryships became a major field for the deployment of these powers. By the time of the Twentieth Party Congress in February 1956, 39 of the RSFSR *obkom* and *kraikom* first secretaries inherited from Stalin had been changed, and by the Twenty-second Congress in October 1961 all but two of the remainder had been replaced.[10] Some of the new secretaries were men who had previously served under Khrushchev when he was party boss of the Ukraine (1938–49) or the Moscow *oblast* (1949–53).[11] Others were local officials picked out by him for promotion. In many cases appointment to an RSFSR *obkom* first secretaryship became a stepping stone for a Khrushchev protégé on the way to senior office in Moscow. At the same time, as Khrushchev's power grew and with it his responsibilities in both domestic and foreign policy areas, he probably left the initiation of *obkom* appointments increasingly to other members of the Central Committee Secretariat, notably A. B. Aristov up to 1960, and F. R. Kozlov from then till 1963.

In his rise to supreme power, regional party officialdom was Khrushchev's most important (though not only) base of support, as it had been for Stalin. In consolidating this support base, Khrushchev employed both the carrot and the stick. His power over appointments enabled him to reward loyal adherents and bind them closer to him, while removing or intimidating into co-operation those whose earlier loyalties had been to other leaders. Furthermore, his policies of decentralizing administration and of involving party bodies more directly in running the economy combined to enhance the significance and authority of regional and republic party officialdom. Thus, it was in the interests of this group to support Khrushchev and oppose those rivals, such as Molotov, Malenkov and Kaganovich, whose power resided mainly in the central government machine. Given the weight of the regional officials in the Central Committee membership, this support evidently proved of great importance to Khrushchev in the 'anti-party group' crisis of June 1957, when he managed to convene the full Central Committee to overrule and purge the hostile majority that had formed against him in the Politburo (then called Presidium of the Central Committee).

Subsequently, however, Khrushchev seems to have alienated this support. His constant reorganizations caused administrative confusion which made it very difficult for regional officials to meet the expectations he had of them, and for this many met with his displeasure and lost office. By the early 1960s something like two-thirds of the RSFSR *obkom* secretaries installed under Khrushchev in the mid-1950s had been replaced. The turnover undoutbedly created a sense of frustration and insecurity which was intensified by the change in the party rules in October 1961, when minimum turnover levels and limited periods in office were prescribed for party committee members for the first time. The final blow was the decision in November 1962 which split a large proportion of the regional party organizations into two, one for industry and one for agriculture, each with its own regional committee (*obkom*), executive bureau and secretariat. This not only created further administrative confusion, but struck directly at the incumbent *obkom* first secretaries by duplicating their offices and thus sharply reducing their individual power and status.[12] Thus, when Khrushchev's lieutenants conspired to remove him in October 1964, they were evidently able to count on his having dissipated the support he had earlier enjoyed among the large bloc of regional secretaries in the Central Committee, support which had proved so valuable to him in 1957.

The *obkom* secretaries clearly had three major grievances at the time of Khrushchev's removal: (1) the bifurcation of their apparatus and organizations; (2) the constant reorganizations and administrative confusion; and (3) their career insecurity. There is evidence that the 'collective leadership' recognized the seriousness of these grievances and immediately undertook to remedy them, thereby showing their concern to win the support and goodwill of regional party officialdom. While it is uncertain whether they entered into any specific commitments at the Central Committee meeting at which Khrushchev gave up office,[13] articles appearing in Central Committee organs in the following weeks made their intentions clear enough.

The leading article in the first issue of *Partiinaia zhizn'* to appear after the plenum, which, without mentioning Khrushchev by name, amounted to a critical review of his errors of leadership, included the following passage:

> Without according assistance to lower-level officials [*rabotniki*], without knowledge of [their] circumstances, a demanding attitude can easily boil down to leadership 'in general', which often leads to the unjustified reshuffling of cadres . . . Indisputably, bad officials must be replaced. The renewal of cadres is a natural phenomenon. Not infrequently, however, there are still efforts to represent frequent changes of them as a virtue.[14]

Subsequent issues of the journal condemned the obsession with administrative reorganization and an appropriate quotation from Lenin was employed to raise the issue to a point of principle:

> Do not start everything over again from the beginning, do not

reorganize right and left, but learn how to make the best use of what has already been created. As few general reorganizations as possible.[15]

And the other major Central Committee journal, *Kommunist*, linked the two issues of reorganization and career security in the following terms:

> Recently, however, work with cadres and the rational employment of them have been subjected to artificial complications [*iskusstvenno uslozhnilis'*]. The frequent restructurings and reorganizations have entailed repeated mass reallocation of officials [*rabotnikov*]. This switching around of cadres has not allowed them to concentrate on the decision of long-term questions of economic development of the *oblast*, *krai* or *raion*, and has imbued officials with a feeling of lack of self-confidence which hinders them from working calmly and fruitfully.[16]

The promise of stability and 'back to normal' conditions implied by such statements must be seen as a response to the confusion, frustration and insecurity generated at all sections of the Soviet bureaucracy by Khrushchev's innovations. Indeed, within a year all the major structural changes he had initiated were reversed. It is striking, however, that the abolition of his regional economic councils (*sovnarkhozy*) and the restoration of the central industrial ministries had to wait eleven months, while a decision on the issue that most directly concerned regional party officialdom, namely, the bifurcation of their organizations, was taken only four weeks after Khrushchev's fall. The decision was promulgated – 'with the aim of strengthening the leading role of the party and its local organs' – at another meeting of the full Central Committee held on 16 November 1964 and prescribed that *oblast* conferences reuniting the split *obkoms* were to beheld during December.[17]

Altogether in the USSR 85 *kraikoms* and *obkoms* had been split, 42 of them in the RSFSR (the 29 RSFSR *obkoms* that were not split were mainly based on national minority areas – autonomous republics [ASSRs] or autonomous regions – or were in sparsely populated areas remote from Moscow). It is particularly revealing of the new leadership's approach to note who became first secretaries in the reunified *obkoms*. In 31 cases (three-quarters) the job was returned to the man who had held it before the split (and who had served as first secretary of either the agricultural *obkom* or the industrial *obkom* in the meantime). Seven of the remainder had already been removed from the *oblast* concerned by Khrushchev (either at the time of or during the split), in most cases receiving other senior positions. In all but one of these *oblasts* the man appointed first secretary of the reunified *obkom* had been serving as either agricultural or industrial first secretary under Khrushchev. The exception was in the Cheliabinsk *oblast*, where the industrial first secretary, F. F. Kuziukov, who 'ought' to have been made first secretary of the reunified *obkom* in this heavily industrialized region, became instead deputy minister for the coal industry. This leaves only four *oblasts* where the pre-split first secretary was serving as either agricultural or industrial first secretary but failed to get his original job back when the *obkoms* were reunited. Three of these were appointed to other positions, two of them clearly involving promotion: F. D. Kulakov (Stavropol *kraikom*) was made head of the Agricultural Department of the Central Committee, and I. V. Kapitonov (Ivanovo *obkom*) was named head of the party organs for the RSFSR Department of the Central Committee; both later became Central Committee secretaries. The third, L. I. Lubennikov (Kemerovo) became deputy chairman of the People's Control Committee of the RSFSR, a post of lesser importance, but his fortunes were already on the wane under Khrushchev.[18] Only one of the four failed to get another post, namely V. V. Skriabin, in the Rostov *oblast*.[19]

Clearly, then, the new 'collective leadership' had instituted a policy of restoring the first secretaryship, in regions where the party organization had been bifurcated, to the original incumbent, or, should he no longer be available, to the 'ranking' party official in the region. And this was a policy of the new leadership as a whole, not just of those members of it who were directly responsible for internal party matters. The relevant decision explicitly assigned to the Central Committee Presidium (rather than to the Secretariat as one would normally have expected) responsibility for 'all organizational questions connected with the creation in the *krais* and *oblasts* of unified party organizations and their leading bodies' – and organizational questions, in Soviet usage, covers personnel as well as structural matters.[20] It is not difficult to see why the members of the Presidium oligarchy insisted on joint control of this operation. The *obkom* first secretaries were the most important cohort of their subordinates, and *who* held these positions was of major relevance to the delicate and fluid power balance in which they operated. This also may partially explain the actual policy that the 'collective leadership' adopted in this matter, that is, to restore the regional leadership as closely as possible to what it had been before Khrushchev's bifurcation measures. As suggested above, the main motive was probably to foster support for their regime within this crucial élite group. Another influential consideration, however, may have been that any other policy would have allowed certain of their number to install their own adherents in *obkom* posts, as well as causing divisive wrangles within the leadership.

Apart from the scrapping of most of Khrushchev's organizational innovations and other 'half-baked schemes', the consensus among the leadership coalition that took over in October 1964 seems to have been limited to one major point: that power and responsibility should be widely shared within an oligarchy dominated by the party Presidium but extending also to the Central Committee Secretariat and the Presidium of the Council of Ministers. Within this oligarchy four leaders clearly carried more weight than the rest, namely, Brezhnev, Suslov, Podgorny and Kosygin, of whom the first three were Central Committee secretaries.[21] But Brezhnev's position as first secretary did not at this time allow him to dominate internal party affairs. It was Podgorny, assisted by his protégé Central Committee secretary V. N. Titov (who had served under Podgorny in the Kharkov party organization), who at first had primary responsibility for party structures and personnel. In the course of 1965, however, Titov and other Podgorny adherents (the 'Kharkov group') were transferred to less strategic posts, and a public (if Aesopian) attack was launched on Podgorny's management of party organizational matters.[22] The attack culminated in December, with Podgorny's transfer from the party Secretariat to the chairmanship of the Presidium of the Supreme Soviet. At the same time I. V. Kapitonov was promoted from head of the Party Organs Department to Central Committee secretary, with responsibility for party organizational affairs. Kapitonov was probably a compromise choice, because he seemed to lack close links with any of the major leaders. With regard to the RSFSR regions, however, he shared his organizational and personnel responsibilities with A. P. Kirilenko who, as first deputy chairman (under Brezhnev) of the Central Committee Bureau for the RSFSR, was Kapitonov's superior in this body. The departure of Podgorny from the Secretariat greatly strengthened Brezhnev's capacity to influence internal party developments, and this capacity was further increased by decisions approved by the Twenty-Third Party Congress in April 1966. Brezhnev was made general (instead of first) secretary, a title previously held only by Stalin and one which emphasized his concern with all aspects of party policy and administration. At the same time the Bureau for the RSFSR was abolished and his protégé Kirilenko was made a member of the Politburo – which the Central Committee Presidium was now renamed (again restoring past nomenclature) – and a Central Committee Secretary.

Against this background of power shifts in the central party command, let us now consider the appointments of *obkom* first secretaries made in the period between the resignation of Khrushchev and the first post-Khrushchev party congress (that is, October 1964–April 1966). Clearly, the operation of reuniting the 42 split *obkoms* and *kraikoms* in the RSFSR, which occupied the first months of this period, was used only minimally to effect leadership changes. In the great majority of cases, the most senior party official already in the *oblast* was made first secretary of the reunified *obkom*, and this was nearly always the pre-split first secretary where he was still serving in the region. The four exceptions to this pattern are, therefore, worth examining.

In the Ivanovo *obkom*, A. N. Smirnov, the chairman of the *oblispolkom* (executive committee of the regional soviet) became first secretary. Smirnov had formerly worked in the light industry area of the USSR government under Kosygin, and his appointment may have reflected the latter's sponsorship, as Kosygin seems to have retained a special interest in this center of textile manufacture. The other three cases, involving men brought in from outside the *oblast*, all present intriguing political facets. The industrially important Cheliabinsk *oblast* was entrusted to N. N. Rodionov, whose career had suffered a serious setback two years earlier at the hands of Central Committee secretary F. R. Kozlov, at that time Brezhnev's principal rival for the succession.[23] The Rostov *oblast,* containing one of the largest party organizations in the

RSFSR, went to M. S. Solomentsev, who had been Rodionov's successor as second secretary of the Kazakh Central Committee. Though there is little in Solomentsev's career to suggest close links with Brezhnev, the subsequent flourishing of his fortunes, which are noted below, suggests sponsorship by someone at the top (Suslov?). His transfer to Rostov was also significant, however, in opening up a senior position in Kazakhstan to which Podgorny's protégé V. N. Titov could later be rusticated. Finally, the change in the Stavropol *kraikom* also killed two birds with one stone, and this time unambiguously to Brezhnev's advantage. On the one hand, it involved bringing up to Moscow F. D. Kulakov, who quickly emerged as Brezhnev's principal lieutenant in establishing his authority over agricultural policy. On the other hand, it created a suitable vacancy for the relegation of L. N. Efremov, a Khrushchev protégé who had been a first deputy chairman of the Bureau of the Central Committee for the RSFSR, leaving Brezhnev's adherent Kirilenko as the only first deputy chairman of this body, with implications which have already been discussed. Thus, even though there seems to have been an understanding among the party leadership to avoid making the reunification of the split *obkoms* an occasion for extensive and necessarily competitive deployment of patronage, it did enable at least Brezhnev and perhaps also Kosygin and Suslov to effect certain advantageous changes.

Following the reunification operation, some seven or eight months elapsed without a single *obkom* first secretary being changed. Between October 1965 and the Twenty-third Party Congress in March–April 1966, however, there were no less than 11 changes.[24] It seems reasonable to hypothesize that these changes were related to the power shifts in the Central Committee Secretariat in the latter part of 1965, which seem to have greatly enhanced Brezhnev's capacity to influence personnel and organizational developments. Indeed, it is likely that the spate of *obkom* leadership changes was in part intended as a demonstration of this enhanced capacity, so that actual or aspiring first secretaries should fully realize that it was *his* favour they should now be seeking. This supposition is supported by the fact that Brezhnev took the unusual step of going in person to preside at the meeting in Gorki, where the most important of these changes was effected.[25] Moreover, the new first secretary, K. F. Katushev, was a young construction engineer who had received his first party appointment only eight years earlier, and was thus living evidence of Brezhnev's capacity for generous promotion.[26] Another of the changes in this period seemed to demonstrate the limited capacity of Kapitonov, despite his role as head of the Party Organs Department, to frustrate changes desired by Brezhnev. In the Orel *obkom*, first secretary N. F. Ignatov, who had earlier been publicly identified in the party press as an associate of Kapitonov,[27] was removed in favour of Brezhnev's candidate T. I. Sokolov, another victim of Kozlov's 1962 purge in Kazakhstan.[28] A second change at this time, which surely must have galled Kapitonov, was the removal of another old associate, I. T. Marchenko, as first secretary of the Tomsk *obkom*.[29] The successor in this case (E.K. Ligachev) is interesting, however, for as former deputy head of the Central Committee Agitprop Department he may well have been sponsored by Suslov.

This chapter does not attempt to explore the patronage and power aspects of all the changes of *obkom* first secretaries in the years since 1965. It does, however, give some attention to these aspects in the account of the early post-Khrushchev period in order better to appreciate the implications of later changes generally. What emerges is that the period in which Brezhnev's influence over the composition of the *obkom* leadership has been dominant should be dated from the latter part of 1965 rather than from 1964. Moreover, to speak of Brezhnev exercising a 'dominant influence' in this matter is not to say that he had a free hand. Changes of *obkom* first secretaries certainly would be discussed by the Secretariat of the Central Committee and would require the endorsement of the Politburo, and despite Brezhnev's increasing pre-eminence within these bodies, there are no grounds for assuming that he has reduced either of them to a mere rubber stamp for his personal decisions. The election in April 1966 of Kapitonov, whom we have characterized as a compromise choice for head of the Central Committee Party Organs Department, as a secretary of the Central Committee probably reflects the concern of Brezhnev's colleagues to hinder the general secretary from too freely disposing of *obkom* appointments. Of course, Kapitonov's promotion was more than offset by the simultaneous elevation to the Politburo of Brezhnev's protégé Kirilenko, thus establishing the latter's clear precedence over Kapitonov in intraparty affairs.

At the Twenty-Third Party Congress in March–April 1966 Brezhnev gave fair warning that further changes of leading party officials could be expected. Although he reaffirmed the assurances contained in the early party statements about the pernicious effects of constant reorganizations and personnel changes, he balanced this by speaking of the need, as he put it, 'to promote young and energetic officials more boldly', and of combining old and new cadres.[30] By the time of the next party congress in 1971 a further 32 regional first secretaries were changed. After that, changes became less frequent and there were only 19 from 1971 to October 1976.

In comparison with the Khrushchev period, the rate of turnover of *obkom* first secretaries has been relatively modest since 1965. Moreover, Brezhnev has by and large avoided Khrushchev's performance of sacking in the second half of his incumbency most of the regional leaders he had installed in the first half. Under Brezhnev, only nine regions have seen their first secretary changed twice, and two of them three times – and several of these were cases where the original first secretary installed under Brezhnev was later moved up to a leading position in Moscow (for example, Katushev, Dolgikh and Riabov, who were all made secretaries of the Central Committee). The majority of the new first secretaries appointed under Brezhnev are still in office, and 26 of the first secretaries inherited by Brezhnev have not been changed. Brezhnev could fairly claim, therefore, that he has kept both his promise of providing stability of tenure and his promise of combining old and new cadres. All the same, two-thirds of the first secretaries now in office were installed under Brezhnev. Thus it seems reasonable to assume that he had succeeded in building up what any leader aspiring to be top man in the USSR must seek, namely, a solid base of support among this crucial body of officials, a point to which we shall return at the end of this chapter.

Another policy pursued by the general secretary which is clearly designed to foster support at the regional level is to recruit a higher proportion of his new first secretaries locally. Under Khrushchev many first secretary appointments were made from outside the region, mainly from those serving as party secretaries or Soviet Executive Committee chairmen in other *oblasts*. It must have been extremely frustrating for someone to work his way up the party hierarchy to one of the leading positions in his region only to find the top job given to someone from the outside. As Table 10.1 shows, 69 per cent of the present *obkom* first secretaries were locally recruited as compared with 53 per cent at the outset of the Brezhnev period.[31]

Table 10.1   *Last position before appointment as RSFSR regional first secretary*

	September 1965	September 1976
Second secretary, same *obkom* (including Moscow city)	15	17
Other secretary, same *obkom*	5	7
First secretary, *gorkom* of *oblast* centre	1	4
Chairman, Soviet Executive Committee (government), same *oblast* (ASSR)	16	21
Chairman, Presidium of the Supreme Soviet, same ASSR	1	1
Total in same oblast	38 (53%)	50 (69%)
Second secretary, republic party Central Committee	2	1
First secretary, other *obkom*	10	5
Second secretary, other *obkom*	7	7
Other secretary, other *obkom*	1	1
First/Second secretary, city party committee, other *oblast*	2	
Chairman, Soviet Executive Committee (government), other *oblast*	4	2
First deputy chairman, Executive Committee (government), other *oblast*	1	
Deputy chairman, Economic Council, other *oblast*	1	
Total from other region	28 (39%)	16 (23%)
Central Committee apparatus:		
Head of department	1	1
Deputy head of department	1	
Head of sector	1	2
Inspector/instructor	1	2
unknown post	2	
Chairman Central Trade Union Council		1
Total sent from Centre	6 (8%)	6 (8%)
Total	72 (100%)	72 (100%)

Sources: The information on the backgrounds and careers of officials analysed in this paper is assembled from the Soviet press and official biographical compilations, particularly the series *Deputaty Verkhovnogo Soveta SSSR* (Moscow, 1962, 1966, 1970 and 1974), and the yearbooks (*ezhegodniki*) of the *Bol'shaia sovetskaia entsiklopediia*. It would be unwieldy to give specific references in the tables, but these can be supplied on request. See note 6 for similar studies by Western scholars.

Brezhnev referred specifically to this policy in his report to the Twenty-Fourth Party Congress in 1971 and earned the applause of the assembled delegates for doing so.[32] The dynamics of this policy can be seen more clearly if actual appointments made within the Brezhnev period are examined. Two-thirds of the first secretaries appointed between October 1965 and March 1971 were selected from within the region, but five-sixths of those appointed between April 1971 and April 1976 were selected locally.

Table 10.1 also indicates that there is something less than a rigid *cursus honorum* for the aspiring CPSU functionary: altogether there are at least 18 different positions from which first secretaries have been selected in the Brezhnev period. Nevertheless, certain lines of transfer or promotion are far more probable than others, and the table shows that there are some half dozen positions from which the great bulk of first secretary appointments are made. Furthermore, there are two jobs – second secretary of the *obkom* and chairman of the Executive Committee of the Regional Soviet – that are by far the best jumping-off points for the first secretaryship. These jobs are, in fact, next in importance to the first secretaryship within the regional party bureau and the two are roughly equal in seniority. If the 1976 figures are compared with the 1965 figures we can also see a tendency to narrow the sources of recruitment to the advantage mainly of men at the second echelon of local officialdom.

Another point worth noting is the small number of people sent out from Moscow to be *obkom* first secretaries, and the fact that these central officials were nearly all transferred from apparatus jobs within the party Central Committee. The one exception – the Trade Union Council chairman – is rather misleading: it was Politburo member Grishin, who stayed in Moscow as first secretary of the City Committee, which has *obkom* status. Contrary to what might be expected, a back-room job in the Central Committee apparatus is *not* a good jumping-off point for top office in the Soviet system. (Georgii Malenkov is the outstanding exception to this.) Because regional experience is generally necessary for party advancement, the transfers from the centre shown in our table probably should not be seen as rustications but rather as cases of *reculer pour mieux sauter*. At the same time such cases are becoming rarer. Between October 1965 and March 1971 only three Central Committee *apparatchiki*

Table 10.2 *New appointments of RSFSR regional first secretaries who were relieved October 1965–October 1976*

Secretary, Central Committee, CPSU	4
Vice-head of department, Central Committee, CPSU	1
Official Party Control Committee	5
Chairman, Central Revision Commission	1
Total central party jobs	11
Chairman, Soviet of Union (of Supreme Soviet, USSR)	1
Deputy Chairman, Council of Ministers, USSR	1
Other positions, Council of Ministers, USSR	6
Junior positions in USSR government	9
First Deputy Chairman or Deputy Chairman, Council of Ministers, RSFSR	4
Other positions, Council of Ministers, RSFSR	3
Junior positions in RSFSR government	2
Total USSR or RSFSR governments	25
Total positions in Moscow	37
Ambassadors	6
Chairman, Presidium of the Supreme Soviet, same ASSR	2
First secretary of different *obkom*	1
Retired on pension	4
Died in office	9
No further information (probably demoted)	3
Total	62

got *obkom* first secretaryships, and from April 1971 to 1976 only one.

Table 10.2 shows what happened to the 62 *obkom* first secretaries replaced under Brezhnev from 1971 to 1976. Nine of the first secretaries died in office and four reached retirement age and went on to a pension – an indication in itself of the trend to normalization of Soviet career patterns. As was mentioned at the beginning of this paper, the *obkom* first secretaries have been, ever since the 1920s, the most important source of high-level appointments at the centre. But for every one who has been promoted there have been several who have fallen by the wayside and disappeared into obscurity. Under Khrushchev this usually meant demotion to some minor post, under Stalin it often betokened something worse. What is most remarkable about the first secretaries replaced under Brezhnev is that only three of them have been so reduced in status that they have disappeared from public view. Most of them have received other honourable positions, usually in Moscow.

Moscow, of course, does not necessarily mean promotion. If an *obkom* first secretary becomes a Central Committee secretary or a deputy chairman of the Council of Ministers that is clearly a move up; if he becomes a deputy minister it is a move down; and if he becomes a minister it is probably a move sideways. However, for any Soviet official a job in Moscow is in itself immensely desirable, not only because there lies the fountainhead of power, but because of the vastly superior conditions of life as compared with Russian provincial cities other than Leningrad. For an *obkom* first secretary whose prospects of further promotion seem poor, a transfer to Moscow, even with somewhat reduced status and responsibilities, can be a most attractive proposition, especially for his wife and children. (In some measure this also applies to ambassadorial appointments, but these are more ambiguous; appointments to minor nonsocialist countries amount to expulsion from the corridors of power; appointment to a Soviet bloc state, however, is more likely to be a lateral movement than a demotion and is not always a dead end – for Yurii Andropov, for example, it led to a Central Committee secretaryship and ultimately to chairmanship of the KGB and membership in the Politburo.) The Moscow appointments also have the great advantage of affording a dual opportunity for the exercise of patronage: comfortable if not always glittering appointments are provided for one set of officials while *obkom* first secretaryships are opened up for another. In the process, functionaries responsive to the general secretary's views can be placed in key central organizations – for example, in the Council of Ministers – and at the same time his support at the regional level can be further reinforced.

Tables 10.3–10.10 contain data about characteristics of the *obkom* first secretaries today (1976) as compared with the outset of the Brezhnev period. There are two respects in which no change has occurred. First, there were no women among the first secretaries in 1965 and there are none today. Secondly, the ethnic composition remains identical: 52 Russians, eight Ukrainians, and 12 representatives of the minority nationalities of the RSFSR. In all other major respects, however, interesting changes may be discerned. Tables

Table 10.3   *RSFSR regional first secretaries: age*

| | Number | | Per cent | |
	Sept. 1965	Sept. 1976	Sept. 1965	Sept. 1976
Up to 45	6	6	8.3	8.3
46–50	20	13	27.8	18.1
51–55	33	14	45.8	19.4
56 +	13	37	18.1	51.4
Unknown		2		2.8
Total	72	72	100.0	100.0

Average age 1965: 52
Average age 1976: 56 (2 unknown)

Table 10.4   *RSFSR regional first secretaries: date of joining party*

| | Number | | Per cent | |
	Sept. 1965	Sept. 1976	Sept. 1965	Sept. 1976
1925–8	6	1	8.3	1.4
1929–32	15	3	20.8	4.1
1937–41	32	20	44.5	27.8
1942–5	16	20	22.2	27.8
1946–53	3	16	4.2	22.2
1954–9		10		13.9
Unknown		2		2.8
Total	72	72	100.0	100.0

10.3 and 10.4 show that although the first secretaries have aged significantly they also contain substantially larger numbers of officials whose initiation to political life dates from as recently as the wartime or postwar periods. In 1965 less than one-fifth of the first secretaries were over 55, by 1976 more than half of them were. Yet, as Jerry Hough has recently argued, the age pattern of this group of officials is not very persuasive evidence of the onset of gerontocracy in the Soviet Union. In 1971 the average

age of the first secretaries was only one year greater than that of the nearest equivalent group in the United States – the state governors.[33] It is also useful to compare the age patterns of *obkom* first secretaries with those of members of the Council of Ministers, the next largest group in representation in the Central Committee. In 1965 the latter group's average age was 56 – what the *obkom* first secretaries average is now – but this had risen by 1976 to 64, and gerontocratic tendencies were unmistakable. Two-thirds of the Council of Ministers in 1965 are still in office today, compared with only one-third of the *obkom* first secretaries. There is some evidence that Brezhnev has long been seeking to introduce large doses of new blood into the Council of Ministers, as he has done in the regional party leadership, but that he has encountered stubborn opposition to this, and has only recently made much headway.[34] Moreover, because of the changes since 1965, men who joined the party during the 1930s no longer dominate the ranks of *obkom* secretaries, although the overwhelming majority are still men who began their political life under Stalin, even if in a quarter of the cases this was during the Second World War, when political orthodoxy was relatively relaxed.

Table 10.5   *RSFSR regional first secretaries, September 1965: education*

Field	Level of education			Total	
	Complete higher	Incomplete higher	Secondary	Number	Per cent
Industry	20	2	1	23	31.9
Agriculture	21			21	29.2
Education	4			4	5.6
Law	1			1	1.4
Military	1			1	1.4
Other/unspecified	4	2	2	8	11.1
Higher Party School	22: of whom HPS only			14	19.4
Total				72	100.0
Possess higher degree (candidate's)				4	5.6

For many years now an official could not hope to gain appointment as an *obkom* first secretary unless he had higher educational qualifications. Most persons aspiring to these positions had professional training – especially as engineers or agriculture specialists –

Table 10.6   *RSFSR regional first secretaries, September 1976: education*

| Field | Level of education | | | | Total | |
	Complete higher	Incomplete higher	Secondary	Unknown	Number	Per cent
Industry	23				23	31.9
Agriculture	23				23	31.9
Education	6				6	8.4
Military	1				1	1.4
Other/unspecified	6	2	2	2	12	16.7
Higher Party School	20: of whom HPS only				7	9.7
Total					72	100.0
Possess higher degree (candidate's)					7	9.7

Table 10.7   *Main areas of RSFSR regional first secretaries' career experience outside party apparatus*

| | Number | | Per cent | |
	Sept. 1965	Sept. 1976	Sept. 1965	Sept. 1976
Industry (management or technical)	23	30	31.9	41.7
Agriculture management or technical)	33	20	45.8	27.8
Education (teaching or administration)	17	17	23.6	23.6
Komsomol apparatus	19	18	26.4	25.0
Soviet (government) apparatus	41	36	57.0	50.0
Armed Forces during War	23	24	32.0	33.3

and if they lacked educational background it was necessary to take a full-time or correspondence course with the Higher Party School. The main conclusions that emerge from comparison of Tables 10.5 and 10.6 are the sharp decline in the number of first secretaries lacking professional qualifications and having only party training, the continued predominance and rough equality in numbers of the industrial and agricultural specialists, and the fact that men trained as school teachers remain the only other significant group of professionals.[35]

When we examine Tables 10.7 and 10.8, however, we get a different picture of the balance between industrial and agricultural specialists. Table 10.7 shows the number of *obkom* first secretaries whose careers include experience in certain major fields of activity. The most commonly encountered areas of experience are the Soviet or governmental apparatus and industrial and/or agricultural production. The only other major areas of experience represented were in Komsomol jobs or in teaching or school administration, both of which are found in about a quarter of the cases in 1965 and 1976.[36]

Table 10.8   *Primary occupation of RSFSR regional first secretaries*

	Number	
	Sept. 1965	Sept. 1976
Industrial specialist	22	28
Agricultural specialist	24	20
Teacher	10	10
Party/Komsomol/local soviet official	8	5
Military/airforce officer	2	1
Railway official		1
Journalist		1
Economist		1
Manual worker	6	3
Unknown		2
Total	72	72

The main change over this period is the shift away from agriculture in favour of industry as the best-represented career component.[37] This shift could not have been predicted from the data on educational patterns but it reflects long-term trends in the preoccupations of the regional party apparatus. The logic of the politico-administrative system as it evolved under Stalin was to orient local party officials more to the problems of agriculture than of industry, most of which was directly administered by the centralized ministries. This tendency was intensified by Khrushchev in his drive to build up agricultural output in the 1950s. The situation is somewhat paradoxical when one considers the urban origins of the party and its role as the spearhead of industrialization.[38] Khrushchev himself seems to have perceived the paradox. His desire to win for the party as effective a role in the running of industry as it enjoyed in agriculture was undoubtedly a major motive in the establishment of the regional economic councils in 1957 and especially in the splitting of the regional apparatus into industrial and agricultural wings in 1962. These measures were later scrapped, but the problem remained, and one of the ways Brezhnev has sought to tackle it is by staffing the party apparatus with men better equipped to handle industrial problems.

The same shift of emphasis is apparent in Table 10.8, which seeks to establish the primary occupational identification of the *obkom* first secretaries, but the relevant information here is incomplete and often difficult to interpret and, of course, the subjective correlates of these career data are not available. Thus, it would be risky to generalize too confidently from the figures shown in this table. For what they are worth, however, the figures do indicate a trend from the primacy of officials best prepared to deal with problems of agriculture to officials best prepared to deal with problems of industry.

This trend raises important questions about the relationship between party officialdom and the 'specialized élites', which have been the subject of considerable speculation and research in recent years. The central issue is to what extent party officials tend to be men formed by their training and experience in a different mould from managerial, administrative, and other groups, and conversely to what extent people who have been closely associated with these specialized fields gain access to the party élite. It has been suggested that this could have a vital bearing not only on the responsiveness of the regime to special interests, but also on the attitudes and values of this crucial body of officials, from whose number the next generation of national leaders will come, and thus have major implications for the pace and direction of sociopolitical change in the USSR.

The problem, which is many-faceted, cannot be discussed adequately in this context, but some light may be thrown on the central issue of fact. As Grey Hodnett remarked in 1965, 'perhaps a qualitative change in the character of the *obkom* leadership depends not so much on how many young men with fresh technical diplomas are drawn into lower party work as on how many older, experienced non-*apparatchiki* transfer to the party apparatus well along in their careers, affecting its character rather than vice versa'.[39] Precisely this question was explored by Frederic Fleron, who established a marked trend between 1952 and 1961 for senior party officials (of whom *obkom* first secretaries formed the majority) to be 'co-opted', as he put it, at a relatively late stage in their careers after working for many years in one of the specialized bureaucracies, rather than being 'recruited' as professional party officials early in their working lives.[40] This trend, despite some contradictory evidence,[41] apparently has been modified in the Brezhnev period, and the importance of specifically *party* experience has been upgraded. Blackwell has noted that 44.1 per cent of the *obkom* first secretaries appointed between November 1964 and 1968 possessed *both* specialized professional training *and* non-party professional experience, compared with 55.5 per cent of those appointed in 1958–64.[42] This trend has continued. Between 1965 and 1976 the proportion of *obkom* first secretaries whose career experience had included managerial or technical work in industry or agriculture declined from 77.7 per cent to 69.5 per cent (see Table 10.7). The percentage change is not great, but takes on significance when one considers changing age patterns (cf. Table 10.3). *Obkom* secretaries appointed in the intervening years have tended to be older than their predecessors, and thus have had greater opportunity to include non-party experience in their careers. Blackwell has shown that for the earlier part of our period the longer 'apprenticeship' of post-Khrushchev *obkom* first secretaries was spent in the party apparatus or jobs closely related to it, rather than in gaining longer or more diverse non-party experience.[43]

Table 10.9   *RSFSR regional first secretaries: date of first party appointment*

	Sept. 1965	Sept. 1976
Up to 10 years previously	6	3
11–20 years previously	24	19
21–30 years previously	31	26
Over 30 years previously	3	16
Data unknown or unclear	8	8
Total	72	72

The *obkom* first secretaries appointed under Brezhnev include some conspicuous examples of 'co-opted' officials – among them the present Central Committee secretaries Katushev and Dolgikh, whose cases have been noted. But the main trend revealed by Tables 10.9 and 10.10 is clearly in the opposite direction. As we see from Table 10.9, the *obkom* first secretaries now in office have had, on the whole, a substantially longer period behind them since their first experience of party work than was the case with their predecessors in 1965. This is not simply a consequence of higher age levels. Table 10.10 shows a clear tendency for *obkom* first secretaries to be chosen from among those officials who have worked their way up from the lower echelons of the party hierarchy. The number whose initiation to party work occurred at the place of work or the district (*raion*) level has increased from 32 to 41. At the other extreme, the number who were appointed to the *obkom* secretariat without any prior experience in the party apparatus has decreased from 12 to three. What this means is that the *obkom* first secretaries of the Brezhnev generation have had, on the whole, less opportunity than their predecessors of the early 1960s to develop a close association with one of the 'specialized élites', and are likely to identify themselves less ambiguously as career party officials. At the same time, the proportion of these officials with some form of professional training has risen from

Table 10.10   *RSFSR regional first secretaries: level of first party appointment*

	Sept. 1965	Sept. 1976
Regional level*	26	17
City level	9	8
District level	23	28
Workplace level	9	13
Other or unknown	5	6
Total	72	72
*Including:		
as first secretary	1	
as second secretary	3	1
other secretary	8	2
Total	12	3

80 to 90 per cent, and the great majority have had some experience working in a specialized field. Consequently, their capacity to intervene in the name of the party in these fields probably has not been impaired.

Despite the policy of 'stability of cadres', the majority of regional party leaders in the RSFSR have been changed under the Brezhnev regime, and the newcomers tend to differ from their predecessors in important respects. Typically they are some years older. They are more likely to have been locally recruited, and have spent considerably longer working their way up the party hierarchy, taking their first party job at a lower echelon. They are even more likely to possess higher specialized education but have spent a smaller proportion of their careers working in specialized non-party organizations, and the most common field of non-party experience is now industry rather than agriculture.

On the face of it the present generation of *obkom* first secretaries has every reason to be grateful to Brezhnev. He has restored their traditional role and status.[44] Unlike Khrushchev, he has not abused his powers over appointments to name constant replacements, nor does he publicly badger and humiliate them. Their sense of security must therefore be much enhanced. Observing the treatment accorded to themselves and their peers over the last decade, they may reasonably count on either retaining their present office or obtaining a transfer to the centre – which, even if not a promotion, will mean a senior position in the privileged circles of Moscow officialdom. Thus the *obkom* first secretaries should be a satisfied and confident group who can be relied upon to back up the general secretary, in contrast to Khrushchev's *obkom* societies on the eve of his removal.

This supposition, however, deserves closer scrutiny. In what sense can these officials be classed as 'Brezhnev's men'? There are four factors commonly found underlying patronage relationships in political or bureaucratic systems: (1) shared loyalties and attitudes arising from common ethnic, local, religious, organizational or professional backgrounds; (2) bonds formed through former work together; (3) shared policies or ideas; (4) the act of appointment itself, in the absence of any previous bonds. Whatever the underlying factor – and in any particular case there may be more than one factor operating – what is involved is a *personal* relationship of reciprocal protection and support.

All four factors are encountered in the Soviet system, although the second seems to be particularly salient.[45] Many cases have been noted where men who had previously served under Brezhnev, especially in the party organizations of the Dnepropetrovsk or Zaporozhe *oblasts* of the Ukraine or of Moldavia, have risen to prominence in recent years evidently because of his patronage. It is striking, however, that there seem to be no such cases among the RSFSR *obkom* first secretaries appointed under Brezhnev since 1965. His record in this respect contrasts sharply with that of Khrushchev, whose rise in 1953–5 was accompanied by the appointment of many former subordinates from the Ukraine and Moscow region to *obkom* first secretaryships. In fact, it is difficult to detect evidence of any of the first three factors listed above operating in the 'Brezhnev generation' of *obkom* first secretaries. Thus, the one basis of a putative patronage link is number 4 – the fact that Brezhnev was in charge at the time of the appointment and therefore presumably approved it even if he did not initiate it. This is in general the *weakest* basis of a patronage relationship, unless the appointment depends in some peculiar way on the 'patron's' good will – for example, the 'client' has suffered at the hands of the 'patron's' predecessors or rivals,[46] or his rise is unusually rapid and involves the by-passing of more obvious candidates. Brezhnev's appointment of K. F. Katushev as first secretary of the Gorky *obkom* in December 1965 and of V. I. Dolgikh as first secretary of the Krasnoyarsk *kraikom* in 1969 are examples of unusually rapid promotion, and both of these men soon moved on to more senior positions in the Central Committee Secretariat. This type of appointment, however is not typical. As was noted in the discussion of Table 10.1, the selection of *obkom* first secretaries under Brezhnev has been increasingly focused on the most obvious candidates from among the *oblast* leadership, that is, the seniority principle has been emphasized. Thus, it is difficult to detect in most of these appointments the presence of personal factors making for a strong patronage relationship.

On the other hand, such a relationship may develop over time. The mere fact that Brezhnev has kept an *obkom* first secretary in office for many years should contribute to a sense of personal loyalty. At the same time, the official's working style and commitments undoubtedly become progressively adapted to working for Brezhnev, even to a point where adjusting to a new general secretary would perhaps be difficult to contemplate. Strongly reinforcing this loyalty is the expectation that a new general secretary would be likely to replace many of the first secretaries to make way for his own men, and this probability increases as an *obkom* secretary grows older. Another aspect of the situation is the position of the first secretary's colleagues and subordinates in the *oblast* leadership. Although they may have taken encouragement from the policy of recruiting more first secretaries locally, it is reasonable to assume that their personal hopes have been increasingly soured by the slowdown in replacements of first secretaries, especially since 1971, and that frustrated ambition must be building up at these levels.[47] Thus, because a potential successor might find ready support in these circles, the dependence of the incumbent first secretaries on Brezhnev is heightened.

There is, however, another aspect to this stability of leadership: frustrated ambition may well exist among the *obkom* first secretaries themselves. Despite the advantages they have enjoyed in being left in office (or when they have been transferred to Moscow) many of them have been marking time in their *oblasts* for a long time and the prospects of achieving major office at the centre – a natural aspiration of any *obkom* first secretary – must seem to be receding as they move into their sixties. Moreover, they may see that those of their number who have been transferred to Moscow have by and large remained on the fringes of power. In fact, only one of the Brezhnev generation of *obkom* first secretaries has achieved full membership in the Politburo, namely, the Leningrad leader G. V. Romanov – and he has so far *remained* in Leningrad. There are likely to be some *obkom* first secretaries, therefore, who would not be averse to a 'new broom' taking over from Brezhnev and effecting changes in the Politburo which might give them their chance.

In summary, the RSFSR *obkom* first secretaries, the most important group of officials in the Central Committee excepting the top leadership, would appear on the whole to be a 'satisfied' group who would be likely to view with apprehension any move to replace Brezhnev as general secretary. On the other hand, the strength of their commitment to him lacks the reinforcement of antecedent personal bonds and the commitment is not without its ambiguities. There may be some potential 'defectors' among their number. How the *obkom* first secretaries would react to a challenge to Brezhnev's leadership is likely to be affected by their varying personal situations, and the balance of relevant factors will change over time.

NOTES

1. T. H. Rigby, 'The Soviet Politburo: a Comparative Profile, 1951–1971', *Soviet Studies,* vol. XXIV, no. 1 (July 1972) p. 18 (this volume, chapter 8). Changes in the *Politburo* since that date have slightly reduced the proportion.

2. This assumes that D. F. Ustinov, who was appointed Minister of Defence in April 1976, remains a member of the Secretariat, from which he has not been formally removed. Ustinov has never been an *obkom* secretary, and his career has been devoted to administration of the defence industry. The other two exceptions are B. N. Ponomarev and N. V. Zimianin, both ideology specialists. Ponomarev made his career entirely within the central agitprop establishment. Zimianin spent some years as a regional and later republican secretary (but not first secretary) in Belorussia before moving to Foreign Ministry and media jobs at the centre. Another somewhat ambiguous case is Chernenko, who worked in the central party apparatus for a considerable period before his promotion to the Secretariat, but he also served for five or six years as a regional party secretary during the 1940s.

3. The criterion for inclusion is whether the party committee concerned comes directly under the Central Committee. The analysis therefore includes the first secretary of the Moscow City Committee (*gorkom*), since this body is not subordinate to the Moscow *obkom*, but excludes the first secretaries of *obkoms* of autonomous *oblasts* which are subordinate to *krai* administrations. By the same token, it includes the *obkom* first secretaries in Autonomous Soviet Socialist Republics; although the state authorities in these areas enjoy a distinctive status, the rights, obligations, and status of their party bodies are indistinguishable from those of 'ordinary' RSFSR *obkoms*. Altogether we are dealing with 72 party committees, comprising six *kraikoms*, 65 *obkoms* (of which 16 are located in ASSRs) and one *gorkom* (Moscow). In terms of their current role and their prospects for advancement to top office, the RSFSR *obkom* and *kraikom* first secretaries have no real equivalent in the other Union republics. The central committees of the other republics are analogous to the RSFSR *obkoms* in coming directly under the CPSU Central Committee, but their first secretaries have no real prospect of promotion to high office in Moscow, with the exception of the Ukrainian and Belorussian first secretary. The second secretaries in the Union republics, who are usually Russians, are more similar in their career profiles to the RSFSR *obkom* secretaries, but it is unusual for men to go *directly* from this post to major appointments in Moscow (the recent appointment of the second secretary in Uzbekistan, V. G. Lomonosov, as chairman of the State Committee on Labour and Wages of the USSR is an exception). Four of the Union republics have *oblast* divisions, but with the exception of the Ukraine, their *obkom* first secretaries exercise responsibilities far inferior

to those of the RSFSR, and their career prospects are effectively confined to their own republic. Ukrainian officials occupy an ambiguous position in these respects. The population and economic resources entrusted to them are comparable with those in an average RSFSR *oblast*, and in certain respects the position of their party organizations is also more analogous (for example, in electing delegates to CPSU congresses) to the RSFSR. Thus certain 'élite' studies group the Ukrainian *obkom* first secretaries with those of the RSFSR. For the present analysis, however, this was felt to be misleading. Relations between the Ukrainian *obkom* first secretaries and the central party authorities are normally mediated through the Ukrainian Central Committee, and it is unusual for them to move to senior office in Moscow without either first (like Podgorny) gaining Ukrainian Republic first secretaryship, or (like Kirilenko) serving for a period in an RSFSR *obkom*.

4. On the role and powers of tsarist provincial governors, see N. M. Korkunov, *Russkoe gosudarstvennoe pravo, vol. 2: Chast' osobennaia* (St Petersburg, 1905) pp. 311–24, V. M. Gribovskii, *Gosudarstvennoe ustroistvo i upravlenie rossiiskoi imperii* (Odessa, 1912), 133–38; and Anatole Leroy-Beaulieu, *L'Empire des tsars et les russes, vol. 2: Les institutions* (Paris, 1882) pp. 97–9. See also John A. Armstrong, *The European Administrative Elite* (Princeton, N. J., 1973). The obvious difference in the career prospects of provincial governors and *obkom* first secretaries is that the former could never achieve the topmost post in the country, whereas the latter may – and two of them, Khrushchev and Brezhnev, have achieved it. Apart from the tsar, however, most other leading positions in the state were filled by appointment, and provincial governors were a major source of recruitment to such positions.

5. Thus George Trevor, *Russia Ancient and Modern* (London, 1862) p. 339, stated that 'a provincial governor in Russia resembles a military commander quartered on a subjugated people, more than a public officer among his fellow subjects'.

6. See Jerry F. Hough, *The Soviet Prefects: The Local Party Organs in Industrial Decision-Making* (Cambridge, Mass., 1969) Introduction. Similar characterizations of the role and status of *obkom* secretaries may be found in other studies of the Soviet political system, and several analyses of the characteristics of *obkom* secretaries are available. While in no case does the coverage permit direct comparison with the data presented in the present study, the following contain many relevant findings and evaluations: Robert E. Blackwell, Jr, 'Elite Recruitment and Functional Change: an Analysis of the Soviet Obkom Elite, 1950-1968', *Journal of Politics*, vol. 34 (1972) pp. 124–52 (covers *obkom* first secretaries in all republics); Robert E Blackwell, Jr, 'Career Development in the Soviet Obkom Elite: a Conservative Trend', *Soviet Studies*, vol. 24, no. 1 (July 1972) pp. 24–40 (same coverage); Peter Frank, 'The CPSU *Obkom* First Secretary: a Profile', *British Journal of Political Science*, vol. 1 (1971) pp. 173–90 (*obkom* first secretaries in all republics in 1966); Grey Hodnett, 'The *Obkom* First Secretaries', *Slavic Review*, vol. 24, no. 4 (Dec. 1965) pp. 636–52 (*obkom* first secretaries of all republics during the bifurcation of 1962–4 and immediately before and after it); Philip D. Stewart, *Political Power in the Soviet Union: A Study of Decision-Making in Stalingrad* (New York, 1968). ch. 7 (covers *obkom* first secretaries in all republics, 1950–66; K. A. Jagannathan, 'The Political Recruitment and Career Patterns of *Obkom* First Secretaries in the Central Committee of

the Communist Party of the Soviet Union' (Ph.D. diss., University of Washington, 1971) chs 4 and 5 (covers all *obkom* first secretaries elected to the Central Committee between 1952 and 1966); and Joel C. Moses, *Regional Party Leadership and Policy-Making in the USSR* (New York, 1974), ch. 6 (covers first secretaries of 25 *obkoms* in the RSFSR and the Ukraine 1955–73). Also useful are several studies of wider groups in the Soviet political élite, especially George Fischer, *The Soviet System and Modern Society* (New York, 1968) (*obkom* first secretaries of all republics comprise two-thirds of the 230 posts analyzed for the early 1960s); Frederic J. Fleron, Jr, 'Representation of Career Types in the Soviet Political Leadership', in *Political Leadership in Eastern Europe and the Soviet Union* , ed. R. Barry Farrell (Chicago, 1970) (covers all members of the CPSU Central Committee, 1952–61); and Michael P. Gehlen, 'The Soviet Apparatchiki', in ibid. (covers all party officials among the full members of the Central Committee elected between 1952 and 1966). Scattered data of relevance may be found in the specialized literature, particularly in articles appearing in the journals *Osteuropa, Soviet Studies,* and *Problems of Communism*, and in the *Research Bulletins* of Radio Liberty; see especially Jerry F. Hough, 'The Soviet System: Petrification or Pluralism?', *Problems of Communism,* no. 2 (1972) pp. 25–45. The information on the backgrounds and careers of officials analyzed in this paper is assembled from the Soviet press and official biographical compilations, particularly the series *Deputaty Verkhovnogo Soveta SSR* (Moscow, 1962, 1966, 1970 and 1974), and the yearbooks (*ezhegodniki*) of the *Bol'shaia sovetskaia entsiklopediia*. It would be unwieldly to give specific references in these footnotes, but they can be supplied on request.

7. A. I. Mikoyan, *V nachale dvadtsatykh* . . . (Moscow, 1975) pp. 26 ff.
8. A. I. Shakhurin, in *Sovetskii tyl v Velikoi otechestvennoi voine,* ed. P. N. Pospelov (Moscow, 1974) vol. 2, pp. 68–9.
9. This discussion assumes, of course, the basic accuracy of Shakhurin's account, and also ignores several important questions, such as Shakhurin's estimate (when recommending Rodionov) of the patronage enjoyed by Rodionov in Stalin's entourage; Rodionov was later executed in the 'Leningrad case', thus being identified as a protégé of Central Committee Secretary A. A. Zhdanov, who was an extremely powerful figure at this time.
10. The exceptions were from the peripheral national minority areas of Tuva and Dagestan. In many cases more than one change of first secretary occurred in these years, as Khrushchev's initial choice proved unsatisfactory or alternatively went on to higher things. Thus 33 RSFSR first secretaryships changed hands twice between 1953 and 1961, 16 changed hands three times, and three changed hands four times. In addition, all five of the first secretaries appointed to new *obkoms* formed after 1953 were replaced by 1961.
11. Thus, in 1955 A. P. Kirilenko (now number four in the *Politburo* hierarchy) was moved from the Ukrainian party organization, where he had made his early career under Khrushchev, to be first secretary of the large industrial Sverdlovsk *obkom* in the Urals and in 1962 was brought up to Moscow to be first vice-chairman of the Central Committee Bureau for the RSFSR. Similarly, A. I. Struev, another of Khrushchev's Ukrainian cadres, became first secretary of the Molotov (now Perm) *obkom* in 1954 and in 1959 was made vice-premier of the RSFSR (he is now USSR minister of trade). E. A. Furtseva, one of Khrushchev's protégés from

the local party apparatus in Moscow, was made first secretary of the Moscow City Committee in 1954 (which had *obkom* status from 1956) and later went on to be Central Committee secretary and then minister of culture. There were numerous other such cases.

12. See John A. Armstrong, 'Party Bifurcation and Elite Interests', *Soviet Studies,* vol. 17 (1965-6) pp. 418-30, especially pp. 425-6. This article provides a valuable analysis of personnel changes and administrative and power relationships involved in the reorganization. It covers the *kraikoms* and *obkoms* of both the RSFSR and the Ukraine, but excludes the *obkoms* responsible for the 16 Autonomous Republics of the RSFSR. See also Hodnett, op. cit.

13. It would appear that the major speech at the October 1964 plenum, given by Central Committee Secretary Suslov, contained a strong critique of Khrushchev's style and methods (see Michel Tatu, *Power in the Kremlin: From Khrushchev's Decline to Collective Leadership* (London, 1969) pp. 416-17). If so, the features that so concerned the *obkom* secretaries would undoubtedly have been mentioned, and an undertaking to remedy them at least implied.

14. *Partiinaia zhizn'*, no. 20 (1964) p. 6.

15. Ibid., no. 23 (1964) p. 4.

16. *Kommunist,* no. 16 (1964) pp. 7-8.

17. *Pravda,* 17 November 1964. The decision also restored the old rural district party committees (*raikomy*) which Khrushchev had replaced by party committees of collective farm/state farm production directorates. The *raikoms* were able to absorb some of the surplus (mainly junior) staff released from the duplicated *obkom* apparatus. In practice, the completion of these arrangements took longer than anticipated by the Central Committee after the November 1964 decision, but the regional party conferences had all been completed before the next plenary meeting of the Central Committee in March 1965 (see *Plenum Tsentral'nogo Komiteta Kommunisticheskoi Partii Sovetskogo Soiuza 24-26 marta 1965 goda: Stenograficheskii otchet* (Moscow, 1965) p. 5).

18. Agriculture is of little relative importance in this region, but at the time of the split Lubennikov had been relegated to the agriculture *obkom*, and it was the man appointed to head the industry *obkom* under Khrushchev, A. F. Eshtokin, who now became first secretary of the reunified *obkom*.

19. This is an intriguing case because Skriabin had worked under Brezhnev in Zaporozhe in 1946-7, and his election as first secretary of the Rostov *obkom* in 1962, at a plenum over which Brezhnev's crony Kirilenko presided, looked remarkably like the installation of a Brezhnev protégé in an area where Suslov is thought by some to retain a special interest (dating from his service there before World War II). In this case, Skriabin's replacement when the Rostov *obkom* was reunified might appear as a concession to Suslov. If this line of speculation had any basis, however, one would have expected Brezhnev to contrive some other position of importance to Skriabin, but this did not happen.

20. See *Pravda,* 17 November 1964.

21. See T. H. Rigby, 'The Soviet Leadership: Towards a Self-Stabilizing Oligarchy?', *Soviet Studies,* vol. 22 (Oct. 1970) pp. 167-91.

22. The sharpest blow in this campaign was a Central Committee decision of 20 July 1965, which assailed 'serious shortcomings' in party recruitment and training in the Kharkov region - Podgorny's (and Titov's) primary patronage base (see *Spravochnik partiinogo rabotnika* (Moscow, 1966) vol.

6, pp. 383–6). For a good summary of the campaign against the 'Kharkov group', see Tatu, op. cit., pp. 499–502.

23.   Rodionov's career has been a curious one. He first rose to prominence under Kozlov in the Leningrad party machine, and in 1960 was made second secretary of the Kazakh Central Committee. In December 1962, however, he was removed from this position at a plenum presided over by Kozlov himself, in a purge of the Kazakh leadership that has been interpreted as an attack on Brezhnev's influence in that republic (see Tatu, op. cit., pp. 155 and 515). For a fuller analysis of political alignments in Kazakhstan at this period, see J. W. Cleary, 'Politics and Administration in Soviet Kazakhstan, 1955–1964' (Ph.D. diss., Australian National University, Canberra, 1967), especially ch. 9. A contrary interpretation by Sidney I. Ploss, in his *Conflict and Decision-Making in Soviet Russia: A Case Study of Agriculture Policy, 1953–1963* (Princeton, N. J., 1965), especially ch. 4, seems to the present author to be less plausible than Cleary's analysis, especially in the light of later events. Rodionov returned to Leningrad, where he received a relatively minor post as deputy chairman of the Regional Economic Council. Whatever his earlier links with Kozlov, the revival of his fortunes after Kozlov's rival Brezhnev assumed the first secretaryship of the CPSU suggests that he had, indeed, forged bonds with the Brezhnev 'camp' that were now being rewarded. Rodionov remained first secretary of the Cheliabinsk *obkom* till 1970, when he was appointed deputy minister of foreign affairs, with responsibility for the 'socialist' countries. He remains a full member of the Central Committee.

24.   It is true that the regional party conferences preceding the CPSU congress provided an appropriate occasion for leadership changes, but the number of such changes is striking coming so soon after the post-Khrushchev reorganization and it is also noteworthy that the majority of them occurred at special 'organizational plenums' held *before* the *oblast* conferences.

25.   Brezhnev's gambit closely parallels Khrushchev's similar display of power, at an equivalent stage in his own rise, when in November 1953 he went personally to Leningrad to preside over the removal of Malenkov's protégé Andrianov and to install F.R. Kozlov as *obkom* first secretary.

26.   Four years earlier, when he was merely party secretary in the Gorki Automobile Works, Katushev had attended the Twenty-Second Party Congress in Moscow: perhaps he caught someone's (Brezhnev's?) eye there. Since 1963 he had been first secretary of the Gorki City Party Committee. He was only 38 years old in 1965.

27.   See Tatu, op. cit. p. 35.

28.   See Cleary, op. cit. Ignatov received the relatively minor appointment of deputy minister in one of the less important machine building ministries.

29.   Marchenko, like Ignatov, had served under Kapitonov when he was first secretary of the Moscow City Committee from 1954 to 1959. He was appointed a minister in the RSFSR government, which was a demotion, though not as drastic a one as Ignatov's.

30.   *XXIII s''ezd Kommunisticheskoi Partii Sovetskogo Soiuza: 29 marta–8 aprelia 1966 goda: Stenograficheskii otchet,* vol. 1 (Moscow, 1966) p. 90.

31.   Moses, op. cit. pp. 230–4, also notes the increasing appointment of 'insiders' to *obkom* first secretaryships, and offers some valuable discussion of the motivation behind it and its effects.

32.   *XXIV s''ezd Kommunisticheskoi Partii Sovetskogo Soiuza: 30 marta–9 aprelia 1971 goda: Stenograficheskii otchet* (Moscow, 1971) p. 124.

33.   Hough, op. cit., p. 40. See also Blackwell, op. cit.

34. See T. H. Rigby, 'The Soviet Government since Khrushchev', *Politics* (Adelaide), vol. 12 (1977) pp.5–22.
35. See Blackwell, op. cit., especially p. 136. Blackwell's data show a marked shift from agricultural to industrial training in appointments of *obkom* first secretaries in the early post-Khrushchev years. Some caution is needed in interpreting the patterns of educational qualifications found among *obkom* first secretaries, for, as Hodnett points out, 'many received their higher education while holding full-time jobs, and many were preoccupied with Komsomol and other extracurricular activities. The circumstances in which a number of diplomas were granted lead one to surmise that not much education, if any, occurred' (Hodnett, op. cit., p. 644).
36. Most government positions held were as chairman of the executive committee of a local or regional soviet, or in some cases as head of its agriculture department. Hodnett (ibid., p. 650) is correct in labelling these as essentially 'party' functions, characteristically performed by officials already well set on a party career. Occupancy of a paid Komsomol office is a common initiation to a subsequent career in the party apparatus.
37. See Blackwell, op. cit., p. 141.
38. One curious aspect here was that in the early 1960s two-thirds of *obkom* first secretaries were of peasant origin, compared with only one-sixth of the party membership at large (see Hodnett, op. cit., p. 643).
39. Ibid., p. 652.
40. See Fleron Jr, op. cit.; and also Frederic J. Fleron, Jr, 'Toward a Reconceptualisation of Political Change in the Soviet Union: the Political Leadership System', *Comparative Politics*, vol. 1 (1969) pp. 228–44.
41. Moses, op. cit., p. 236, found an increase in the proportion of 'co-opted' first secretaries in 1965–73 as compared with 1955–64, which is contrary to the evidence adduced by Blackwell and the present chapter. This contradiction does not seem to be more than partially explicable in terms of definitional differences. An important factor may be the different periods of comparison. As Blackwell's evidence shows, there was a marked increase in the proportion of 'co-opted' officials appointed as first secretaries in the period 1958–64 as compared with 1953–7. It is possible, however, that the contradictory findings may be partly due to differences in the groups studied. As mentioned earlier, the present chapter is based on appointments in all RSFSR *kraikoms* and *obkoms* and the Moscow *gorkom*, and Blackwell's analysis relates to all *obkoms* in all republics, while that of Moses is based on a sample of 25 *obkoms* in the RSFSR and the Ukraine: perhaps the sample was not entirely representative with respect to the variable under consideration.
42. Blackwell, op. cit., p. 144.
43. Blackwell, op. cit. Blackwell further demonstrates that greater party or party-related experience is the main factor in the longer careers of those first secretaries he designates as 'specialists' (having both specialist training and career experience) and 'semi-specialists' (having one of these), as well as those designated as 'professional politicians' (having party and party-related experience only) (ibid., pp. 36–38).
44. In this connection it is worth considering the representation of first secretaries of RSFSR *obkoms* (including the six *kraikoms* and the Moscow *gorkom*) in the Central Committee and the Central Auditing Commission (membership of which mostly goes to officials next in standing to those elected to the Central Committee). In the Central Committee formed in 1966 there were 36 RSFSR *obkom* first secretaries among the full members,

31 among the candidate members, and five among the members of the Central Auditing Commission. In the Central Committee formed in 1971 these numbers were respectively 41, 29 and two, and in that formed in 1976 there were 60 among the full members and the remaining 12 were candidate members of the Central Committee. To put the figures in perspective, however, it must be noted that there was a considerable expansion in these bodies over this period – the full members of the Central Committee, for example, increasing from 195 in 1966 to 287 in 1976. Thus the *obkom* first secretaries grew from 18 to 21 per cent of the full members of the Central Committee over the decade. The other major group of officials who improved their Central Committee representation over the same period were the members of the Council of Ministers who increased from 22 to 24 per cent of the full members. Of course, the RSFSR *obkom* first secretaries are not the only category of party officials in the Central Committee, although they are the largest of them. Altogether 42 per cent of the full members in 1976 were party officials. The proportion of RSFSR *obkom* first secretaries among them increased from 43 per cent in 1966 to 50 per cent in 1976.

45. See T. H. Rigby, 'Politics in the Mono-organizational Society', in *Authoritarian Politics in Communist Europe: Uniformity and Diversity in One-Party States,* ed. Andrew C. Janos (Berkeley, Calif.: Institute of International Studies, University of California, 1976) pp. 55–60. Under Soviet conditions cases of patronage based on shared policies or ideas are difficult to identify, but this factor may be present more often than is supposed.

46. This was a factor in Khrushchev's early patronage of Brezhnev himself, and in Brezhnev's patronage of the Kazakh first secretary Kunaev, whose previous demotion had involved Brezhnev's rival F. R. Kozlov.

47. See Moses, op. cit. pp. 229–40.

11. Central leaders and local cadres under Gorbachev

It was no part of Lenin's vision to install a new structure of social and political inequality in his socialist republic. Yet the oft-remarked élitist potential embedded in the theory and practice of Lenin's 'revolutionary vanguard' began to engender such a structure from the very first months of the Bolshevik regime. We have seen how quickly the loose hierarchy of quasi-autonomous Bolshevik committees was transformed into a bureaucratic élite which, in imposing the structures and processes of the new 'socialist' order, simultaneously laid the foundations of their own collective power and privilege. The composition of this new élite soon began to reflect its social functions, with proven effectiveness in running the new bureaucratic structures progressively replacing standing in the revolutionary movement as the key criterion for promotion, and education and administrative experience generally, albeit acquired under the old order, taking on growing importance.

In this emergent 'socialist' order, the delegitimation and marginalization of traditional and market structures rendered administrative command the predominant mechanism for the acquisition and distribution of goods and services, indeed of the conditions of life itself. Bureaucratic office, which afforded access to this mechanism, therefore became the most valued social good of all, and the pattern of relationships within the office-holding 'class' and between it and the rest of society became the chief determinant of social structure. Two ostensibly contradictory, but in practice symbiotically related factors, namely interpersonal bonds of reciprocal favour and support on the one hand, and increasingly regularized and centralized procedures (the nomenklatura system) on the other, emerged as the chief determinants of bureaucratic careers within the first decade, and have remained so ever since. The formal and informal links between central leaders and regional cadres became a major element in Soviet bureaucratic politics, as we have seen in the cases of Stalin, Khrushchev and Brezhnev.

The configuration of power within the central leadership has varied widely over the seven decades of more of Communist Party rule. For much of the time it has been a weakly institutionalized oligarchy, with a potential, tragically actualized by Stalin, to collapse into a system of personal dictatorship. At the same time we have noted a definite trend, albeit subject to occasional regression, for the powers, functions and mutual relationships attaching to particular structures and offices to become more clearly defined and more consistently observed: in other words, a process of institutionalization of the oligarchical structure of supreme power.

The mono-organizational system, in which the power and privileges of Soviet political élites and the bureaucratic 'class' as a whole are rooted, has been the vehicle of vast social changes in its more than two generations of existence; the industrialization, urbanization and educational 'revolutions' have transformed the profile of the Soviet population, and with it of the political élites themselves. The political traumas that have taken repeated toll of these élites – the Civil War, the factional struggles of the 1920's, Stalin's purges, the Second World War, and the post-Stalin succession struggles – opened the way to successive brands of 'new men'. The revolutionary notables of the earliest period were soon sharing power with bureaucratized younger revolutionaries and post-revolutionary recruits; junior cadres (like Nikita Khrushchev) were provided with technical training, often leading to rapid promotion in the party, government and managerial bureaucracies; younger ones (like Leonid Brezhnev) trained in the early 1930s, were rocketed to senior office in their tens of thousands in the course of the purges later in the decade; some of these survived the shake-outs of the war and post war years to dominate the leadership by the 1960s, while others gave way to a new and often better-educated generation (that of the Gorbachevs and Ryzhkovs), predominant amongst leading local cadres by the 1970s.

Such, in broad outline, are some of the main themes which we have examined in detail in the preceding chapters. It remains now for us to pursue these themes into the Gorbachev era, and to consider the character of Soviet political élites, at the centre and in the provinces, on the eve of the 1990s.

RENEWAL AND REJUVENATION

To say that this is a leadership 'in transition' may tell us little, since 'transition', as we have seen, despite slower turnover in the late Stalin and Brezhnev eras, has been its normal condition. Yet there are two aspects of the present transition that give it exceptional significance: its scale, and its circumstances.

The significance of the first aspect was analyzed in two important books written before the death of Brezhnev by Jerry F. Hough and Seweryn Bialer.[1] The sharply reduced turnover during the 1960s and 1970s, and the consequent ageing of the Soviet political élites meant that change, when it came, would be massive, and would bring into high office large numbers of officials of a new generation, whose education and life experience would differ markedly from those of their predecessors, and perhaps dispose them quite differently towards issues of policy and structural reform. Not everyone was convinced by this prognosis. It was pointed out that rising forty- or fifty-year-old officials were not necessarily typical of their generation, and might in fact have gained the confidence of their older superiors, and promotion at their hands, for precisely this reason; in any case, two or three decades working in the party-state bureaucracy would have thoroughly domesticated them to its entrenched structures, processes and mores.

This was an issue that only the future could settle, though not, perhaps, definitively, for were this new generation indeed to start behaving in new ways it might arguably be due to quite other causes than their generational proclivities. And this brings us to the second special aspect of this leadership transition, namely, the circumstances in which it is taking place. These circumstances are, of course, what Gorbachev has described as the 'pre-crisis situation' in which the Soviet Union found itself by the early 1980s and the 'revolutionary' changes he and his colleagues have launched in an attempt to deal with that situation. This called for a culling of senior officials too set in the comfortable ways of Brezhnev's 'era of stagnation', and accelerated advancement of vigorous and imaginative protagonists of *perestroika*.

The predicted massive turnover in the political élites has duly eventuated. By the beginning of 1989, less than four years since the election of Gorbachev as General Secretary, newcomers made up over four-fifths of the top party leadership, more than nine-tenths of the top government leadership, and nearly three-quarters of the republic and regional party bosses. The scale of these changes appears all the more remarkable when we note that substantial replacements had already been made between Brezhnev's death in November 1982 and Gorbachev's accession in March 1985. No less than four full members of the Politburo died during this period and three new ones were appointed, along with a member of the Secretariat and three new members of the government Presidium, while no less than 21 new RSFSR regional first secretaries were appointed, 16 of them under Brezhnev's immediate successor Yuri Andropov (partly explaining why the turnover at this level has subsequently been somewhat less than at the centre).[2]

Table 11.1   *Turnover in political élites, 1985–9*

	Number 1 Jan. 1989	New since March 1985	Per cent new under Gorbachev
Full members Politburo	12	9	75
Candidates Politburo	8	8	100
Members CC Secretariat	10	8	80
Presidium Council of Ministers	14	13	93
First Secretaries Republic CCs	14	12	86
Regional first secretaries RSFSR	72	50	69

Note: The biographical data on which the tables in this chapter are based were obtained from successive issues of *Ezhegodnik BSE* and *Deputaty Verkhovnogo Soveta*, and from information appearing in Soviet central and republican newspapers.

Has this massive renewal of the élite since 1982 brought a marked shift in generational representation? At the top level, it clearly has. Shortly before Brezhnev's death the average age of Politburo members passed 70 and that of the government Presidium was only two years less. By the beginning of 1989 both party and government leadership averaged a decade younger: the voting members of the Politburo 62.3, the candidate members 57.9, the CC secretaries 60.5, and the government Presidium 58.4. A leadership aged in its prime had replaced one largely past its prime. No less pertinent, perhaps, they were born,on average, some eighteen years later, and made their early political careers not in the 1930s but in the late 1940s or 1950s. This meant substantial differences in life experience which might be expected to make for significant differences in what Bialer terms their 'role predispositions.'[3] Some caution is called for here, however. The leadership was still composed mostly of men who had received their education and political socialization under Stalin, and been picked out for high office by Stalin-era veterans of the Brezhnev generation. Perhaps Bialer is right in arguing that 'the real turning point may occur only when the post-Stalin political generation enters the élites in large numbers and high positions'.[4]

In this context Gorbachev, in 1989 still, at 57, the *youngest* voting member of the Politburo, could perhaps be seen as a transitional figure. He had his schooling and early university training, joined the party and began his career as a Komsomol organizer, during Stalin's final, obscurantist, terror-laden years. On the other hand, he experienced the post-Stalin thaw as a law student at Moscow University and rose rapidly as a full-time official during Khrushchev's 'years of hope'. Moving to the next level down, among the eight candidate members of the Politburo there were now two clear 'representatives' of the post-Stalin generation: Central Committee Secretary responsible for internal party organization and cadres (and Gorbachev protégé) G. P. Razumovsky, and First Deputy Chairman of the Council of Ministers and Chairman of Gosplan Yu. D. Maslyukov: the former was aged 17 at the time of Stalin's death and the latter aged 16. Three of the party first secretaries of non-Russian republics were younger: S. G. Arutyunyan of Armenia (born 1939), S. A. Niyazov of Turkmenia (born 1940) and G. G. Gumbaridze, the Georgian leader appointed in the wake of the bloodily suppressed Tbilisi demonstration of April 1989 (born 1945). A number of regional first secretaries in the RSFSR are of like vintage. As we noted in Chapter 9, this last category of officials, though not exempt from the general process of ageing of the élites in the Brezhnev era, was subject to substantial turnover and never became a gerontocracy;

by the same token the rejuvenation process in the post-Brezhnev years has not been so spectacular as in the central élite.[5]

The Soviet political élite at the turn of the 1990s, and especially its inner core, is thus substantially younger than it was a decade earlier. Nevertheless, it is older than it had been at any time up to the early 1970s. The lowering of the average age of voting Politburo members from just on 70 in 1982 to 62.3 in 1989 looks impressive, until we recall that it was 61.1 in 1971 and 55.8 in 1951. The same pattern is discernible at lower élite levels, both at the centre and in the provinces. Compared with the late Stalin period, today's élite does not look at all youthful. In 1950, for example, the Council of Ministers Presidium averaged 53 and the RSFSR party first secretaries 43.[6] Rejuvenation of the élite cannot, in itself, tell us much about the turn to radical reform under Gorbachev. Changing patterns of life experience making for different role predispositions may be a more influential factor, but since the post-Stalin generation is only now beginning to enter the political élite, it can scarcely yet be the major one. Surely the explantation must be sought elsewhere, in the 'pre-crisis situation' in which the mono-organizational system found itself by the early 1980s.[7] It is this that moved the Politburo veterans to choose their vigorous and imaginative youngest colleague as General Secretary in 1985, and that provided a favourable context for the massive renewal of the élite in the years since then. Of course, the whole pattern of causality must be far more complex than this statement suggests, but there seems little doubt that its main thrust lay in this direction, not the reverse.

LEADERS OF A NEW TYPE?

Apart from age, does the Soviet political élite in the era of *perestroika* display other characteristics that distinguish them from their predecessors? Let us start with gender. There is now a woman in the central leadership for the first time since Khrushchev's protégée Furtseva died in 1974. Aleksandra Biryukova, a career trade-union functionary, was made a CPSU Central Committee secretary from 1986 to 1988, when she was appointed a candidate member of the Politburo and Deputy Premier responsible for welfare administration. She is, however, the only woman (in 1989) in the almost one-hundred-strong Council of Ministers; there are no women among the secretaries and department chiefs of the Central Committee; and no women among the 14 first secretaries of republic Central Committees and 72 first secretaries of regional party committees in the RSFSR. She is thus the one female among the top 200 or more of the Soviet political élite. While it would be presumptuous, given the lack of specific information, to refer here to 'tokenism', it is obvious that the present leadership has not departed seriously from established standards and priorities with regard to gender representation in the élite. Turning to ethnicity, the most noteworthy development is the reduced representation of non-Russians in the core élite, which continues a long-term trend. In considering Table 11.2, we should bear in mind that the percentage of Russians has been declining over the period covered both in the general population and in the overall party membership, and now amounts roughly to 50 per cent and 60 per cent respectively. In the late Stalin era the number of Russians among full members of the Politburo was roughly in proportion to their weight in the party as a whole, and the other members were drawn from precisely those three nationalities that were most 'over-represented' in the party, for historical reasons.[8] Under Khrushchev the chief development was the co-option to the Politburo of several Ukrainians, men linked with him from his long years as party boss in Kiev, and a reduced predominance of Russians. The effect of this carried over into the 1970s but has been progressively reversed since the later Brezhnev years. Under Khrushchev and Brezhnev the non-Slavic membership was also recruited from non-traditional sources. In the late 1980s the 'over-representation' of Russians has steadily grown, as has the 'under-representation' of Ukrainians and non-Slavs.

This trend is even more marked among the candidate membership of the Politburo. Khrushchev used the latter mainly to give a voice without a vote to party leaders from some of the non-Russian republics, a pattern that persisted at a declining level under Brezhnev and his immediate successors. Thus non-Russians made up four of the five non-voting members in 1961, five of the eight in 1966, three of the six during most of the 1970s, and two of the seven in 1983. By 1987 there were none left. In January 1989 Russians made up 85 per cent of the total (voting and non-voting) membership of the Politburo, other Slavs 10 per cent, and non-Slavs 5 per cent.

Table 11.2   *Ethnicity of voting Politburo Members, 1952–89*

	Jan. 1952	Jan. 1972	June 1984	Jan. 1989
Russian	7	8	8	9
Ukrainian		4	2	1
Belorussian		1		1
Jewish	1			
Georgian	2			1
Armenian	1			
Azerbaijani			1	
Kazakh		1	1	
Latvian		1		
Total	11	15	12	12
Per cent Russian	64	53	67	75
Per cent Slav	64	87	83	92

A similar picture is found in the Presidium of the Council of Ministers. In the mid 1970s it comprised seven Russians (54 per cent), three Ukrainians, a Belorussian, a Jew and a Bashkir.[9] In 1989 there were 12 Russians (86 per cent) and two Ukrainians. In the Central Committee Secretariat non-Russians have long been a rarity. In January 1989 nine out of ten secretaries were Russians, the other one (N. N. Slyun'kov) being a Belorussian.

It would be rash to conclude from these changes that Great-Russian nationalism has come to predominate in the Soviet political élite. At the very least, however, one must acknowledge that in co-opting officials to top party and government positions the Gorbachev leadership has shown no greater concern for equity in ethnic representation than they have for equity in gender representation.

One issue of major practical as well as symbolic importance relates to the leadership of the non-Slavic republics. The long-established pattern is that the topmost posts in party and state (the Central Committee First Secretary, Chairman of the Council of Ministers, and Chairman of the Presidium of the Supreme Soviet) are filled by local nationals, but certain organizationally strategic posts are either in effect reserved for Russians or other Slavs (especially the post of Second Secretary of the Central Committee) or at least commonly staffed by them (for example, Head of the Party Organs Department, Chairman of the KGB). In the Baltic and Central Asian republics, with their substantial Slavic minorities, the latter usually get a share of other senior posts as well. This has remained the common pattern under Gorbachev, but with some significant nuances.

In the Central Asian republics, all of which were subjected to massive purges of their corrupt establishments, Russians began to be appointed to certain posts which had previously been reserved for local nationals.[10] Up to 1986 the three topmost posts remained taboo, but in that year Moscow removed the Brezhnev protégé (and Politburo member) Dinmukhamed Kunaev from the post of Party First Secretary in Kazakhstan, and replaced him by the Russian Gennadi Kolbin from the Urals, who had earlier spent eight years as Second Secretary in Georgia. Kazakhstan had had a Russian First Secretary before, namely Brezhnev himself, but that was in the mid 1950s, and in the intervening decades the Kazakhs had grown enormously in national consciousness and self-confidence. Against this background and in the context of growing freedom of expression and association the appointment was a serious miscalculation. It provoked widespread indignation, culminating in a large scale and bloodily suppressed riot in Alma-Ata, and although Moscow speedily restored control and did not yield on the matter at issue, it deepened ethnic resentments and provided a salutory lesson on the dangers of violating established conventions on the ethnic distribution of top republic posts. In 1989 Kolbin was replaced by a Kazakh.

By 1988, with its unprecedented assertion of minority national concerns, particularly in Transcaucasia and the Baltic republics, the pressures on these conventions were running strongly in the opposite direction, even calling in question Moscow's practice of posting imported Russians to organizationally strategic posts, including the key 'watchdog' post of Second Secretary. This issue came out into the open at a plenum of the Lithuanian Central Committee on 20th October 1988, which endorsed Moscow's proposal to replace the First Secretary R. B. Songaila by A. M. Brazauskas. Several speakers demanded that the Russian Second Secretary N. A. Mit'kin should go too, that he should be replaced by a native Lithuanian, and that the 'watchdog' role of the Second Secretary should be done away with.[11] Brazauskas persuaded the Committee to defer a decision on the Second Secretary till the next plenum, and when this was convened seven weeks later he produced a nice compromise, no doubt worked out in discussions with Moscow. Mit'kin was indeed replaced by another Russian, but one, Vladimir Berezov, who was educated in Lithuania, was married to a Lithuanian school teacher and had spent his whole working life there, albeit most recently as head of the Central Committee's Department of Organisational-Party Work – one of the key channels of Moscow control.[12] Moscow's concessions in this case were far from radical, but the incident signalled that the Kremlin could no longer treat such appointments as purely administrative decisions and must be prepared to enter into a *political* process to ensure the choice of officials amenable to its purposes.

Finally, how do the Gorbachev-era recruits to the Soviet political élite compare with their predecessors in terms of their education and career experience? At the topmost level, the most significant trend has been towards greater diversity. Khrushchev's victory over the 'anti-party group' in 1957 had introduced into the Politburo a predominance of men, who, like him, had spent long years as the Kremlin's 'prefects' in the provinces, that is, as first secretaries of *oblast, krai*, or republican party committees. This predominance persisted after Khrushchev's removal, but its decline began in the early 1970s and has accelerated under Gorbachev. Whereas at the beginning of 1972 13 out of the 15 voting members of the Politburo had worked for at least four years as first secretaries of regional or republican party committees, by mid-1984 the proportion was down to 8 out of 12 and by early 1989 to 6 out of 12, a reduction from 86 per cent to 67 per cent and now to 50 per cent.

But the drift to heterogeneity is even greater than these figures suggest. From the 1950s to the mid-1970s the great majority of those co-opted to top jobs in Moscow after years spent as provincial party bosses had other things in common as well: a technical education (usually in some branch of engineering) and shop floor and/or managerial experience in industry. This is no longer the case. Only three of the 1989 Politburo fully fit this pattern, namely Vorotnikov, Ligachev and Shcherbitsky. A

Table 11.3   *1989 Politburo main career components*

| | Higher education field | Party Posts | | | Komsomol | Central govt. | Industry[e] | Police[f] | Academia |
		incl. as Reg. 1st Secs[c]	incl. CC App[d]	Total					
									Years employed in
Gorbachev	law[a]	8		25	7				
Vorotnikov	industrial	6		18					
Zaikov	industrial[b]	3		7	5		32		
Ligachev	industrial	18	4	34					
Ryzhkov	industrial			3		11	29		
Chebrikov	industrial			16				21 (K)	
Shevadnadze	history	13		16	15			8 (M)	
Shcherbitsky	industrial	23		34					
Slyunkov	industrial	4		8		9	19		
Yakovlev	history		21	24					2
Nikonov	agriculture	2		15		6			
Medvedev	economics		12	17					22

Notes   a later also agriculture   b engineering economics
   c Regional: *oblast, krai,* republic CC   d App (aratus): excludes work as CC Secretary
   e all mostly managerial   f K = KGB, M = MVD

fourth, Slyun'kov, spent four years as First Secretary in his native Belorussia, but *after* serving for nine years in Moscow as Deputy Chairman of Gosplan. Gorbachev and Shevardnadze spent long years as local party bosses but lacked both a technical education and work experience in industry.

As we see in Table 11.3, which shows the main components in the career experience of 1989 Politburo members, they now manifest a variety of quite distinct paths to the top. True, there is one basic feature they all share: advancement has been won by successive promotions up one or more of the official hierarchies within the framework of the nomenklatura system: outside this framework there is no path to high office under mono-organizational socialism. Furthermore, all present voting members of the Politburo have had some period of their careers in full-time party posts. But there the uniformity ends. The three members (Ligachev, Vorotnikov and Shcherbitsky) who followed the once-stereotypical path of technical education – work in industry – regional party secretary - Moscow, are now matched by three 'technocrats' (Council of Ministers Chairman Ryzhkov and Central Committee Secretaries Zaikov and Slyun'kov – Zaikov is simultaneously First Secretary of the strategic Moscow City Committee), each of whom rose to high office after a quarter-century or more of work in industrial management and the government economic administration, and only then were co-opted into senior party posts. Two more (Gorbachev and Foreign Minister Shevardnadze), lacking technical training, got their entrée into the regional party élite after climbing to senior posts in the Komsomol, in the case of Shevardnadze supplemented by nearly a decade in the MVD (Interior Ministry) police. Chebrikov,now a Central Committee secretary, worked for many years in provincial party jobs, though never in a key line (first secretary) post, and was *then* transferred to the KGB leadership. CC Secretary Nikonov, trained as an agronomist, has made most of his career in the administration of agriculture. And finally, political economist Medvedev and historian Yakovlev have risen to the top via the ideological apparatus, the former largely within academia and the latter mostly in the CC's Propaganda Department. These summaries do not do justice to the varied experience enjoyed by several of these leaders (for example, Yakovlev has also been an exchange student at Harvard and served as a journal editor and as Soviet ambassador to

Canada). Nor is this the place to go into the varied patronage links and political orientations that helped determine their careers. The point here is to note the unprecedented heterogeneity of their paths to the top and the consequent richness of skills, knowledge and experience which they bring to their collective deliberations – along, perhaps, with divergent convictions and commitments.

It is worth asking whether any comparable trend is observable in the government élite. In the late Stalin era most of the dictator's chief lieutenants were made deputy chairmen of the Council of Ministers responsible for particular areas of government activity, so that the membership of the Council of Ministers Presidium largely coincided with that of the voting members of the Politburo. Even at that time, however, the occasional 'technocrat', who had made his career exclusively in industrial management and administration, reached the top echelons of the government machine, without acquiring membership of the Politburo. This was later to become the predominant pattern, although the decisive breakthrough came not with Stalin's death in 1953, but with Khrushchev's victory in 1957 over the 'anti-party group', most of whom were party leaders holding top positions in the Council of Ministers. By the mid-1970's all but two of the 13 members of the Council of Ministers Presidium were 'technocrats', most of whom had made their whole careers in the spheres over which they were now presiding (the exceptions were First Deputy Chairman Mazurov and Deputy Chairman for Agriculture Nuriev, both of whom were posted to the central government after careers in the provincial party machine).[13]

Although the overlap between the government Presidium and the party leadership remains small, the predominance of 'technocrats' in the former body has been significantly diluted under Gorbachev. Nine of the 14 1989 members could be so classified (Chairman Ryzhkov, First Deputy Chairman Maslyukov and Deputy Chairmen Silaev, Voronin, Batalin, Kamentsev, Tolstykh, Belousov and Talyzin). One, Deputy Chairman for social questions Biryukova, made most of her career in the trade-union apparatus, as noted above. And four others, First Deputy Chairman for agriculture Murakhovsky and Deputy Chairmen Shcherbina (fuel and energy), Gusev (chemical industry) and Vedernikov (heavy industry), had previously been pursuing standard party careers, including substantial periods as regional first secretaries. There have thus been complementary trends in the composition of the top party and top government élites. Both have become more diverse, and whereas half the former in 1989 have pursued careers other than as party line-executives (namely, as either 'technocrats' or 'ideologists') the latter has become less a preserve of 'technocrats', primarily to the benefit of former party line executives. These developments, like all matters touching the exercise of power at the top, have had little comment from Soviet leaders, scholars and journalists, and we are left to speculate on how far they are fortuitous and how far intended; and if intended, by whom and why. Their implications may perhaps be better appreciated when considered in relation to the structural changes examined below.

REGIONAL ELITE: INS AND OUTS

Lack of biographical data on a number of the new men appointed since 1987 prevents an adequate trend analysis of the educational and career characteristics of Gorbachev's regional first secretaries, although available data suggests little marked change in these respects compared with Brezhnev's appointments in the 1970s. The big change in this important category of officials (they constitute the largest single group among the voting members of the Central Committee) relates to the positions from which they are recruited and their subsequent fate after replacement. Khrushchev made very active use of his power over senior appointments to reward his friends and punish his enemies, and this involved frequent shake-ups of regional élites, cross-switching of key personnel and the despatch of new brooms from Moscow. As we saw in Chapter 10, under the Brezhnev regime, with its tacit social compact of live and let live and its explicit policies of 'stability of cadres' and 'trust for cadres', tenure was lengthy and new first secretaries were chosen more and more from among the close local associates of their predecessors. Andropov began to reverse this, and the reverse was sharply intensified immediately after Gorbachev's takeover in March 1985. Between 1976 and 1982, when Brezhnev died, the average annual turnover among the 72 regional first secretaries in the RSFSR was a little over three; in 1983–4 it rose to ten; during Gorbachev's first year it soared to 24, a third of all regional leaders; following the Twenty-Seventh Party Congress in March

Table 11.4   Source of RSFSR regional first secretaries under Brezhnev and Gorbachev

Previously held position	In office as of Sept. 1976		appointed Mar. 1985– Dec. 1988	
Same region				
Second Secretary, same *obkom* (inc. Moscow city)	17		6	
Other secretary, same *obkom*	7		1	
First secretary of *oblast* centre	4		1	
First secretary subordinate *obkom* (in Krai)			1	
Chairman soviet executive committee (E. C.) (or government), same *oblast* (or ASSR)	21		5	
First deputy chairman, soviet E. C.			1	
Chairman Presidium Supreme Soviet, same ASSR	1		1	
Total in same region	50	(69%)	16	(29%)
Other region or republic				
Second CC secretary, other republic	1			
First secretary, other region (includes one in *obkom* under a *kraikom*)	5		4	
Second secretary, other region	7			
Other secretary, other region	1			
Chairman soviet E. C. other region	2			
Total from other region	16	(23%)	4	(7%)
Central Committee apparatus				
Secretary CC			2	
Head of department	1		4	
Deputy head of department			5	
Deputy head of sub-department			1	
Head of sector	2		5	
Inspector or instructor	2		13	
Total from CC apparatus	5	(7%)	30	(54%)
Other central posts				
Chairman CC trade unions	1			
Minister USSR government			3	
Deputy minister			1	
Head of chief directorate in ministry			1	
Ambassador			1	
Total from other central posts	1	(1%)	6	(11%)
Total cases	72		56	

1986 it subsided for a time, but gradually regained momentum, and there were 14 changes in 1988.

Table 11.4 shows where the new first secretaries have come from. Those directly promoted from within the local élite have been reduced from over two-thirds under Brezhnev to less than a third under Gorbachev; the relatively small proportion transferred from other regions has been further reduced; and the number sent out from jobs at the centre has soared from 8 per cent to 65 per cent. These figures testify to the determination of the new Moscow leadership to break the power of the regional cliques and bend local wills to central purposes. The neglect of home-grown cadres has not been as great as at first seems: 11 of the 30 Central Committee officials posted as regional first secretaries had previously worked in the region concerned and had then served in the CC apparatus for a relatively short period – sometimes for just a few months – before being returned to their region to set it to rights. This system of 'probation' (*stazhirovka*) was pioneered in Georgia in 1983–4, by the then Republic First Secretary Eduard Shevardnadze, who spoke enthusiastically of its effectiveness for the purposes we have mentioned.[14] It also, of course, presents excellent opportunities for the exercise of patronage. It would be simplistic, however, to see here only the hand of Gorbachev. In 1985–6, when by far the largest number of such 'probations' were served, most of them with the rank of 'Central Committee Inspector', 'Second' secretary E. K. Ligachev would undoubtedly have been involved. But throughout the period the Department of Organisational-Party Work, responsible for administering the CC's cadres policy, was headed by G. P. Razumovsky, believed to be a close adherent of Gorbachev, and with whose promotion to the rank of Secretary in March 1986 Ligachev's increasing involvement in other matters, and Gorbachev's growing personal authority,it is likely that the latter acquired a predominant influence over appointments at this level. Although he seems to have made only limited use of this to advance officials closely linked to him in the past, new first secretaries are likely to see their future prospects as substantially dependent on his approval and adjust their conduct accordingly. A final point worth noting is that, whereas in 1985–6 12 out of the 17 officials posted from the central party machine to regional first secretaryships had the most junior rank of CC Inspector, in 1987–8 all but one had held

Table 11.5   Subsequent fate of replaced RSFSR regional first secretaries

	Replaced Oct. 1965– Oct. 1976	Replaced March 1985– Dec. 1988
Central party positions		
Secretary CC	4	1
Head department CC		3
Deputy head department CC	1	
Official Party Control Committee	5	
Chairman Central Revision Commission	1	
Total central party positions	11	4
Other central positions		
First Deputy/Deputy Chairman USSR Council of Ministers	1	2
Other positions USSR Council of Ministers	6	5
More junior positions under USSR Council of Ministers	9	3
First Deputy/Deputy Chairman RSFSR Council of Ministers	4	2
Other positions RSFSR Council of Ministers	3	
More junior positions under RSFSR Council of Ministers	2	
Chairman Central Consumer Cooperatives Union		1
Chairman Soviet of the Union	1	1
Ambassadors	6	3
Total other central positions	32	17
Local positions		
Chairman, Presidium of Supreme Soviet, same ASSR	2	
First secretary CC, other republic		1
First secretary, other region RSFSR	1	3
Total local positions	3	4
No subsequent position		
Died in office	9	2
Removed in disgrace		1
Retired on pension	4	28
Total no subsequent position	13	31
No further information (possibly junior position)	3	
Total	62	56

more senior ranks involving as a rule more extensive experience at the centre. The 'probation' system was being run down, but the Central Committee apparatus remained the most important recruiting ground for regional party leaders.

The contrast between the Brezhnev and Gorbachev periods in the subsequent fate of replaced regional first secretaries was no less marked than the contrast in their provenance, as we see in Table 11.5. The table compares the first (almost) four years of Gorbachev's primacy with an 11 year period under Brezhnev, the two periods yielding a comparable number of replacements (56 and 62 respectively). Under Brezhnev few regional leaders were pensioned off. Some went on to greater things, but otherwise they tended to stay put until they died in office or, more commonly, were brought up to a comfortable job in Moscow, often carrying lighter responsibilities. Under Gorbachev the proportion transferred to jobs at the centre has gone down from 70 per cent to 37 per cent, while the proportion retired has increased sevenfold, accounting for over half of all first secretaries replaced. In 1985 the Vologda first secretary Drygin was made something of a public hero for *voluntarily* choosing retirement.[15] Far more numerous, no doubt, were those who retired under pressure or duress: I have identified only one, the Bashkir first secretary Shakirov, who was removed with public ignominy,[16] although others were later to be criticized for mismanagement or worse. It was constantly stressed that the touchstone of whether regional party leaders, like other categories of officials, deserved to retain office, was their will and capacity to advance *perestroika* in their bailiwicks. Under Gorbachev, as under Brezhnev, Khrushchev and Stalin before him, the style and priorities of the General Secretary gave a distinct character to the relationship between central and local party leaders, and one reflection of this was the source of recruitment of the latter and their subsequent fates.

THE RULING OLIGARCHY UNDER GORBACHEV

We return then, to the top political élite, considered now not for their background and career characteristics, but for their roles and mutual relationships as a ruling oligarchy.

The 'dictatorship of the proletariat' established in 1917 was from the first, in effect, a dictatorship of the party leadership, a dictatorship which, by entrusting every field of legitimate social activity to official organizations subject to its direct command, came to exercise an unprecedented power over the lives of the population. Contrary to widely-held assumptions, it was from the first a collective rather than a personal dictatorship, that is, an oligarchy, and it mostly has remained such, with the egregious exception of the two decades or so of Stalin's absolute rule. However, in common with many - perhaps most – oligarchies, it is fluid and unstable in its internal structure, which tends to drift alternately towards an immobilizing diffuseness and towards a tyranny-threatening concentration. As we saw in Chapter 9, the oligarchy has gradually learned how to moderate these tendencies, through various conventions, understandings and *ad hoc* correctives, and this has engendered a measure of institutionalization, however incomplete, of the oligarchical structure of power. Certain long-existing formal structures and roles have served as the building blocks of this institutionalization process.

The key structures are:

(1) an inner executive body within the party central committee, known (except for 1952–64) as the latter's Political Bureau (Politburo);
(2) a subordinate administrative body known as the Secretariat of the Central Committee; and
(3) an inner cabinet within the government, know since the late Stalin era as the Presidium of the Council of Ministers.

Key members of the latter two bodies also sit on the Politburo, so that all three operate as an interlocking executive of some 30 odd persons. Each of these bodies meets as a rule once a week. The Secretariat, as well as administering the several-thousand-strong central party machine and the hundred-thousand-or-so-strong party machine in the provinces, decides a great deal of second-order business coming up to the leadership through party channels, referring only the most important or contentious issues to the Politburo. The Council of Ministers Presidium directs the 80 odd ministries, state committees and other agencies of the central government through which most of the economic, social and cultural activity of the USSR is run, and also decides a great deal of second-order business not warranting referral to the Politburo. It does not, however, deal with substantive matters coming from the foreign relations, police and military branches of the government, which go directly on to the Politburo's agenda.

With the exception of the earliest years and also partially the late Stalin and early post-Stalin years, the post of General Secretary has been the most authoritative one, conferring a greater or lesser primacy within the ruling oligarchy. Usually second in importance is the Chairman of the Council of Ministers. Then, as a rule, one of the other CC secretaries (commonly, though not officially, referred to as the 'Second Secretary') also assumes special importance, exercising on behalf of the Politburo *vis-à-vis* the party Secretariat much the same role as the Chairman of the Council of Ministers does *vis-à-vis* the government. And fourthly, there is the Chairman of the Presidium of the Supreme Soviet, that is, the state presidency. In the last thirty years the incumbents of these posts, and these only, have had in effect *ex officio* membership of the Politburo. Its other full and candidate members will comprise officials drawn from the following categories:

(1)   additional members of the government Presidium and CC Secretariat;
(2)   heads of key government bodies effectively autonomous of its Presidium (i.e. Defence Minister, Foreign Minister, KGB Chairman);
(3)   Deputy Chairman of the Supreme Soviet Presidium;
(4)   RSFSR officials: Chairmen of its Council of Ministers and Supreme Soviet Presidium, first secretaries of Moscow city and Leningrad regional committees;
(5)   first secretaries of Central Committees in non-Russian republics;
(6)   Chairman of the Trades Union Council (not since the 1950s).

The oligarchy, then, in its most obvious aspect, is an inter-locking network of collective decision-making bodies. In another aspect, however, it functions as the apex of a complex hierarchical structure of command, embracing all fields of legitimate social activity, and this is manifested in an internal hierarchy both within the interlocking executive as a whole and within each of its constituent parts. In its broadcast terms this hierarchy puts the full members of the Politburo at the top, followed by the candidate members, the CC secretaries not in the Politburo, and finally the Council of Ministers members not in the Politburo. Within the Politburo itself the *ex-officio* members stand at the top, usually in the order listed above. In the Secretariat, the hierarchy is General Secretary, 'second secretary', other full members of the Politburo, candidate members, and non-members of the Politburo. There is a line of command that runs General Secretary – secretary responsible – head of CC Department – head of sector responsible/secretary of republic or regional party committee. In the Council of Ministers there is a similar hierarchy based on the level, if any, of Politburo membership, and a line of command that runs Chairman of the Council of Ministers – first deputy chairman – deputy chairman – minister, and so on.

Both these aspects, the collective and the hierarchical, are necessary to the operation of the central political élite as an effective executive, but there is also an inbuilt tension between them. Under Stalin the hierarchical aspect totally took over and virtually eliminated the collective. At other times hierarchical lines have become dysfunctionally blurred and weak. There is another tension as well, discussed in Chapter 9: that between the need for an authoritative 'chief executive' within the core éite, and the danger that a powerful chief executive might accumulate dictatorial powers, given the weakness of social and political constraints on the power of the ruling oligarchy generally.

A final point: a General Secretary seeking to enhance his power and authority and to assert a more effective chief-executive role will find it useful, if he can, to gain appointment to other key positions. In terms both of status and of executive control the most desirable such position is obviously the chairmanship of the Council of Minsters. This post was taken over by Stalin after crushing all resistance in the 'Great Terror', and by Khrushchev after his defeat and expulsion of the 'anti-party group'. The lesson was not lost on Khrushchev's successors, who agreed to try and limit the power of future General Secretaries and had the Central Committee vote to ban joint tenure of the General Secretary and Government Chairman posts. Brezhnev eventually achieved the next best thing: the chairmanship of the Supreme Soviet Presidium, which brought him more authority but not

Table 11.6   *Membership of key executive bodies, March 1989*

Name	Polit-buro	Secre-tariat	Presid-ium C. of M.	Post(s) held
Gorbachev, M. S.	M	M		Gen. Sec. Ch. Pres. SS, Chr. State Defence Council
Vorotnikov, V. I.	M			Ch. Pres. SS RSFSR
Zaikov, L. N.	M	M		Sec. CC, 1st Sec. Moscow *gorkom*
Ligachev, E. K.	M	M		Sec. CC (agriculture)
Medvedev, V. A.	M	M		Sec. CC (ideology)
Nikonov, V. P.	M	M		Sec. CC (agriculture)
Ryzhkov, N. N.	M		M	Ch. C. of M.
Slyun'kov, N. N.	M	M		Sec. CC (socio-economic)
Chebrikov, V. M.	M	M		Sec. CC (legal, police)
Shevardnadze, E. A.	M			Min. Foreign Affairs
Shcherbitsky, V. V.	M			1st Sec. CC Ukraine
Yakovlev, A. N.	M	M		Sec. CC (international)
Biryukova, A. P.	C		M	D. Ch. C. of M. (social)
Vlasov, A. V.	C			Ch. C. of M. RSFSR
Lukyanov, A. I.	C			1st D. Ch. Pres. SS
Maslyukov, Yu. D	C		M	1st, D. Ch. C. of M. (planning)
Razumovsky G. P.	C	M		Sec. CC (cadres)
Soloviev, Yu. F.	C			1st sec Lennigrad *obkom*
Talyzin, N. V.	C		M	D. Ch. C. of M. (Comecon)
Yazov, D. T.	C			Min.Defence
Baklanov, O. D.		M		Sec. CC (defence ind.)
Murakhovsky V. S.			M	1st D. Ch. C. of M. (agriculture)
Batalin, Yu. P.			M	D. Ch. C. of M. (construction)
Belousov, I. S.			M	D. Ch. C. of M. (defence ind.)
Vedernikov, G. G.			M	D. Ch. C. of M. (heavy ind.)
Voronin, L. A.			M	D. Ch. C. of M. (supplies)
Gusev, V. K.			M	D. Ch. C. of M. (chemical ind.)
Kamentsev, V. M.			M	D. Ch. C. of M. (foreign trade)
Silaev, I. S.			M	D. Ch. C. of M. (machine-building)
Tolstykh, B. L.			M	D. Ch. C. of M. (science & techn.)
Shcherbina, B. E.			M	D. Ch. C. of M. (energy)

Note: M = full member, C = candidate member, Sec. = secretary, Ch = chairman, 1st D. Ch = first deputy chairman, D. Ch. = deputy chairman, Min. = minister, Pres. = presidium, SS = Supreme Soviet, Ctte = committee, *gorkom* = (party) city committee, *obkom* = (party) regional committee, ind. = industry.

Policy areas for which CC secretaries and deputy premiers are responsible are shown in brackets.

much power, as well as the State Defence Council, which certainly did add to his power. His short-serving successors Andropov and Chernenko succeeded in assuming these positions quite quickly, suggesting that they were now accepted as appropriate prerogatives of the General Secretary.

It is in the light of these factors, and against the background of the evolution of the oligarchy as a political executive since Stalin's day, that we should consider the shape it has come to assume under Gorbachev. Table 11.6 shows the membership of key executive bodies and positions occupied by the ruling oligarchy in March 1989, just four years after Gorbachev assumed the General Secretaryship. The first thing to note is that the present General Secretary had also followed his three predecessors in becoming Chairman of both the Supreme Soviet Presidium and the State Defence Council. True, there was a long delay in his assuming the former post, whether due to the concern of his colleagues to restrain the build-up of his power and authority, to his own self-restraint, or in order to facilitate a gain in the substance of power at the cost of its formal trappings (the evident *quid pro quo* for his supporting Gromyko's assumption of the Presidium chairmanship was that Gorbachev's junior ally Shevardnadze took over from Gromyko as Foreign Minister). When Gorbachev was at last endorsed as Chairman of the Supreme Soviet Presidium, on 1 October 1988, it was in the context of a radical reorganization of the Central Committee apparatus and an associated reshuffle of top officials, which are generally believed to have substantially strengthened Gorbachev's power base. It also occurred against the background of decisions on constitutional changes which would convert the Presidium chairmanship into an executive state presidency, in keeping, allegedly, with measures to enhance the authority of the elected soviets over the government apparatus.

The second point to note in Table 11.6 is the far stronger representation of Secretariat members than of Government Presidium members in the Politburo. The significance of this can be better appreciated if we relate it to past patterns of Politburo membership. As we see in Table 11.7, the balance has varied enormously in the post-Stalin period. The low-point of Secretariat membership was immediately after the dictator's death, when most of the voting members held government office. Khrushchev's rise went hand in hand with the rise of the party machine, and the only time the Politburo has contained slightly more CC secretaries than it does today was immediately after his defeat and expulsion of the 'anti-party group' in 1957. (The comparison may be pertinent, as some observers have styled the leadership changes of 30 September – 1 October 1988, which raised the predominance of the Secretariat to its present point, as Gorbachev's 'coup'.) In Brezhnev's later years the balance again shifted substantially in favour of the Secretariat, though not nearly so far as under Khrushchev. In the first couple of years of Gorbachev's incumbency Secretariat and Government Presidium were roughly in balance, and the subsequent dramatic enhancement of the former's salience has gone hand in hand with the growth of the General Secretary's personal authority.[17] I return to this in the final section.

Table 11.7   *Posts held by Politburo members in 1989 and selected past years*

| | Full members + Candidate members in | | | |
Posts held	March 1953	Oct. 1982	March 1986	March 1989
CC Secretariat	1 + 0	6 + 2	4 + 1	8 + 1
USSR Presidency	1 + 0	1 + 1	1 + 0	1 + 1
USSR Government	8 + 1	3 + 1	4 + 3	2 + 4
Trade unions council	0 + 1	0 + 0	0 + 0	0 + 0
Party and government RSFSR	0 + 0	2 + 1	1 + 2	2 + 2
Party CCs other republics	0 + 2	2 + 4	2 + 1	1 + 0
Total members	10 + 4	13 + 9	12 + 7	12 + 8
Posts held	10 + 4	14 + 9	12 + 7	14 + 8

Note: In 1982 and 1986 the Chairman of the Party Control Commission held full membership, included here in the CC Secretariat. Chairmanship of the State Defence Council, held by every General Secretary since Brezhnev, is not shown here as a separate post.

One further development observable in Tables 11.6 and 11.7 is the greatly reduced representation of leaders from the non-Russian republics in Gorbachev's Politburo and the increased number of officials from the Russian Federal Republic. It is worth reflecting on this in relation to the increased predominance of ethnic Russians in the Soviet core élite remarked on earlier.

While this book has been in production, several further changes have been made in the ruling oligarchy, which maintain and in some respects deepen the trends analysed in this chapter. An updated account will be presented in our companion volume *The Changing Soviet System*. Here, however, we must turn in conclusion to the processes and underlying socio-political structures on which the character of Soviet political élites ultimately depends.

AN END TO THE NOMENKLATURA SYSTEM?

It is not part of my task here to attempt a general account and evaluation of the changes in Soviet society under Gorbachev, and the present chapter is concerned only with those changes directly pertinent to the subject of this book.[18] It will be necessary, however, to recall some of those broader changes if we are to understand the significance of the developments discussed in this final section. The evidence of deepening economic decline and worsening social problems must have been apparent to many in Soviet ruling circles at least by the early 1980s, but the system had to move further into crisis before, by early 1985, a sufficient consensus evidently emerged that bold and possibly painful and risky measures were unavoidable. To spearhead such a programme they chose Mikhail Gorbachev, a man who had demonstrated his commitment to the system in his long years as a regional boss, his capacity for sensible within-system reform in his work as CC Secretary for agriculture, and his leadership skills while standing in for the ailing Chernenko as chairman of the Politburo – a role in which, according to Andrei Gromyko, he 'performed brilliantly'.[19]

The first measures of the Gorbachev team focused on restoring order and discipline: tough campaigns against corruption, drunkenness and slackness on the job, which hurt and alienated many, workers and officials alike, and which provided the context for the extraordinary turnover of regional leaders in Gorbachev's first year which we noted earlier. These campaigns were seemingly aimed at putting new strength and vigour into the traditional mono-organizational system, but at the same time there was much talk of a more radical *perestroika* or revamping of the system, and measures were not long in coming which began to eat into the edges of that system, notably the revival of private (individual and co-operative) enterprise in the service industries. Deeper economic changes followed; an industrial reform aimed at making enterprises autonomous market actors rather than merely the base units in a ministerial command structure, and later an agricultural reform fostering family and co-operative farms on a leasehold basis. A transition to some kind of 'market socialism', a concept earlier rejected by Gorbachev, was evidently now in process.

By 1988 this was being associated with an explicit repudiation of the established 'command-administrative system' of centralized management of all social processes, a concept closely akin to my 'mono-organizational socialism'.[20] For it was the whole socio-political order, not just the economic system, that was to be transformed, and striking changes were already evident in important areas, notably in the relaxation of politico-administrative controls over the dissemination of information (*glasnost'*), over culture and public expression generally and over non-official association for a wide range of purposes and activities. It was acknowledged, moreover, that this would entail unprecedented limitations on the arbitrary powers of party and state officials, and that 'socialist pluralism' would need the protection of a 'socialist *Rechtsstaat*' (*sotsialisticheskoe pravovoe gosudarstvo*).

At the time of writing, few Soviet or foreign observers believe that these changes have reached the point of no return, and opinions differ widely as to how far (and what proportion of) the Soviet leadership is committed to their proclaimed broader goals, or what prospects they have of success. One thing that is already clear, however, it that any substantial and lasting move from 'mono-organizational socialism' to 'socialist pluralism' will have fundamental implications for the matters considered in this book. If the creation and distribution of material and non-material values is no longer to depend entirely on administrative decisions taken within a single centralized organizational structure, the 'bureaucracy' will lose the basis of its 'ruling class' status as characterized in Chapter 1. If the constituent units of society are to be autonomous of party-controlled administrative direction, they will need to find their own leaders rather than having them assigned to them under the universal nomenklatura system of personnel administration. If governing the county is to involve accommodating leaders' purposes to a plurality of interests and opinions acknowledged as legitimate, rather than simply finding the best administrative measures to implement leaders' goals, the rulers, both central and local, must cease to be simply bureaucrats (or 'partocrats') and learn to be politicians.

These three aspects are inextricably intertwined, and all three have found reflection in official discussions and official policies. The crucial element is the nomenklatura system, which for over 60 years has dispensed access to power and privilege in the USSR and constrained local and specialized élites to subordinate the interests of their 'constituencies' to those of the ruling oligarchy. The origins of that system were examined in Chapter 3 and its operation in the late Stalin era described in Chapter 4. It changed little under Khrushchev and Brezhnev, serving their differing purposes equally well, as we saw in Chapters 6 and 9. In the 1970s and early 1980s party training literature encouraged wider consultation and less highhandedness in making nomenklatura appointments,but left no doubt as to where the power and responsibility ultimately lay. For example, a handbook on internal party procedures published as late as 1987, referring to nominally elective positions, states that the party body on whose *nomenklatura* the position stands, 'as a result of collective discussion makes a decision to recommend the most suitable candidate for election. After he has been elected, the higher party body confirms him in the post'.[21]

By now, however, change was on the way. Addressing the Central Committee on personnel policy in January 1987, Gorbachev declared that elections should cease to be an empty formality, that alternative candidates should be allowed to stand for election as local and regional party secretaries, and that elective procedures should be used in the selection of managerial personnel as well. Although the Central Committee did not include his most radical proposals in its resolution,[22] they were soon beginning to be implemented.[23] Altogether in 1987 120 out of the 909 new first secretaries of district and city party committees were chosen in contested elections.[24] While earlier examples reported merely offered a choice between candidates who would in any case have been on the official 'cadre reserve' for these posts (for example, between the second secretary and soviet executive committee chairman for the position of district first secretary), later cases frequently involved far less predictable candidates, and it was clear that, with encouragement from the Centre, local party organizations in at least some regions were playing a more genuine part in choosing their own leaders. Revised instructions on party elections issued in August 1988 strengthened the secret ballot provisions, making it easier for local conferences to reject candidates recommended by higher levels.[25] In the round of local party conferences towards the end of 1988 1117 district and city secretaries (evidently not just *first* secretaries) were elected against alternative candidates, as well as a number of regional party secretaries.[26] In January 1989 the Turkmen CC was given the choice of two candidates for a vacancy on its Secretariat, in what was apparently the first case of contested election for a post at this level.[27]

Meanwhile, it was not only in the party machine that moves were afoot to democratize the choice of leaders and representatives. In the 1987 elections to the local soviets a very limited element of choice was allowed in a minority of electoral districts, employing a device that allowed practically all candidates to gain election. By contrast, the elections to the new Congress of People's Deputies in March 1989, despite all their limitations, provided widespread and genuine opportunities for voters to influence outcomes, with results, especially in cases where senior officials failed to gain election, that could precipitate élite personnel changes, at least at the regional level. In many cases the workforce is involved in the choice of factory management, directors now often being chosen from applicants responding to job advertisements. In Moscow a school director was reported to have been similarly selected.[28] Far more politically sensitive, contested elections have become usual in the 'creative unions' (writers, artists, and so on) and the party preferred candidate is not always elected.[29]

It is impossible in the space available to consider these developments in the detail they deserve. The chief point to be made here is that between 1987 and 1989 choice 'from below' came to play a significant and sometimes decisive role in a wide range of cadre decisions. Since a large proportion of the two million or more posts on the nomenklaturas of party committees are in form elective, and this includes nearly all the more senior positions, it is obvious that this development places in question the whole nomenklatura system. This is widely recognized within the educated Soviet public. Yet it is by no means clear at the time of writing that the party leadership's intention is to phase out the system, or merely to render it more sophisticated and flexible, perhaps at some point dropping the discredited term 'nomenklatura'.[30]

An authoritative article on party elections published in September 1988 reported that over half the new first secretaries of district and city committees chosen over the previous year had to be co-opted on to the committees they were to head because they were being posted to these jobs from outside by decision of higher echelons. While stressing that this was excessive and should be reduced under the new election procedures, which prescribe a secret ballot on such co-optation proposals, the article nevertheless denied that the practice could be dispensed with. 'One needs to resort to it when selecting (*pri izbranii*) for elective posts graduates of the CC CPSU's Academy of the Social Sciences and of party schools, when recommending as secretaries of party committees officials of higher-level organs, or when transferring (*pri perestanovke*) cadres "horizontally", in the interests of their more rational allocation (*rasstanovki*)'.[31] The implication is obvious: there are still those who have the responsibility for matching party officials to party jobs,elective or not, for 'rationally' 'recommending', 'transferring' and 'allocating' them. There is no sign here of the party machine abdicating its powers under the nomenklatura system. As Central Committee secretary Ligachev put it in a speech in Rostov in December 1988, 'the electiveness of leaders in no wise divests party committees of the responsibility for selecting and training cadres'.[32] That this is not mere rhetoric is indicated by the fact that the sharp reduction in the party apparatus associated with its late 1988 reorganization scarcely touched those sections concerned with personnel administration.[33]

In a meeting with Moscow city officials (the *aktiv*) in January 1989 Gorbachev was asked about the nomenklatura, and his reply, although as reported somewhat evasive, likewise assumed the retention of that 'responsibility'. His rider was that it must be exercised 'democratically'. This entailed 'consulting with the collective, with the *aktiv*', before making personnel recommendations.[34]

So says the General Secretary in Moscow, and the same blend of new-style 'democratization' and traditional 'cadres policy' is observable deep in the provinces. Typical is the following extract from a February 1989 Kirgiz Central Committee resolution on 'strengthening the political guidance of *perestroika*':

The Bureau and departments of the (republic's) CC and the regional, city and district committees of the party are to implement undeviatingly a cadres policy appropriate to the tasks of the current phase of *perestroika*. Party committees are to carry out systematically the work of training a high-quality (*polnotsennyi*) reserve, and testing them in practical tasks. They are to make provision for applying active measures for training party officials and the *aktiv* and for advance planning (*prognozirovanie*) of the promotion (*dvizhenie*) of leading cadres, making wide use of democratic forms of selecting cadres on an alternative basis [i.e. with elective choice – T. H. R.] and subsequently go over to this practice in all party organizations.[35]

It is pertinent to recall here that even under Brezhnev party organs were being exhorted to consult with the *aktiv* and the 'collective' of organizations before 'recommending' who they should elect as their leaders; and that even in Stalin's time the usually empty voting procedure was occasionally activated to reject persons 'recommended' as secretary of base party organizations (but never at higher levels) when they were particularly unpopular.[36] The effect of allowing a genuine vote at two (and sometimes three) further levels up the party hierarchy is to put teeth into the injunction to consult. Those responsible for making 'recommendations' (that is, those on whose nomenklatura the post stands) are now expected to find two or more acceptable candidates, and to face the possibility that, if they choose badly, an 'outsider' nominated from the floor will gain election. Thus, 'the nomenklatura', as an editorial article in the Central Committee's organizational journal put it in November 1988, 'cannot serve as armour for those who are not capable of doing their job on the level of the demands of the time, and who have lost the confidence of the masses'.[37] It is claimed that this will make for a more rational personnel administration, and it is also clearly designed to help lend some credibility, both domestically and internationally, to the Soviet Union's democratic credentials. It entails some risk of surprises, not always pleasant, but the leadership is evidently confident that these can be contained within safe limits, with the help of appropriate 'political methods of leadership'.

So far as positions on the Central Committee's own nomenklatura are concerned, there is no evidence of a willingness to expose their 'recommended' candidates to the risk of rejection. Reports of the election of regional first secretaries, always conducted under the eye of a representative of the Central Committee (usually an official of its Party Structures and Cadres Department) never mention more than the one name. At the October 1988 meeting of the Lithuanian Central Committee, at which members called for the replacement of the Russian Second Secretary, the clinching argument advanced by the new First Secretary Brazauskas for deferring action was the following: 'You all know what the status of the second secretary is. Whether you like it or not, it exists. It's on the nomenklatura of the Politburo'.[38]

This incident will serve to introduce a further important aspect of current cadres policy: the need to adapt it, devising appropriate 'political methods', to the now sharply divergent political circumstances in different regions, which are due largely to the impact of increased freedom of expression and association. While substantial political diversity is discernible even within the RSFSR and other republics, the differences between republics are far more striking, as developments in the Transcaucasus and Baltic areas most graphically demonstrate. One example must suffice to make the point: that of the election in December 1988 of the leading sociologist Mikk Titma to the Secretariat of the Estonian CC. Estonia had been among the front-runners in extending the practice of contesting elections in a variety of spheres,[39] as well as in the emergence of influential voluntary associations. It was in Estonia that the first Popular Front for the Support of *Perestroika* was formed, in 1987, to be emulated later in a number of other republics and regions, and Titma played a leading role in the Popular Front from its inception. When the relatively conservative Estonian First Secretary Vaino was replaced in June 1988 it was as a consequence of mounting *public* pressure spearheaded by the Popular Front and by the Estonian 'creative unions', which in effect repudiated his authority and appealed over his head both to their own people and to Moscow. This was the context in which Titma, a scholar who had never before held a party post, or any other administrative office, was made ideology secretary a few months later. At the Central Committee meeting which elected him, three other persons were nominated, two of them experienced city party secretaries and the other the editor of the CC's chief Russian-language newspaper. All three withdrew, and Titma, who had to be co-opted to the Central Committee for the purpose, was duly elected, 97 voting for him and 16 against.[40]

While there could be little doubt that Titma's nomination had at least been cleared both with the new First Secretary Vyalyas and with the Central Committee in Moscow, his achievement of high political office was clearly the consequence not of the normal operation of nomenklatura-based cadres policy, but rather of the importance of his role in an unofficial – and in the republic context, quasi-oppositional – political movement. There are so far no close parallels to this case, but the question nevertheless arises: is it a foretaste of how leaders will be generally chosen in the future – in which case the nomenklatura system is doomed – or is it merely an exceptional case deemed appropriate in exceptional circumstances?

In December 1988 the gifted and influential Soviet sociologist Academician Tatyana Zaslavskaya, replying in *Izvestiya* to readers' letters provoked by an interview she gave some months previously, addressed a question which was raised in the introductory chapter to this book: 'Is it correct to call the bureaucracy, or putting it differently, the social stratum of "nomenclatured workers" (*nomenklaturnykh rabotnikov*), a class?' Her answer, in essence, was 'not quite': this stratum possesses, she said, the three basic characteristics of a class cited by Lenin, namely, (1) a special relationship to the means of production (enjoying almost unlimited disposal over them); (2) a special place in the organization of social labour (it administers it); and (3) it differs from the rest of the population in the sources of its share of social wealth. But Lenin also insisted on a fourth element in any structure of classes, namely the economic exploitation of certain classes by others, and on this point she stated:

> What we have recently learned about the structure and functioning of our society in the periods of Stalinism and Brezhnevism provides us, it seems to me, a basis for speaking, at the very least, of indirect exploitation by the nomenklatura stratum of the remaining mass of the population (I wish particularly to stress that I am speaking precisely of a stratum). But even if one considers that this stratum did not succeed in decisively transforming itself into a class, it was, in any case, confidently marching in this direction.[41]

Although the nomenklatura system had come under criticism, Zaslavskaya considered that 'it is far from having given up its positions'. Nevertheless, she closed on a hopeful note: the laws already enacted or in process of adoption 'are calculated to effect the breaking-up of this special stratum, and to ensure that it is unable to further consolidate itself'.

SOME FINAL REFLECTIONS

The changes referred to by Zaslavskaya threaten not only the continued dominance of the nomenklatura 'stratum', but the whole mono-organizational system of which it is the cornerstone. They thereby call in question every aspect of the structure and character of the Soviet political élite which we have identified in the preceding pages. For it is, of course, the directing and co–ordinating role of the party apparatus within the mono-organizational system that has made the corps of regional first secretaries the most important élite group outside the top leadership, and its 'command economy' that has made ministers and heads of other central government agencies the next most important. The reorganization and drastic pruning of the party apparatus launched at the September 1988 CC Plenum weakens its capacity to exercise this directing and co-ordinating role, especially in the key area of the economy, and thereby not only strikes at the roots of the regional first secretaries' power but also signifies role changes with obvious implications for their selection criteria: the predominance of engineers is already beginning to look an anachronism.

Changes in the political sphere are likely to have no lesser impact than those in the running of the economy. The elevation of the elective soviets over 'their' administrative élites, if it becomes a reality following the republic and local soviet elections in early 1990, will markedly alter the profile of local political élites, whether or not the earlier suggestion that the posts of chairman of the soviet and local party first secretary should normally be held by the same person is implemented.

So far as the central élite is concerned, the 30 or so officials constituting what I have called the ruling oligarchy, current economic and institutional reforms will have profound implications, some of which were already becoming manifest by the first half of 1989. The process of institutionalization of patterns of authority, office-holding, structural overlap and operational procedure within the ruling oligarchy,which we recalled earlier in this chapter, can be best understood as an adaptation of top-level leadership and decision-making to the functional requirements of a mature mono-organizational social order. Those patterns may well become dysfunctional if the social order is indeed to be transformed into one with a substantially marketized economy and democratized polity. One must be alert to this contingency and avoid the uncritical interpretation of current changes in terms of past patterns and the political dynamics which they have embodied.

An important case in point is the greatly increased overlap already noted, in the membership of the Politburo and the CC Secretariat, to a level seen before only once, and that briefly, in the wake of Khrushchev's victory over the 'Anti-Party Group'. Since this coincided with the growing primacy of General Secretary Gorbachev, one could be tempted to view it, on past experience,as a 'takeover' of the Politburo by the Secretariat. Yet the sharp reduction in the Central Committee apparatus and the subordina-tion of most of it, in September 1988, to a half dozen Commissions consisting of CC *members* (not officials) each chaired by a Politburo member, suggested that some other interpretation was required. Meanwhile reports emerged that the Secretariat's weekly meetings had been discontinued, while the commissions had not yet established a pattern of regular meetings.[42] Apparently one of the three key decision-making bodies at the centre was now no longer functioning, its collective deliberations having been absorbed by the Politburo, and its day-to-day operations placed effectively in the hands of the commission chairmen and their department heads, answerable ultimately to the General Secretary. If this interpretation is correct, it would lend fresh significance to the increased ideological *and* technocratic expertise now available within the Politburo membership itself.

A more obvious case is that of the changes in the state presi-dency. As we have already noted, it would be fatuous to interpret Gorbachev's belated assumption of the chairmanship of the Pre-sidium of the Supreme Soviet as simply the reassertion of a quasi-institutionalised 'prerogative', since it occurred in the con-text of a radical transformation of the role and structure of the Supreme Soviet. With his election in May 1988 to the new position of Chairman of the Supreme Soviet, Gorbachev acquired not only unprecedented formal executive powers but also a new and potentially very demanding public political role.

This brings us to a further dimension of change with major implications for the composition of the Soviet political élite. It has been a basic (and noncontroversial) proposition of this book that the Soviet political élite is essentially a *bureaucratic* élite. Except at the very summit, where interpersonal power relations can assume overwhelming importance, the power, standing and rewards enjoyed by élite members have been a function of the *office* to which they have been appointed, of their formal position within one or other of the bureaucratic hierarchies. This reflects the fact that the political process has been concentrated overwhelmingly within the closed bureaucratic sphere, and only marginally overflowed into the public domain.

By 1987 this state of affairs was being significantly modified. The liberalization of public expression and association allowed many thousands of citizens to participate, through the media, informal groups, public meetings and demonstrations, and even the meetings of official organisations, in activities aimed at influencing public attitudes and ultimately public policy. Some of these activities met with marked success, notably on environmental issues and issues of nationality rights. A number of individuals assumed leadership roles within this public political process that bore little or no relationship to their current employment: individuals as disparate as sacked Politburo member Boris Yeltsin, social scientist Yuri Afanasiev and leading nuclear physicist (and lately exiled dissident) Andrei Sakharov. The first phase of this re-emergence of open politics in the USSR culminated in the elections to the Congress of Soviets in May 1989, the complex arrangements for which ensured a majority of docile deputies while admitting a generous minority of radical activists in various causes, and in the subsequent debates in the Congress and the election there of the new 'working' Supreme Soviet.

If this line of development continues and becomes entrenched, it will be necessary to re-conceptualize the Soviet political élite in terms which embrace leaders in this public political process as well as the élite of career officialdom. Indeed the distinction may become blurred as individuals in the first category achieve executive office (the sociologist Mikk Titma mentioned above being an early example) while others in the latter category acquire skills helpful for surviving and prospering in the public political process (as several party officials in the Baltic and Transcaucasian republics have done, along, one might argue, with Boris Yeltsin and even Mikhail Gorbachev). Such skills include those of public advocacy and pressure, but also those of conciliation and compromise.

This opens up a prospect attractive to the liberal mind, but at the time of writing it can be offered only on the level of speculation, not of prediction. Indeed a view current among some Soviet intellectuals is not implausible, namely that the revival of a public political process was intended as a short-term measure aimed at shaking up existing structures, disarming domestic and foreign critics, and creating favourable conditions for Gorbachev and his followers to consolidate their power, after which it could be constrained within well controlled channels, serving then merely as a less transparent facade of democracy veiling the traditional bureaucratic command system. Of course if such was the intention it might not prevent this public political process from developing a momentum of its own which threatened to run out of control-some have argued that precisely this had happened by the middle of 1989. At the same time it is not difficult to imagine circumstances that would provoke the suppression or drastic winding down of open politics, even if this were not originally intended, most obviously a widespread breakdown of order provoked by either ethnic or socio-economic grievances.

It is, however, the obstacles to successful economic reform that place the largest question mark against the prospects for a vigorous public political process in the USSR and the attendant changes in the character of the political élite. By mid-1989 it was being openly argued by Soviet officials that the reform measures had so far only worsened the performance of the command economy without providing a working alternative to it. Regional party leaders complained that the situation still required them to exercise their traditional roles in the economy but they were decried as 'bureaucrats' if they attempted to do so.[43] It is thus premature to assume that a transition to something like market socialism can or will be successfully completed, let alone that it will prove an effective cure for the ills of the Soviet economy if it is.

Failure, whatever form it took, would leave little alternative to a return to the old 'administrative-command methods', no doubt with some structural and procedural modifications. In that case it is unlikely that much would survive of the other components of Gorbachev's reform programme, particularly those making for genuine political liberalization and democracy. Whatever the outward forms, the foundation elements of the mono-organizational system, softened up in recent years, could be expected to recongeal. Should this happen, the recent modifications we have observed in the recruitment and composition of the Soviet political élite may prove to be only modest and ephemeral departures from the patterns whose origins and evolution we have traced in this book.

NOTES

1. Jerry F. Hough, *Soviet Leadership in Transition* (Brookings Institution, Washington, 1980), and Seweryn Bialer, *Stalin's Successors. Leadership, Stability and Change in the Soviet Union* (Cambridge University Press, Cambridge, New York, etc.,1980).
2. Further on élite changes under Gorbachev and his immediate predecessors, see David Lane (ed.), *Elites and Political Power in the USSR* (Edward Elgar, Aldershot, 1988, and Gower, Brookfield Vermont, 1988), especially ch. 2 by Thane Gustafson and Dawn Mann, 'Gorbachev and the "Circular Flow of Power" ', and chapter 3 by Ronald J. Hill and Alexander Rahr, 'The General Secretary, the Central Party Secretariat and the Apparat'. See also T. H. Rigby, 'The Soviet Political Executive, 1917-1986', in Archie Brown (ed.), *Political Leadership in the Soviet Union* (Macmillan, London, 1989) ch. 2, and R. F. Miller, J. H. Miller and T. H. Rigby (eds.), *Gorbachev at the Helm: A New Era in Soviet Politics?* (Croom Helm, London, 1987) especially ch. 1 by T. H. Rigby, 'Old Style Congress – New Style Leadership?', and ch. 3 by J. H. Miller, 'How Much of a New Elite?'.
3. See Bialer, op. cit, pp. 99–101. Cf. Hough, op. cit., ch. 3.
4. Bialer, op. cit., p. 102.
5. See also Hough, op. cit. p. 70. We cannot yet calculate an average age for the RSFSR regional first secretaries in 1989 owing to the lack of data on several recent appointees.
6. Ibid., p. 70.
7. I consider this in *The Changing Soviet System: Mono-organisational Socialism from its Origins to Gorbachev's Restructuring* (Edward Elgar, Aldershot, forthcoming), ch. 8.
8. See T. H. Rigby, 'Communist Party Membership under Brezhnev,' *Soviet Studies*, vol. XXXVIII, no. 3 (July 1976) p. 326.
9. See T. H. Rigby, 'The Soviet Government since Khrushchev,' *Politics*, vol. 12, no. 1 (May 1977) p. 16.
10. This was initiated under Andropov, and in 1983-4 a number of regional party posts in the Central Asian republics were entrusted to Russians for the first time for decades.

11. See *Sovetskaya Litva*, 27 October 1988.

12. See *Sovetskaya Litva*, 10 December 1988. The same plenum also elected a junior secretary responsible for industry, and he was a Lithuanian whose wife's name was Tatyana, unmistakably a Russian.

13. See T. H. Rigby, 'The Soviet Government since Khrushchev', loc. cit, and *Der sowjetische Ministerrat unter Kosygin*, Bericht no. 21 (1977) des Bundesinstituts für ostwissenschaftliche und internationale Studien (Cologne, 1977).

14. See *Zarya Vostoka*, 8 April 1984.

15. See *Pravda*, 23 September 1985.

16. *Pravda*, 23 June 1987.

17. For greater detail on the historical background to the matters examined in this section, see T. H. Rigby, 'The Soviet Political Executive, 1917-1986', ch. 2 in Brown (ed)., op. cit.

18. See Archie Brown, 'Power and Policy in a Time of Leadership Transition', ch. 6 in ibid. On the socio-economic and political context of Gorbachev's emergence and first year in power, see Timothy J. Colton, *The Dilemma of Reform in the Soviet Union*, rev. edn (Council on Foreign Relations, New York, 1986).

19. For Gromyko's remarkable panegyric to Gorbachev in supporting his nomination as General Secretary, see *Kommunist*, no. 5 (March 1985) pp. 6-7.

20. These developments are examined at greater length, and relevant sources cited, in Chapter 8 of my book *The Changing Soviet System*, op. cit.

21. *Slovar'po partiinomu stroitel'stvu* (Moscow, 1987) pp. 156-7.

22. For Gorbachev's report and the Central Committee resolution, see *Kommunist*, no. 3 (February 1987).

23. For examples of elections of local party secretaries with a choice of candidates, see article by Kemerovo *obkom* first secretary N. S. Yermakov, *Sovetskaya Rossiya*, 10 February 1987, *'Plenum raikoma izbiraet pervogo sekretarya'*, *Partiinaya zhizn'*, no. 5 (March 1987) pp. 32-5, and *'Novyi podkhod k vyboram pervogo sekretarya'* ibid., no. 9 (May 1987) pp. 72-3.

24. *Partiinaya zhizn'*, no. 17 (September 1988) p. 11.

25. *Partiinaya zhizn'*, no. 16 (August 1988) pp. 30-5. See also *'Osnovy demokratizatsii izbiratel'nogo protsessa v partii'*, ibid., no. 17 (September 1978) pp. 8-15. For a valuable exegesis, see John Löwenhardt, 'Democratization of Party Elections in the Soviet Union. The Central Committee's Instructions on Elections 1937-1988', paper presented at a conference in the Bundesinstitut für ostwissenschaftliche und internationale Studien, October 1988. Among the few substantive innovations in the new instructions is a provision limiting tenure of any particular party office to ten years.

26. *Partiinaya zhizn'*, no. 4 (February 1989) p. 16.

27. The candidates, both district first secretaries, made speeches presenting their programmes, a discussion followed in which 13 CC members took part, and this was followed by a vote which the successful contender won by a margin of 65 to 58. See *Turkmenskaya Iskra*, 27 January 1989.

28. See *'Konkurs doveriya'*, Pravda, 9 January 1988.

29. The most frequently cited case here is that of the Film-makers Union. For an extensive account of the election of their first secretary by the Moscow writers' organization, see *Literaturnaya gazeta*, 21 October 1987, pp. 1-2.

30. A report of the first meeting of the CC's new Commission on Questions

of Party Construction and Cadres Policy stated that party organs should desist from a 'formal nomenklatura approach' to the selection and assignment of cadres. See *Pravda*, 28 February 1989.

31. *Partiinaya zhizn'*, no. 17 (September 1988) p. 13.
32. *Pravda*, 25 December 1988.
33. For example, while the Estonian CC apparatus lost all told 30 per cent of its apparatus, its Department of Organizational-Party and Cadres Work went down by only 8 per cent (from 25 to 23). See *Sovetskaya Estoniya*, 23 December 1988. On the other hand, it seems likely that many posts are being devolved on lower-level committees, while others are removed from party nomenklaturas altogether and entrusted to the relevant state authorities. In Kazakhstan the CC nomenklatura was more than halved by March 1989. See *Kazakhstanskaya Pravda*, 12 March 1989.
34. *Pravda*, 10 January 1989.
35. *Sovetskaya Kirgiziya*, 25 February 1989.
36. See my 'Party Elections in the CPSU', *Political Quarterly*, vol. 35 no. 4 (1964) pp. 420–43.
37. *Partiinaya zhizn'*, no 22 (November 1988) p. 10. The point is illustrated by a case cited in a *Pravda* editorial *('Oblastnye i kraevye partkonferentsii'*, *Pravda*, 6 December 1988), where a district first secretary in Orenburg region long protected with impunity by the regional first secretary Balandin failed to receive sufficient votes to be elected to the party committee (and thus to retain his post) in the secret ballot at the district party conference.
38. *Sovetskaya Litva*, 27 October 1988.
39. For early examples, see V. Belousov and V. Shirokov, *'Vam vidnee'*, *Pravda*, 1 March 1987.
40. *Sovetskaya Estoniya*, 8 December 1988.
41. *Izvestiya*, 24 December 1988. Compare David Lane, 'Ruling Class and Political Elites: Paradigms of Socialist Societies', ch. 1 in David Lane (ed.), *Elites and Political Power in the USSR* (Edward Elgar, Upleadon, 1988). See also E. O. Wright, 'A General Framework for the Analysis of Class Structure,' *Politics and Society*, vol. 13 no. 4 (1984) pp. 383–424.
42. This has apparently not yet (October 1989) been reported in any Soviet publication, but it has been mentioned to Western specialists by several senior Soviet officials and scholars.
43. A number of the speeches at the April 1989 CC Plenum are instructive in this connection; see *Pravda* 27 April 1989.

Index